W9-CGM-099

Praise for CONNECT

"Carole Robin and David Bradford are masters at helping people bring IQ and EQ together to satisfy both and be successful. I recommend this book."

—RAY DALIO, founder of Bridgewater Associates and author of *Principles: Life and Work*

"It's never been clearer that meaningful relationships are critical to a fulfilling and healthy life. *Connect* is a practical and timely book I highly recommend that shows us that by learning to connect with ourselves, we can more easily connect with others and build thriving relationships."

—ARIANNA HUFFINGTON, founder and CEO of Thrive Global

"At LinkedIn, we made 'Relationships Matter' one of our core values because the personal connections you make persist across jobs, companies, and careers. *Connect* offers a compelling and highly accessible road map for building relationships that lead to professional success and personal fulfillment. I highly recommend this book."

—REID HOFFMAN, co-founder of LinkedIn and co-author of *Blitzscaling* and *The Alliance*

"Learning to connect across differences and develop relationships in which we can actually see and hear others for who they are is becoming an imperative for nations and individuals alike. *Connect* is a carefully structured set of concepts and practices that readers can apply to everything from their marriages to their management challenges. It's a treasure!"

—ANNE-MARIE SLAUGHTER, CEO of New America

"One of my goals, and the reason I founded MasterClass, is my fervent commitment to democratizing access to the world's best. I am thrilled that the immensely valuable lessons in *Connect* are now available to millions of people. I encourage anyone who cares about developing stronger and more meaningful relationships anywhere in their life to read this book."

—DAVID ROGIER, founder and CEO of MasterClass

"I owe most of what I have accomplished in both my career and my personal life to the lessons I learned in the course on which *Connect* is based. I can't wait to give a copy of *Connect* to my teammates, my family, and my friends."

—DARA TRESEDER, CMO of Peloton and board director of PG&E

"Decades in business have shown me that building high-trust relationships is one of the most important keys to success, whether in negotiations or on the basketball court. With practical insights into relationship building in both personal and professional environments, *Connect* is the best book in its class."

—IRV GROUSBECK, entrepreneur, co-owner of the Boston Celtics, and professor at the Stanford Graduate School of Business

"Carole and David's classes have been an invaluable resource—what a gift to have their insights and lessons in a book. I would recommend it to anyone who wants to feel happier and more fulfilled, and to anyone who wants a better, smarter future for our world."

—DR. JENNIFER AAKER, co-author of *Humor, Seriously* and *The Dragonfly Effect*

CONNECT

CONNECT

BUILDING EXCEPTIONAL RELATIONSHIPS WITH FAMILY, FRIENDS, AND COLLEAGUES

DAVID BRADFORD, PhD

CAROLE ROBIN, PhD

CURRENCY
NEW YORK

Published in the United States by Currency, an imprint of Random House, a division of Penguin Random House LLC, New York.

Currency and its colophon are trademarks of Penguin Random House LLC.

Library of Congress Cataloging-in-Publication Data

Names: Bradford, David L., author. | Robin, Carole, author.
Title: Connect / David Bradford, Ph.D., and Carole Robin, Ph.D.
Description: New York : Currency, [2021] | Includes index.
Identifiers: LCCN 2020025313 (print) | LCCN 2020025314 (ebook) |
ISBN 9780593237090 (hardcover) | ISBN 9780593237106 (ebook)
Subjects: LCSH: Interpersonal relations. | Interpersonal communication.
Classification: LCC HM1106 .B735 2021 (print) | LCC HM1106 (ebook) |
DDC 302—dc23
LC record available at https://lccn.loc.gov/2020025313
LC ebook record available at https://lccn.loc.gov/2020025314

Printed in the United States of America on acid-free paper

crownpublishing.com

9 8 7 6 5

Figures by Mapping Specialists, Ltd., Fitchburg, WI

To Eva and Andy—

our heroic spouses who love and accept us

for who we are and whose patience and support

sustained us throughout this journey

CONTENTS

CONNECT

1

SEEKING EXCEPTIONAL

This book is about a special type of relationship we call *exceptional*. You may have one or two exceptional relationships already—maybe even more. In these relationships, you feel seen, known, and appreciated for who you really are, not an edited version of yourself. Your hundreds of Instagram friends might know what you ordered for dinner at that fancy restaurant last week, but the person you have an exceptional relationship with knows that you've actually been struggling with food issues for years, or that this was the dinner when you and your partner talked about starting a family, or that the impetus for the evening was to discuss the pros and cons of leaving your job. Those subjects are off-limits to the friend you haven't seen since high school who follows your feed. They rarely come up with the person you carpool with. They are not germane to the aunt you check in on every so often. But someone you're in an exceptional relationship with knows what's really going on for you because that someone really knows *you*.

Relationships exist on a continuum. At one end you experience contact without real connection, while at the other end you feel known, supported, affirmed, and fully accepted. In the middle of the continuum, you feel attached to people in your life, but with many, you want closer connection. The question is, *How?* How do you move along this continuum? We have dedicated our lives to answering this question for thousands of students and clients, and now, for you.

Exceptional relationships *can* be developed. They have six hallmarks:

1. You can be more fully yourself, and so can the other person.
2. Both of you are willing to be vulnerable.
3. You trust that self-disclosures will not be used against you.
4. You can be honest with each other.
5. You deal with conflict productively.
6. Both of you are committed to each other's growth and development.

Let's unpack these a bit.

THE FIRST THREE center around self-disclosure. Why are we still talking about this, when many would say we've become a culture of oversharers? Because there is a difference between a presented image and sharing who you really are. Oscar Wilde, among others, wryly commented, "Be yourself, everybody else is taken." Too often, we edit what we disclose out of fear of being poorly judged.

Social media has created a world where we're pressured to spin everything into a positive. Your Facebook posts might show you smiling in front of the Eiffel Tower, but in reality, the trip was a disaster. Silicon Valley CEOs we know talk about the incessant need to describe everything in terms of how much they are "crushing it," but fatigue, fear, and burnout are very real in the Valley. It's exhausting to keep up these false fronts. Editing and spinning who you are not only costs you your ability to be authentic but leads others to create their own spin. We're not suggesting you have to reveal everything to one single person. But you do have to share the parts of yourself that are important to that specific relationship. And what you share needs to be the real, wholly authentic you, not one obscured by a smiling vacation picture or cheery holiday greetings.

The last three hallmarks have to do with feedback and conflict. Challenging someone can actually be a powerful way of supporting them, and yet few people feel confident they can do it well. Someone with whom you have an exceptional relationship calls you on behaviors that really bother them, and when they do, you know it's a chance for learning, not something against which you have to put up your guard. They know that in helping you understand the impact of your behavior, they are showing commitment to your relationship *and* helping you grow.

Fights happen, even in the best of relationships (as you'll see, the two of us are proof of that!). But a fear of conflict can lead you to bury irritants that, if raised and successfully dealt with, could actually deepen the relationship. Conflicts left unspoken can still cause harm. In an exceptional relationship, it's easier to raise and resolve issues so that they don't lurk and result in long-term damage. You see such challenges as opportunities to learn, which decreases the chance that these same difficulties will appear again.

WE HAVE SPENT our careers showing people what it takes to build and maintain strong, functional, and robust relationships in both personal and professional settings. We invite you to join the thousands of students and clients who have learned that, and more, from us. Our passion comes from results we've observed in our coaching, teaching, and consulting careers. We don't just study and teach the concepts in this book—we *live* them. Sometimes imperfectly;

David's wife of over fifty-five years has told him, "You teach this stuff—why aren't you doing it!" Carole's husband, Andy, has expressed similar sentiments to her. But we have always sought to live what we teach, and it has shaped our lives for the better.

Even so, we almost lost our exceptional relationship with each other. There was something that David did (or, more accurately, didn't do) that caused Carole to get to the point where she wanted to write him off and have nothing more to do with him. We'll go into the details in chapter 17, but the critical point is that even though we were at the brink of a total collapse of our relationship, we were able to come back and repair it. This allowed us to write this book together and, in the process, to develop an even more exceptional relationship. We are living proof that mistakes and misunderstandings happen, and repair and recovery are possible.

The two of us are teachers but will be the first to tell you that some lessons have to be experienced; that's why the focus of this book is on application. We worked in the business school of one of the world's most prestigious universities, but what we have to say has even more relevance outside the business sphere. And while the course we devoted decades of our lives to, Interpersonal Dynamics, is affectionately called "Touchy-Feely," there's nothing squishy about it. Soft skills require a lot of hard work.

The conceptual material in this book is based on social science research, especially interpersonal psychology, as well as decades of our own experience. David came to Stanford University's Graduate School of Business over fifty years ago to develop the Interpersonal Dynamics course and today is known as the "Father of Touchy-Feely." Carole joined twenty years ago, became known as the "Queen of Touchy-Feely," and helped expand the program, doubling its size.

Touchy-Feely remains, far and away, the most famous and popular course offered in the MBA program. Over 85 percent of students enroll, and they often have to place it high on their class ranking to get in. Students frequently report the experience as "transformational," and alumni regularly say that it was the most impactful course they took and one that they continue to use in their personal and professional lives. Lifelong friendships and even marriages have been forged among the students. It's been written about in bestselling books like *Creative Confidence* by David Kelley, featured on the *Today* show, written about in *The New York Times,* and featured in *The Wall Street Journal*—all of which noted the importance of these skills in today's organizational life.

As students quickly learn, just because the class is affectionately known as "Touchy-Feely" that does not mean it is easy. When they sign up for the course, they are placed in a twelve-person group known as a T-group, which meets for about sixty hours over the ten-week term. The "T" in T-group stands for "training," not "therapy," and its purpose is to provide a learning laboratory in which students can practice class concepts—such as the importance of self-disclosure, how to give and receive feedback, how to connect across differences, and how to influence one another—by interacting with one another and learning from the reactions of their peers. We firmly believe that the best way to learn to be more interpersonally effective is to engage with others in real situations and in real time rather than through lectures, readings, case studies, or, yes, even a book. While *Connect* covers everything that we teach during class, you will need to use the relationships in your life as your laboratory to get the maximum benefit. Throughout the book, we provide specific suggestions to show you how.

For students who are used to crunching numbers and muddling through problem sets, it can be initially jarring to sit in a group exploring who feels more connected to whom and why. But over the years, countless students who didn't initially grasp what all the hype was about have left the class as true believers. (And no, it's not a cult!) The class's impact doesn't come from brilliant comments from the faculty, as good as we might be. Our function is simply to build conditions in which students learn how the way they behave impacts others—and what that might mean to their success as future leaders.

Experts have come to recognize that interpersonal / soft skills are fundamental to professional success. A central belief we hold is that people do business with people, not just with ideas, machines, strategies, or even money. Touchy-Feely provides the best opportunity to develop the soft skills that have become crucial to leadership success, such as connecting, building trust, and gaining influence. But students gain something even more profound, best captured by what one student said years ago: "I knew if I went to any top business school, I would learn how to be a better manager and leader. But I also believed if I came to Stanford, because of this class in particular, I would become a better human being—and that would in turn make me much more than a good leader."

Whether at reunions or in all the emails we have received over the years, we hear, "This course saved my career / marriage ten years later." "I use what I learned in Touchy-Feely at work almost every day." "I know I am a better parent, spouse, and son / daughter, not to mention work colleague, as a result of this course." A recent participant from an executive program said, "Surprisingly, this program didn't explicitly focus on improving my leadership. It mostly taught me how to be a better person . . . and as a side effect, I'm a more effective leader, with improved self-awareness, compassion, vulnerability, and communication."

Mastering these soft skills takes hard work, but they can be learned by anyone. That's why it's not just MBA students who benefit from the principles of Touchy-Feely, nor is it just a California woo-woo phenomenon. Similar groups with much more diverse participants have been conducted around the world—in Europe, Africa, the Middle East, Asia, and Latin America—with similar outcomes.

Beyond our academic experience, we have both been consultants and executive coaches in hundreds of for-profit and nonprofit organizations in many countries, in multiple industries, and for companies ranging in size from Fortune 100s to startups. We jointly developed a very successful one-week executive version of the course for Stanford that senior managers from around the world attend. Carole now applies the same principles and process to developing Silicon Valley CEO/founders and investors.

One of the most striking observations we've had over the years is that deep, fulfilling, personal connections can happen with a wider range of people than we normally think possible. We can develop an exceptional relationship with someone whom we seem, outwardly, to have little in common with. We've seen it happen, again and again, in both personal and professional settings. What it takes are the skills to move beyond surface conversations. These don't necessarily require a lot of time, but they do require a commitment to truly learn about ourselves and about the other.

You won't develop them with everybody. That isn't possible, because these deep connections require a great deal of effort. What's more, it's not necessary. You probably have a range of people in your life, like tennis partners, people you go to movies and concerts with, or those you have over for dinner occasionally. You may have colleagues who offer great professional collaboration but who are not your closest friends. These relationships provide partnership, social interaction, intellectual stimulation, professional validation, and fun. They're less intense, and that's perfectly fine. What's more, you need them. Not every dessert can be chocolate soufflé, and not every interaction has to be with someone who knows you deeply.

Still, let's say you have some relationships in your life that you know could be stronger. You're not sure they'll ever reach "exceptional," but you know there's room for growth. Perhaps you'd like to learn how to go from casual to a bit more personal, from detached to somewhat more connected, from dysfunctional to functional, or from competitive to collaborative. Or perhaps you already have some relationships that feel special and deep but that you sense could be even richer. The concepts in this book can help you move forward anywhere along the continuum.

We aren't promising you the "five easy steps to deep connections" because such steps don't exist. One size does not fit all. What works for you might not work for someone else, and something that helps grow one relationship might fall flat in another. Exceptional is also not an end state, because relationships can always grow deeper. Instead, think of exceptional relationships as living, breathing organisms that are always changing, always in need of tending, and always, *always* capable of taking your breath away.

We're straightforward about the effort required to build more meaningful relationships and just as straightforward about the benefits. We have seen its unequivocally profound impact on friendships, marriages, family systems, and work colleagues. We know that using what we teach results in stronger, happier, deeper relationships with less unnecessary conflict. When you have a sense of safety and honesty with another person, the opportunities for growth are unlimited. When your interactions with another person are at their most authentic, there is a paradigm shift. And in the end, an exceptional relationship is about more than a collection of skills and competencies; it's fundamentally about a different way of being. And therein lies something that feels magical.

2

A WORLD-CLASS COURSE, ONE CHAPTER AT A TIME

We know what Interpersonal Dynamics has delivered to generations of students. We've turned to the skills we teach time and time again when helping others deal with relationship challenges and when dealing with our own. Our students have urged us repeatedly to put the class material in book form so that they can refer back to it or share it with their friends, spouse, or business partners. Beyond that, we have a personal dream of bringing the benefits of this course to many thousands of people beyond Stanford and have long pondered the question of how to make these lessons available more widely.

There are challenges. The course this book is based on relies on close, experiential learning with a small group of students. Each student is committed to being in the same face-to-face group for ten weeks, so even if the going gets tough, there's no quitting. Conflicts work out in the groups as people get to see more nuanced sides of one another. Second, students get assistance from others in the group. If an interaction between two people doesn't go well, others step in and say, "Hey. What's going on here?" or "I'm feeling protective of Gabriel and want to make sure he's doing okay." And third, the class has cultural norms that support learning, including confidentiality and the idea that the only mistake is refusing to learn from our mistakes. The latter reframes problems as learning opportunities.

These three factors certainly don't exist in a book. Yes, we can provide the same concepts, stories, and material covered in our lectures and readings, but we can't provide a group of eleven other peers to support your learning and keep you engaged. And we can't influence the cultural norms of your particular relationships. We like to think of ourselves as a pretty capable duo, but even so, we have our limits. There's also the challenge of helping you convert a conceptual understanding into actual behavior. After all, it's possible to *know* what to do without being able to actually do it. With experiential learning, you try something first and *then* learn about it.

So for this to work, first and foremost, we need your active involvement. In our classes, we say that those who sit back and observe will gain the least, while those who roll up their sleeves and really engage with one another will learn the most. In this book, we have created five scenarios that run throughout, each featuring two people at an inflection point in their relationship. The pairs we feature cover a wide gamut—from a daughter trying to change a decades-old way of relating with her father, to a married couple weighing their shared responsibilities against their individual needs, to work colleagues whose relationship is deepened and tested over time. All cases are an amalgamation of real relationships we have had or seen, and we ask that rather than reading the book passively, you work to imagine yourself in each situation.

In reading of their travails and putting yourself in their places, reflect on how you would feel and act. What does that say about what you do well and how you might limit yourself? Are there some competencies you need to develop? Then, when we describe ways that these situations could be handled, assess how easy that would be for you and what would be challenging. Explore what insights you can gain about yourself from your reactions. Taking an active stance will help you personalize the material.

Second, put what you're learning into practice. Each chapter ends with self-reflection questions and suggestions for ways to apply your learning. Take the time you need between chapters to use these lessons, just as our students do between classes. Putting this material to work is not simple. You'll notice that in lieu of solid answers, we often give you options, because the specific solutions depend on you—on the sort of outcome you want, on your abilities, and on the risks you're willing to take.

Since relationships are co-determined, the right course of action also depends on the other person: What do they want? What can they handle? What's the context for the relationship? Instead of being constraining, this kind of flexibility is liberating. Though there's no guarantee you'll always succeed in getting the connections you want, you can learn from trying. In fact, if we had our druthers, you would read a single chapter, apply its lessons to your life, and then read the chapter again.

Third, fine-tune two crucial personal "antennae." One of these needs to look outward, and the other needs to focus inward. If you only have the latter, you can't understand the other person, and if only the former, you lose yourself. In listening to both, you are more likely to act in ways that best fit the situation and your collective needs. Keeping those antennae highly tuned will help you see every interaction with another person as an opportunity to learn. A friend of ours has suggested the Stanford course should actually be called Interpersonal Mindfulness, because in order to engage with another in the ways we describe throughout the book, you have to become acutely aware of what's going on for you as well as for the other.

No, we're not grading you. But stick with it anyway.

The Arc of Relationships—and of This Book

All relationships vary, but most develop in a similar pattern. They often start with a common interest, like music or hiking. At other times, people might have complementary interests—one likes to make plans and initiate activities, while the other finds it a chore. In this process, the two must learn how to relate to and influence each other. To what extent can the second person say no to plans the first suggests? To what extent can the first state when they are feeling used and push some of the scheduling responsibility onto the second?

This might be as far as you go with some people, and that's perfectly fine. For example, let's say you and a buddy both like basketball and have built an easy friendship, and that's enough of a bond for an enjoyable game every other weekend. Usually you talk about movies and current events (with certain contentious topics avoided), and that's satisfying to you both. In this relationship, neither of you feels the need to discuss your deepest worries or biggest dreams. As we said in chapter 1, not every friendship needs to be the equivalent of chocolate soufflé.

However, there are relationships that you want to take deeper. You move past these initial stages of getting to know each other and begin to communicate more openly and personally. As you do, mutual knowledge and understanding grow and you find more areas in which to connect. As trust builds, you're each increasingly willing to take risks about what you disclose, becoming even more vulnerable. The cycle continues and is reinforced, and the relationship develops. This deeper relationship allows you to discuss issues like difficulties at work or conflicts with your teenager that you wouldn't raise with a more casual friend.

As you become more important to each other, the relationship also becomes increasingly complex. Obligations and expectations build, as do potential points of contention. How will you deal with inevitable annoyances? If you can face and resolve them well, the relationship becomes even stronger. That in turn encourages each of you to surface what you want from the other and what's getting in the way. Openness and honesty grow. As the healthy relationship develops, you avoid power imbalances, so that you each get roughly the same amount of satisfaction.

As you negotiate your evolving relationship, you each learn how to influence the other. You build interdependence that makes it easy to ask for help when you need it and to turn it down when it's not useful. Challenges and conflict don't go away, but you know how to deal with them. When a relationship reaches this stage, each person can be of great support to the other. You can discuss issues openly, give and receive feedback, and grow as a result.

However, if the relationship is to progress even further, you have to significantly increase your level of disclosure and risk-taking. There is even greater risk since you both now have skin in the game. Sometimes the relationship deepens and reaches exceptional almost seamlessly, through years of joyful shared experiences, layered disclosures, and ever-increasing trust. But in most cases, one or more critical issues transform it. Let's suppose a major conflict emerges with the potential to tear the fabric of the relationship. You might decide it's better to let sleeping dogs lie and avoid the issue altogether. The relationship survives but plateaus. Facing the issue tests the relationship and might end it. But fully resolving the conflict strengthens the connection—you are moving toward exceptional territory.

Deep relationships take time—there is no instant intimacy. You can influence the speed and direction of a relationship's trajectory—and we'll show you some ways to do just that. But it takes two to tango, and so what develops in a relationship will also depend on the other person, including their willingness and ability to take these steps toward growth. You may be able to influence that, but you can't control it. The arc of development also isn't necessarily linear. A relationship may stay where it is for a while or even regress and then start growing again.

This book is structured to follow the rough arc of deepening relationships and is divided into two parts. In part I, we examine the six hallmarks of exceptional relationships described in the first chapter. These concepts are key to *all* functional, robust relationships, whether they end up becoming exceptional or not. We talk about how to be more fully yourself and how to help others do the same. We cover the question of balance in a relationship and mutual influence. We examine how to deal with minor annoyances and more significant disagreements, and we ask what gets in the way of offering and hearing feedback. We explore the knotty question of whether people can change, and we look at the role curiosity plays in resolving conflicts.

In part II, we look at how relationships transition from very good to exceptional. What does it take to successfully resolve a major conflict and, in the process, deepen the connection? How do you set boundaries while still remaining close? We also look at the issue of entanglement, which can happen when personal issues for one person trigger pain for another. While not all relationships need to be tested to become exceptional, we've found that it's often in the testing stage that bonds become deeper and individuals become more skilled at forging and maintaining them.

When a relationship doesn't reach exceptional status, that doesn't mean you've failed, and it doesn't mean the relationship will never be exceptional. How to handle this tricky territory is the subject of chapter 16. And finally, the last chapter of the book discusses how our own relationship faced a crisis that almost ended it and how we pulled all of the learning in this book together to not only salvage what we had but deepen it. It was scary, and it is humbling to admit that even we who teach this stuff could so thoroughly screw up.

A Learning Mindset

Reportedly, as the French Impressionist painter Auguste Renoir lay dying at seventy-eight, his last words were, "I think I'm beginning to learn something about it." What a wonderful, open, exploratory mind. We have our own, saltier take on the same idea. Whenever we face challenges, we think, "Well, that's an AFOG"—which is short for "another f**king opportunity for growth."

We cannot stress enough how important such a learning mindset is, whether you go with Renoir's words or with ours. You can't significantly develop a relationship (and certainly can't reach exceptional) unless you're open to learning. This mindset isn't limited to new skills and competencies but also applies to a willingness to look within. In the 1970s there was a cartoon character, Pogo, who said, "We have met the enemy and he is us." It's easy to blame another when things go wrong, but it's necessary to also be willing to reflect on whether part of the enemy "is us."

A learning mindset has several characteristics. One is a willingness to let go of the idea that your way of doing things is always best. Another is being game to try new things and take the risk of making mistakes. And a third is seeing mistakes as learning opportunities rather than something to be embarrassed about and hide. Curiosity is key. Thinking, *I wonder why this isn't working,* is much more productive than blaming another person when something goes awry.

Having an open mind for continuous learning is a wonderful way to live. It means you're open to your own development, which includes acquiring the skills and competencies this book describes, reflecting on assumptions you hold that might limit you, and reconsidering behaviors that aren't serving you well. As Alan Alda said, "Your assumptions are your windows on the world. Scrub them off, every once in a while, or the light won't come in." Some changes might be relatively easy to make, and some might be very challenging, but it's all part of the magic of relationships.

When the going gets tough, there's a temptation to say, "I can't. That's not me." True, that may not be you *now,* but can it *never* be you? Perhaps it's not you *yet,* as described by psychologist Carol Dweck's work on growth mindsets. None of the skills and competencies we suggest are so esoteric that they can't be acquired. We say that with certainty because we have seen so many participants in the Interpersonal Dynamics course make the "I can't" disclaimer, only to learn the competencies by the end of the term. In every case, their mindset had to first shift from "I can't" to "I see I have a choice, even though it's hard." And while it is legitimate for different people to make different choices, we must all acknowledge we've made a choice.

This is hard work, no doubt. But it's worth it. Good luck, and may you make many rich learning mistakes.

Introduction to Deepen Your Learning

To make the material in this book personally relevant, your first task is to select four or five relationships—with family, friends, or work colleagues—that you would like to significantly deepen. At the end of each chapter you will find a recurring "Self-Reflection" section in which we ask you to consider how the chapter content relates to those relationships. Regardless of what category of relationship you choose, keep in mind that the lessons learned in each chapter apply across all of them. In the recurring "Application" sections, we suggest ways to apply the material toward making those relationships stronger.

We encourage you to share your goals with the people you have chosen so that they have some context and understand why you will be asking them for help. You may want to stress that you see this as an opportunity to make the relationship you already value even stronger rather than only a learning opportunity for *you*. Hopefully, they will join you in your learning journey.

The third recurring section, "Making Sense," asks you to reflect on what you learned from "doing." Experiences have the most value when you try to make sense out of them. We'll ask you, as we ask our students, What was it like *applying* the concepts to a key relationship? What did you learn about yourself and about building stronger connections?

SELF-REFLECTION

The first chapter listed the following six characteristics of an exceptional relationship:

1. You can be more fully yourself, and so can the other person.

2. Both of you are willing to be vulnerable.

3. You trust that self-disclosures will not be used against you.

4. You can be honest with each other.

5. You deal with conflict productively.

6. Both of you are committed to each other's growth and development.

Take each of the key relationships that you have selected. For each one:

- Which one(s) of these six characteristics is strongest?
- Which one(s) of these six would you most want to improve on?
- What is it about what *you* (not the other person) do—or don't do—that contributes to the limitations you identified?

APPLICATION

Take one of the people you selected and initiate a conversation about what you would like from the relationship. Share your assessment from the self-reflection exercise above (including what you think you do and don't do), and find out whether they assess you, themselves, and the situation the same way.

MAKING SENSE

How did it go? What did you learn about yourself and about how you raise issues? How receptive were you to the other person's comments?

In this chapter, we covered some of the ways we block our learning. Did any of those limitations come up for you? What did you learn about the *process* of building stronger relationships?

NOTE: You might want to consider keeping a journal of what you learn from the "Deepen Your Learning" activities throughout the book. You will be returning to these relationships in subsequent chapters, and it will be interesting to see how they develop. Our students are required to keep a journal throughout the course, and while many of them hate it at the time, most thank us afterward!

PART I

GETTING TO THE MEADOW

CLIMBING THE MOUNTAIN

AS A TEENAGER and into his twenties, David spent summer vacations near the White Mountains in northern New Hampshire and would frequently climb Mount Washington, in the Presidential Range. Its multiple trails made it his favorite destination, but it's also a dangerous mountain. Although not the hardest ascent in North America, it holds the record for the most fatalities, as its sudden climate changes in the middle of the summer leave many weekend climbers unprepared. It might be a beautiful, warm, clear day, but in a matter of minutes clouds can sweep in, suddenly dropping the temperature and making it difficult to see the next trail marker. David would never climb alone, partially because he liked having company but also because he never knew when he might need help.

Climbing Mount Washington with a partner is akin to building an exceptional relationship. Relationships begin on an easy, well-worn trail of light conversation. Soon the climb becomes a bit more challenging, and you begin to have options. The trail splits and you disagree about which fork to take, a disagreement that requires resolution. Then you're at the difficult, steep headwall, and the choices multiply. How much should you offer to help your partner? Will they welcome the offer or be insulted? What if you want to take a break but your partner doesn't?

It's exhilarating as you climb together over the headwall. A beautiful meadow lies before you with summer flowers. You lay your knapsacks down so you can rest and take in what you have accomplished. You could decide to just stay there and enjoy each other's company. The boulders look bigger ahead, the climb more demanding.

All five pairs we'll meet in the next ten chapters of the book arrive at the meadow, each in their own way. What they achieve is huge—they find their way to more robust and meaningful relationships, and as individuals, they have learned and grown. All relationships have to get here first, before they have any hope of reaching the summit of becoming exceptional. Some will remain at the meadow, and some will go on. But make no mistake—even getting to the meadow will be challenging, though rewarding.

3

TO SHARE, OR NOT TO SHARE

Elena and Sanjay—Work Colleagues, Parts 1 and 2

Most of us have countless interactions each day with people who don't really know us well. You say hi and exchange pleasantries with your local grocer. Your neighbor may know how many children you have and where you work, maybe even where you last vacationed, but not much else. You have friends with whom you periodically have dinner, and they know you better, but there are still vast aspects of your life they don't know. At times, you may yearn for deeper and more meaningful connections, but you don't always know how to get there.

Letting yourself be more fully known is crucial to developing exceptional relationships. Self-disclosure creates more opportunities to connect and increases trust. It is also enormously validating to be accepted for who you *really* are. That said, it's not risk-free.

Carole once led a retreat with a dozen Silicon Valley executives where she felt flat and disconnected. She was distracted by outside important events going on for her and was finding it hard to concentrate. Not only were these significant clients, but as the "teacher" she felt especially vulnerable. What if it didn't go well? How would she be seen? What would happen if she admitted what was going on for her? Rather than trying to fake it, which she might have done earlier in her career, she decided to live what she teaches and disclose all that she was feeling—including the fact that she felt vulnerable sharing these feelings. The moment she opened up, she felt more connected. Some executives thanked her for breaking the ice and said they were also feeling flat and disconnected.

In this chapter, we cover what it takes to be really known by someone else, which isn't as simple as it may seem. What happens if you're authentic and open but then misunderstood? Or what if your openness overwhelms the other person? What role do emotions play in self-disclosure? What are you willing to risk in order to be better known?

Elena and Sanjay, Part 1

Elena felt conflicted as she left her desk to meet her colleague Sanjay for lunch. She'd had an issue with a co-worker in the morning—the co-worker had tried to push something back onto Elena's plate that he'd agreed to do weeks before. Elena had held her ground, and the co-worker had gotten upset and snapped at her. She wanted to get Sanjay's take on it, but she worried that he might think that she hadn't handled the situation well, or that she was overreacting.

Even though they worked in different departments, Elena and Sanjay had gotten to know each other when they were each assigned to the tech review task force a year before. Elena loved working with Sanjay, whom she found to be a creative problem-solver and generous team member. They were able both to build on each other's ideas and to disagree in productive ways.

After the task force's work had ended, they'd started having lunch together periodically so they could catch up. They were both avid outdoors people and would compare notes on gear deals and the best camping spots. Sanjay enjoyed camping with his family, and Elena was an avid white-water kayaker.

Elena really valued her friendship with Sanjay. She had a lot of friends outside of work, but she couldn't "talk shop" with them, and they couldn't grasp all of the nuances of her workplace. In her last position, she'd stumbled—and lost her job—because she'd been direct and open about her opinions, which didn't fit the company culture. In her new position, she wanted to find somebody she trusted for advice, someone who knew the ins and outs of how things got done. She thought Sanjay might be that person.

But what if Sanjay took any overtures the wrong way? They were both married, and all she wanted was a friendship. Also, what would happen if she told Sanjay what had occurred at her old company, some of which she wasn't proud of? She decided she'd better be careful.

They got their food at the cafeteria line and found an empty table. "How's your week going?" Sanjay asked.

"Well, the usual ups and downs," Elena said, still unsure what to share.

Sanjay didn't pick up on her statement and instead, with much enthusiasm, talked about his weekend camping trip. "You were right about that campsite—it's amazing," he said. "But I want to go back when I'm not chasing a toddler around the whole time."

Elena thought perhaps it was a good thing she hadn't told Sanjay about her morning conflict. He hadn't picked up her cue or pressed for more information. Elena also felt a twinge of envy about Sanjay's weekend with his kids, because she'd been trying to get pregnant. She decided against disclosing that, since it felt far too personal. Instead, she offered more tips about other campsites.

When the conversation shifted to company issues, Elena decided to go for it and share a few details about her morning. "As much as I enjoy working here," she said after she'd given him a summary of the morning's incident with her co-worker, "moments like that make me a bit crazy."

Sanjay listened intently. "I've had that happen to me, too, and it drives me up a wall," he said. "In fact, it happened with one of my direct reports just yesterday." He shared a few further details, and Elena felt relieved and a bit closer to him.

She considered asking his advice about how to deal with her

somewhat difficult boss but decided against it for fear it would lead her inadvertently to disclose her past experience of having been fired. She felt relieved when the conversation shifted to their reactions to a recent announcement from the CEO. As Sanjay and Elena got up to bus their dishes, they each said how much they'd enjoyed the lunch.

ELENA PLAYED IT pretty safe, which we get. Every time you disclose something personal, you risk being misunderstood; the fear that the disclosure will result in judgment or rejection is very real. We all filter information through our own past experiences, some of which can be so significant they distort how we respond in the present. For instance, we consulted for a Fortune 500 company where a senior VP would rarely speak up in meetings. Turns out, several years before, he had been summarily fired after taking a firm stance on an issue. He'd been rehired the next day, but he felt so burnt that he never disagreed or offered a strong opinion again. Others are impacted by judgmental statements by parents ("You are a lazy person") that they hold on to for years, causing them to be extremely sensitive to any comment that might reinforce that judgment.

Fear of disclosure can pop up anywhere along the arc of a relationship, because you share more as a relationship grows. However, the fear is particularly acute early on. When the other person doesn't know you well, they don't have the context with which to understand the full meaning of your actions. Will they read more into what you've said or done than what's there? Even worse, will they get locked into an opinion about you, or a judgment, and not take in any new disconfirming information? There's an old adage: "To know all is to forgive all." If someone knew all the circumstances that led you to behave a certain way, they would be more likely to forgive what might initially seem egregious. But it's not necessarily so simple. You can't share everything about yourself at once or too early in the process of becoming known.

For example, in the third week of an Interpersonal Dynamics class David taught, he was still building a connection with the students. The topic that day was the importance of getting help from others. He wanted to model more openness and shared the value he found in therapy. One student responded, "I respect you less because I see that as a sign of weakness; I think people should solve their own problems."

In a similar vein, Carole once mentioned to a client that Judaism provided her with a "user's manual for life." He was taken aback and said, "I can't believe a person as intelligent as you would fall for that religious BS. It makes me question whether you can be as helpful to me as I thought."

In both situations where our disclosures created bumps, we initially felt defensive and misunderstood, but our greater concern was that they would limit our effectiveness. Would the student stop listening to David and maybe get less out of the course? Would the client be resistant to Carole's coaching? Fortunately, neither of those concerns came true, because there was continued contact in the class and in the coaching engagement. Both the student and the client grew to know us more fully, overriding their initial skepticism. But not all situations allow the luxury of continued contact and a chance to adjust early impressions.

We also had the benefit of knowing how our student and client had reacted to our statements (as disconcerting as those reactions were) because they told us. That's often not the case. Particularly early on in a relationship, you may not know how the other's reacting. They're unlikely to say, "What you just said really bothered me." Generally, all you have to go on is body language or tone, which can be ambiguous. Their furrowed brow could be a sign of disapproval—or maybe they're just unhappy about something in their life and their reaction has nothing to do with you.

The point is, it's a risk. But there's also risk in playing your cards too close to your vest; unfortunately, the closer I hold my cards, the closer you are likely to hold yours. You can't get to deeper relationships without disclosure.

So how much should you disclose? And when? There are no definitive answers to those questions, but in our experience, people are generally too cautious—they could be sharing more, sooner than they think.

The 15 Percent Rule

Consciously or unconsciously, you're always assessing what's appropriate to share in any given interaction. Those decisions are highly dependent on the context, how you feel about risk, and, especially, the state of the relationship.

Elena's decision *not* to share the circumstances under which she was fired or her difficulties in getting pregnant made sense, given the situation. If Elena had mentioned her firing to Sanjay, he could potentially have judged her negatively, not knowing the specifics of the situation and not knowing her that well. Similarly, Sanjay might have felt uncomfortable if she'd shared her fertility fears, as that is quite personal territory. However, Elena played it *very* safe by talking about camping and the CEO's announcement—there was little personal disclosure in that. Yes, she dipped her toe in the water by mentioning a disagreement with a co-worker, but she didn't press it very far. Their lunch conversation, although friendly, probably didn't significantly help to build the sort of relationship she wanted. Discretion may be the better part of valor, but most people err, like Elena, on the side of caution, causing the relationship to stagnate.

How to address this dilemma? One way is what we suggest to students: "Try the 15 Percent Rule." Consider three concentric rings that represent decreasing safety as you move out from the center. The smallest ring, in the middle, is the *Zone of Comfort*. This refers to what you say or do that you don't think twice about and with which you feel completely safe. The outermost ring is the *Zone of Danger*—things you wouldn't consider doing or saying given the high likelihood that the outcome would be negative. The ring between "Comfort" and "Danger" is known as the *Zone of Learning* and is where you are unsure about how another will respond. That is typically the zone in which people learn. In response to students' concerns about venturing into Learning at the risk of unintentionally ending up in Danger, we suggest testing the waters by stretching into the zone of learning by 15 percent as shown below. The downside of this moderate approach is not likely to be disastrous and, if the interaction is successful, can help you be further known. With that success, you can then consider venturing out another 15 percent from there.

The 15 Percent Rule is not an absolute; its value is in helping you consider possible choices. Imagine you're with a friend and wonder how that person feels about you. You can stay within your comfort zone by saying something relatively safe, like, "Sometimes I worry about what others think of me." Somewhat riskier and 15 percent outside your comfort zone might be, "I made a comment about our mutual friend Michael last week and have been worrying about how you felt about me ever since."

Going outside your comfort zone is fundamental to learning. For example, when you first begin to ski, you start on a "bunny slope," not a double black diamond. Once you've mastered the bunny slope, you can't become a better skier unless you move to a more challenging run (15 percent). At the top of that new run, you might feel afraid or exhilarated—or maybe both at once. But after you spend enough time there, you'll find your comfort zone has expanded, and you are ready to move to the next harder run (the next 15 percent), and so on. Sure, if you want to avoid that feeling of fear, you could stick to the bunny slope. But that won't make you a better skier. The same process of continuously stretching yourself is key to building relationships and serves as the basis for continuous disclosure.

So what could 15 percent have looked like for Elena? She didn't have to reveal that she'd been terminated in her previous job (that might have actually been an example of stepping into the danger zone), but she could have talked about what she found unpleasant about her previous company. Instead of just describing her co-worker's annoying behavior that morning, she could have asked Sanjay how he would have handled that situation. Or she could have taken more of a risk and shared that sometimes she fears she's too rigid. It's unlikely there would have been disastrous consequences from any of these disclosures, and they might have moved the relationship beyond just discussing camping.

There are a few important caveats to the 15 Percent Rule. First, it's subjective: a 15 percent move for me might seem low risk for you and extreme for a third person. Talking about therapy might be in your 15 percent zone if you're thirty-five years old and live in New York but well outside your 15 percent zone if you're a fifty-five-year-old in rural England. Second, you have to take into account the impact of your disclosures on the other person. For example, you wouldn't want to share a detailed argument you had with your mother with someone who had just lost her own. And third, you have to gauge the situational appropriateness. What might work in a one-to-one conversation might not at a larger dinner party.

What Emotions Have to Do with It

Sharing facts starts to build a larger picture of who we are but only goes so far. What tends to have more impact is sharing feelings. The important distinction is between cognitions (thoughts), which tell *what is,* and emotions (feelings), which tell *how important it is*. (Even though they are not exactly the same, for simplicity we use "feelings" and "emotions" interchangeably in this book.) Two people who experience the same event can have very different emotional reactions. They both might have been fired from their job, yet one is devastated, while the other feels challenged.

The other benefit of emotions is that they actually give meaning to facts. Elena could find kayaking exhilarating or frightening. It can be empowering because she initiated the adventure or disempowering because her friends coerced her into doing it. The objective event carries totally different information depending on the emotions attached to it.

Feelings also can indicate the intensity of an experience. In reacting to another's behavior, you could be slightly *bothered, annoyed, upset, angry,* or *furious.* These different degrees are crucial in human interaction; they illustrate a lot about who you are. Emotions provide color, drawing others to us in a way that being utterly unemotional and rational does not.

Think of it as music. What makes an opera piece rich is the variety of tones, ranging from high sopranos to deep baritones. In the same way that a great musical score requires both high treble and lower bass notes, to communicate well we must express thoughts/cognitions *and* feelings/emotions.

What would Sanjay and Elena's interaction have been like if she had expressed emotions in addition to thoughts? Elena had roughly twelve different feelings in the moderate-to-strong range over the course of this lunch, yet she expressed none of them.

THOUGHTS/COGNITION	FEELINGS ELENA HAD
Elena's sharing perceptions of the company	*Connection with Sanjay, reassurance that she wasn't alone in her feelings*
Elena's not sharing being fired	*Concern/apprehension about how Sanjay might judge her*
Elena's difficulty in getting pregnant	*Sadness because she doesn't have a child of her own, envy at Sanjay's having a child, fear of sharing any of this as being too personal*
Elena's disagreement with her colleague	*Worry about how Sanjay might see her, relief at how he responded, closeness to Sanjay because of that*
Discussion of the CEO's memo	*Relief that the conversation shifted away from her*
Sanjay's saying he enjoyed the lunch	*Happiness that Sanjay also liked the lunch, anticipation about their next meeting*

This is *not* to argue that Elena should have shared every one of these emotions. The 15 Percent Rule applies to emotions, too; it would probably be too far to go, for instance, for her to express her sadness, envy, and fear over her difficulty conceiving. But there were plenty of other options to choose from and ways to stretch herself if she wanted to be closer to Sanjay. What might have happened if Elena had expressed some of her feelings?

After Elena told Sanjay about her morning conflict and he disclosed similar interactions, she felt increasingly at ease. Let's revisit their conversation and imagine that Elena expressed her feelings, telling Sanjay:

"I'm feeling *reassured* by our conversation. I thought I was the only one who felt this way. I really *appreciate* your openness and it puts me more *at ease*."

Sanjay smiled at her and said, "Great! Glad to hear that."

Elena had also been thinking about how much better this company was than her old one, but disclosing that she had been terminated was beyond her 15 percent comfort zone. To verbalize her emotions, she could have said:

"Aside from the stuff that bugs us, Sanjay, I'm really *enjoying* working here. It's so different from where I worked before, which was toxic, and I sometimes felt scared to speak up. And it didn't turn out well."

In saying this, Elena stepped outside her comfort zone. The conversation might now unfold in a number of different ways:

a. Sanjay says, "That's too bad," and changes the subject. Elena has a choice whether to proceed or just drop the topic.
b. Sanjay responds by asking, "What was that like?" Elena starts by saying, "It was really awful and I'm just glad I'm out." She can now assess his response and stop there or continue to make subsequent disclosures.
c. Sanjay expresses a feeling in response, being a bit more personal but within his comfort zone. "That sounds really tough; I'm sorry you had to go through that." Elena is now at another decision point and has many options. She can take a breath, take a 15 percent higher risk, and reveal what happened in the past. Or she can decide that's enough and say, "I don't need to go into more of the details right now, but I can't tell you how much I appreciate your empathy."

To give another example, when Sanjay talked about his recent camping trip and Elena felt the twinge of envy, she could have said:

"That sounds like fun to me, and I have to admit I'm a little *envious*. My husband, Eric, and I have been hoping to get pregnant, and frankly I can't wait."

This scenario, like the prior one, could unfold in a number of different ways, depending partly on how Sanjay reacts and partly on how much of a risk Elena is willing to take.

Sanjay might be quiet for a moment or change the subject. Again, Elena has choices: She could drop the issue or continue. However, if Sanjay responded with something like "Yeah, my kid is a lot of fun," Elena could share her hopes and expectations. Let's say he stepped outside his comfort zone with some personal statement, such as, "He's both fun and a lot more work than my wife and I ever expected; I sure hope I'm doing right by him." Elena could then increase the reciprocal self-disclosure by talking about the frustrations she and her husband have been feeling, and perhaps disclosing that they're considering seeing a fertility specialist. Eventually, they might even move to a level of comfort in which she might talk about how the issue is even more charged and difficult for her to talk about given that women in the workplace are sometimes put in a "mommy/less ambitious" bucket when they have or want to have children. Sanjay's reaction to that would undoubtedly impact how much more she'd be willing to share. Elena's two antennae, tuned to Sanjay's reactions and her own, can inform her choices.

Why Emotions Get a Bad Rap

If emotions are so valuable, why do we downplay them? In many cultures, logic and rationality hold sway as the coin of the realm. This is true in most education; one doesn't earn an A in math by saying, "I feel better by selecting twenty-three." Likewise, in many work settings, managers say, "Leave feelings out of this"—even though they refer to their own emotions constantly ("I am *annoyed* that this report is late"; "I am *excited* that we were awarded the new contract"; "I am *worried* that we're going to lose this customer").

We also tend to stigmatize "being emotional" and are advised not to "wear our emotions on our sleeves." Men, in particular, are socialized not to display emotion, while women who work in male-dominated environments often feel conflicted about how much emotion to show for fear of being seen as too sensitive and insufficiently tough, or as "dramatic." Fortunately, norms are changing. An important influence was Daniel Goleman's seminal work on emotional intelligence, which showed that being in touch with one's emotions and expressing them appropriately was a key determinant in leadership success. In the past, many men considered it taboo to express emotions, but nowadays, it is more acceptable—and even desirable. Still, many of these stereotypes persist.

Emotions sometimes appear contradictory, which also works against our willingness to share them. You can be *excited* about a conversation and a bit *apprehensive* about where it might lead. You may feel *hurt* by someone's feedback but also *grateful* that they've taken the risk of raising a difficult topic. In those situations, you may go silent as you try to determine what the right feeling is.

For example, imagine that it's Friday, you've had a stressful week, and you're barely holding yourself together. All you want to do is collapse on the couch with a good book. Your significant other greets you at the door and announces plans for an exciting evening out at a special restaurant, followed by dancing. Normally, you would welcome a plan like this, but right now it sounds like torture. However, you're appreciative of your partner's attempt to perk you up.

What do you do? You could suck it up and go along—maybe you would enjoy it, but probably you'd end up feeling frustrated and even more exhausted. You could decline, but that runs the risk of your partner's feeling rejected—and your feeling guilty for spoiling the fun. Neither choice is ideal. But there is an alternative: We call it Hamlet's quandary, "to share, or not to share." Rather than trying to resolve the problem by deciding whether to go along or not, why not just *name the dilemma*? "Honey, I really appreciate what you've planned. It shows me how much you care that I've had a tough week. But I'm so exhausted and don't want to go along just because of your effort. Could we figure out something that would work for both of us?" That opens up a range of possibilities that could meet both parties' needs.

Elena, too, could have shared her dilemma. Instead of shutting down the discussion of her past job, she could have said, "It was something that I might not have handled well. I've been hesitant to share it out of concern about what you'll think of me and worry that it would damage our working relationship." Sharing both sides of the quandary allows a fuller expression of the issues. The other learns more about not only what's important to you but also what is blocking you. Yes, this disclosure increases your vulnerability, but that's the price of potentially deepening the connection.

We have one more important point to make about expressing feelings, and it's all about the language we use to do so. Both of us are fanatical about how the phrase "I feel" is used, because it can be used in two different ways—one useful, and one misleading. It can be used to express an emotion, as in "I feel *upset* by your comment," or it can express a thought/cognition, as in "I feel like you want to dominate this conversation." Because we place such high value on emotions in interpersonal relations, we drive our family and friends crazy by constantly reminding them to use the term "feel" only to express an emotion.

There are two ways to tell whether your "I feel" statement is really expressing an emotion. The first is paying attention to the word that follows "I feel." If that word isn't an adjective describing an emotion (such as "sad" or "angry"), you should be skeptical. If it is "like," "that," or "as," you are unlikely to be describing an emotion. It's grammatically impossible (at least in English) to express a feeling when you say, "I feel that" or "I feel like." We don't say "I feel that angry." Or "I feel like sad." You can also try a simple substitution. If you can replace "feel" or "feel like" with "think" and the sentence still makes sense, then you haven't expressed an emotion. For example, "I feel that you want to dominate" and "I think you want to dominate" convey the same meaning—because both are cognitions, not feelings.

This may seem overly precise, but stick with us, because it's important. Think of the difference between "I feel irritated and dismissed" and "I feel that you don't care." The shift in language might be subtle, but the impact is profound. "I feel that you really don't care about my opinion" contains no feeling words, although it is likely that there are some strong feelings unstated! (Note that you could drop the "I feel that" and the sentence would not change.) "I feel irritated and dismissed" is a statement about me whereas "I feel that you don't care" is an accusation that is likely to cause defensiveness.

A Wealth of Choices

An idea that's central to this book is that in any given situation, you have many choices about how to respond. You may feel limited by the impression you want to make, but you still have a choice. You may be influenced by the other's response—but that, too, is a choice. Even though Elena might be *impacted* by how Sanjay reacts, her responses need not be *determined* by that reaction. Sanjay's responses along the way will make it easier or more challenging for Elena to decide whether to further disclose or not—but it's always ultimately her call.

Social scientists call the belief in our ability to act in the world "having agency." Too often, people think they have no choice in how to respond to what has happened to them. Throughout this book, you'll see a variety of approaches that describe how we have more agency and can be more impactful than we initially think. This is an important mindset because moving to deeper, more meaningful, and exceptional relationships will require challenging choices.

Our emphasis on choices, having influence, and acting with agency is not to imply that you can build an exceptional relationship on your own. Relationships are co-determined. Nevertheless, you can take steps that increase the chance that the other will join you in this journey. Nor does having a choice deny the impact of external factors. Elena and Sanjay, for example, are impacted by conventional business culture norms that discourage friendships at work that are "too personal," particularly if there is the possibility of anything romantic. That said, external factors can also *encourage* us to move outside our comfort zone, as happened with Elena a couple of months later.

Elena and Sanjay, Part 2

Sanjay and Elena continued to meet for lunch, usually every Thursday, and got to know each other better. One Thursday, Elena was especially looking forward to their meeting because she'd had a troubling incident with her boss. She asked if Sanjay would help her think it through, and he said he would be happy to.

"I'm not sure how well you know Rick," she began, "or if you've ever worked with him."

"I don't know him very well at all. Why? What's going on?"

"He gives me assignments that sound like he wants me to look into something," Elena began, "but then he's unhappy when I suggest an approach he doesn't like. A while ago he asked me to research whether we should invest our trade show budget in local, regional, or national shows. I spent a good chunk of time doing the research, including speaking to all the stakeholders. Yesterday, I made the recommendation at our staff meeting and he immediately shot it down, saying it wasn't the recommendation he was looking for. He thanked me tersely and dismissed my analysis. That's just one example, but he's done that several times over the last few months."

"That sounds frustrating. Maybe you could go talk to him and let him know that it's becoming a problem that you want to address before it gets any bigger?"

Elena hesitated. "Yeah, I could . . . but I don't think so."

"Why not?"

"I just don't think it would end well."

Sanjay, wanting to understand more about Elena's resistance, asked, "How do you know? What's holding you back?"

"I'm not sure Rick would be very open, and he might get upset."

Sanjay, being the intuitive guy Elena likes so much, said, "Sounds like there's more to that."

Sanjay, of course, was right. Elena was on the verge of self-disclosure and was scared. She worried that telling Sanjay about what had happened at her last job would change his opinion of her. But she realized that if she was going to have the relationship she really wanted with Sanjay, she had to take the risk of being even more vulnerable.

Sanjay could tell Elena was struggling with something. He sat patiently, waiting for her to continue.

Elena took a deep breath and finally said, "This feels really risky for me to share. You've heard me talk about how toxic the culture was at my old company. What I haven't told you is the difficulty I had with that boss. I could never seem to please him, and when I went to see him to talk about it, I got into trouble. The discussion started off civilly enough, but then he made one excuse after another, and the more he did that, the more upset I got. Here I was, trying to work it out, and he was just brushing the whole thing aside. I lost it and started yelling at him. I rarely ever raise my voice, but I was just so frustrated. And then I was fired."

Sanjay nodded sympathetically. "That really sounds tough."

A bit reassured, Elena continued, "I guess I'm still unnerved about that incident. As I said, I'm usually composed, but I guess that I'm afraid of going to Rick and having this thing happen again."

Sanjay leaned forward and quietly said, "But that was that boss in that company, and this is a different boss."

Elena nodded thoughtfully. "I've been worried about telling you this. I didn't know if you would think I'm too emotional or not competent. And I was afraid it would damage how we relate to each other. I just feel so crummy about what happened. It's really hard for me to talk about. And I really don't want to put you in an awkward position."

"Wow, Elena, I had no idea you were sitting on all this, and I'm so sorry you held that back. I don't see you as overly emotional—you certainly weren't that way on the tech task force. Actually, I admire your courage in telling me. It must have been hard to say all of this."

Elena breathed a big sigh of relief. "You have no idea how much your response means to me, Sanjay. I worry about being stereotyped as the emotional female. That's what my previous boss accused me of, when I think I had a good reason to be mad."

Sanjay nodded vigorously. "Seems like you're carrying a lot over from that past experience. Be careful of that in dealing with Rick. Generally, you can be fairly direct with managers here." After a pause, Sanjay said, "It makes me realize there are things I've held back from you, too, not knowing how you would react."

"Really? You worry about that, too?"

"Yeah, definitely. I really value our friendship; I don't have many like it in the company and especially with any women. I'm a happily married man, and you know how much I love Priya. But we can't always talk about my work, because she can't fully relate, you know? Just because I like talking with you doesn't mean I'm looking for anything inappropriate—but it makes me nervous what others might think or even what you might think. Talk about feeling vulnerable! Just saying all this is weird," he said with a nervous smile.

"I know exactly what you mean," Elena said. "I feel nervous about our friendship, too. I'm so glad we can talk about this."

The Vulnerability Question

During past lunches, Elena had started to disclose more, but gingerly. The day she told Sanjay about being fired, she took not just one move outside her comfort zone but several. It could have been because of an increase in trust, or because she really needed to talk with someone about Rick, or because she realized that if she wanted a closer work relationship, there was no better time. Whatever the reason, Elena again had choices. And she chose to be vulnerable.

Now, there is vulnerability and there is *vulnerability*. Early in our experience with T-groups, we were struck by the fact that some disclosures had more impact than others and wondered why. Then David got some feedback that suggested an answer. Early in his professional life, David saw the power of being more open and had a relatively easy time divulging personal information. Then one day a friend said, "You do a good job of revealing things about yourself, but you are rarely vulnerable." At first, David felt hurt and misunderstood. Then he put it together with what he'd observed with students.

What feels risky and most vulnerable is when you are especially uncertain about the impact of your disclosure. If you have disclosed something (even if it is very personal) multiple times in similar settings and you have a pretty good sense of how others are going to react, even if it's negatively, you'll feel far less vulnerable than if you are sharing something you have never said to anyone. David knew his students felt the most vulnerable when they didn't know whether they would be accepted or rejected, praised or pitied. That kind of vulnerability brought others closer.

That was what made their self-disclosure truly vulnerable. And it was only when David understood that distinction and was able to make himself known in a much riskier way that he found others trusted him more fully.

For instance, David once taught a session on self-disclosure in a Stanford executive program, with some university faculty also in attendance. He wanted to model what he was teaching, so he swallowed twice and disclosed that years before he had been turned down for tenure. Though David had shared that fact before, what made the disclosure particularly vulnerable was that there was a tenured professor among the participants and David worried he would lose credibility. Then David took his disclosure a step further and revealed his feelings of worry and insecurity about sharing that fact. Carole remembers thinking about how gutsy that was, and many participants commented that it gave them a much more visceral sense of how disclosure builds connection. (In fact, to take this even further, David has some concerns about sharing this information in a book for all to see. That, friends, is vulnerability!)

One common concern people have about disclosure—especially when it involves revealing things that might appear as defects—is that others will see them as weak. We see it differently. It takes fortitude and internal strength to self-disclose. That's what Sanjay responded to when he told Elena, "I admire your courage in telling me. It must have been hard to say all of this."

Leaders, especially, are often afraid to reveal personal information that defies the perception that they totally have their act together—what if others respect them less? If the disclosure casts doubt on the person's competence to do the job, then sharing that information *can* cause a loss of influence and respect, but otherwise it helps the leader be seen as more human. We will return to this in more detail in the next chapter, but a leader who is not willing to be vulnerable sets a norm that does not encourage any others in the organization to do that either. The only way for a leader to legitimize self-disclosure is to model it.

David once facilitated a retreat for the executive team of a Fortune 500 company. Over dessert the first evening, conversation turned to the pressures the members were under. Some of these were work related and some were personal. Everybody knew that Frank's wife was very ill, but they were ignorant of the details. He hesitantly shared how painful the situation was and started to tear up. He quickly apologized as he tried to gain control. "No, no, that's all right!" his colleagues exclaimed. They then shared how moved they were by his disclosure and how impressed they were by how he was handling his wife's situation.

In her work with CEO/founders in Silicon Valley, Carole repeatedly hears how thirsty they are for this type of authenticity, how afraid they are to be vulnerable, and how deeply ingrained their beliefs are that demonstrating any of this will result in their being seen as weak. And yet, over and over, they feel reassured when they stop spinning their image and discover that others in their life see them as stronger and more (not less) credible when they take that risk.

The Costs of Silence

Even safe or bland comments are not risk-free. In the absence of data, people will make stuff up. Everybody draws conclusions when interacting with others. The less we reveal, the more others will fill in the blanks in order to make sense of what they see. When we are too reserved with our feelings, we actually lose control over how we are seen.

A different kind of silence occurs when we only share an image of ourselves—in those cases, the other can't see or know who we really are, including the parts that are more interesting. Even if we are successful in selling our image, this is a hollow victory. It just confirms that the real me is undesirable. Furthermore, as the noted French author François de La Rochefoucauld once said, "We're so accustomed to disguising ourselves to others that in the end we become disguised to ourselves."

Just as bad, once we've come to be known a certain way, we often feel bound to behave consistently, becoming less and less truly known. The cost is more isolation and what we call "the Creeping Constraint of Secrets." Important parts of ourselves are often related to other aspects of who we are. Hiding one part can lead to hiding much more, resulting in progressive impoverishment of what we show and, ultimately, of our relationships.

This was dramatically illustrated by a friend who is gay and talked about his life before he came out. "There were major parts of myself that I had to keep secret," he told us. "Obviously being gay, but also topics that might be related, no matter how tangential. I had to be circumspect about whether I was romantically involved with anybody. I couldn't have any pictures of my partner on my desk. I had to be very careful talking about what I had done on my recent vacation because I might slip and mention 'we' or, God forbid, 'he.' I didn't encourage social engagements with co-workers. I avoided political discussions that might lead to topics like gay marriage, so many of my conversations remained at rather superficial levels. And, worst of all, I had to force myself to keep quiet if somebody made a homophobic comment. As time went on, others came to know a smaller and smaller piece of who I am."

Constraints like these are everywhere. Even though Stanford tries to enroll students from a wide range of socioeconomic backgrounds, students from affluent families feel comfortable booking getaways to Napa Valley for wine tasting or talking about all the countries they've visited. This means that those who are on full scholarship are often silent about their background, go into further debt so as to participate in renting ski houses, and tend to be quiet when others share their globetrotting adventures. Devoutly religious students often feel constrained from sharing their religious beliefs out of concern for others' judgment.

It's not until these students find themselves in the Interpersonal Dynamics group that they feel safe enough to share their values, their background, their fears, and their hopes and dreams. That's often when they recognize the costs they have paid for not sharing more about who they really are. Every time we observe this awakening, we double down on the importance of building exceptional relationships—because while we can't all be in a T-group, we all can learn to create a safer space to self-disclose and become more known.

Why More Is Sometimes Better Than Less

What comes first, safety or disclosure? It can be easy to think, "Until I know I can trust that person and be accepted, I'm not going to take the risk of disclosing. I need to first know how they're going to respond." We argue that the causal direction has to be reversed—that risking a 15 percent disclosure is what builds safety. If each person waits for the other to take a risk, little progress is ever made.

To make matters more challenging, one disclosure may not get the result you want. That happened with Elena when she hinted at something by saying, "Well, the usual ups and downs." Sanjay did not pick up on that, and Elena didn't elaborate. Too often, people put their toe in the water with a small disclosure and then stop in the absence of a response. You might need to take a slightly more noticeable risk before the other person responds. That occurred when Elena later risked sharing what led to her being fired and her fear that it might happen again. She was fully 15 percent out of her comfort zone. What if Sanjay had instead responded, "That's unlikely to happen here and maybe you should just let go of the past." If he had, here again Elena would have had choices. She could have shrugged off his comment and changed the conversation to another subject, or she could have taken another risk and gone back to saying more about the problems with her boss.

It would no doubt have stung if Sanjay hadn't responded positively, but it's unlikely that Elena would have dissolved in a puddle. People are rarely that fragile. And taking the risk when you don't know the outcome is central to building deep personal relationships. On this journey, you have to trust the process, believing that in the long run, *by disclosing first,* you are more likely to build trust, gain acceptance, and achieve the relationship you most want. This is what "having agency" is all about.

Deepen Your Learning

SELF-REFLECTION

1. Put yourself in Elena's position. *You still feel bruised from being fired in your previous job, and the last thing you want is to have it happen again. Part of the problem is that you didn't know the culture. You*

like Sanjay and enjoyed working with him on the task force. Could he be a person you could be open with and who could help you learn how to succeed in this company? You would like a relationship where you can share what is important, but will he negatively misjudge you?

- How do you think you would go about letting yourself be more fully known? Consider the different choice points that Elena had in this chapter. What would you have said? What does this say about your ease (or difficulty) in letting yourself be more fully known in professional situations like this?

2. Being Known: More broadly, how easy is it for you to let others know what is important to you? What do you find most difficult to share? What are your concerns about sharing that?

3. Key Relationship: Take one of the key people whom you listed in the last chapter. Are there things about you *that are relevant to that relationship* that you haven't fully shared? What are your concerns about disclosing these?

4. Disclosing Emotions: How easy / challenging is it for you to share your emotions? Look over the Vocabulary of Feelings in Appendix A. Are there some feelings that are more difficult than others for you to express?

APPLICATION

In number 3 above, you identified some issues relevant to that relationship. What could you share that would be 15 percent outside your comfort zone?

Note that there are two areas of potential self-disclosure. The first is content, but the second is your feelings and concerns about sharing the content. Elena disclosed both levels in her self-disclosure. To what extent did you share both in the conversation above?

This coming week, in conversations with friends and acquaintances, try dropping your level of personal disclosure to share things beyond your comfort zone that you might not normally have shared. These could be facts, opinions, or feelings.

MAKING SENSE

What did you learn from your self-disclosure with the one person you chose above? In your self-reflection, you were asked what concerns you might have about disclosing. How have those changed? What did you learn about yourself from doing this, and how did it impact the relationship?

What was it like being more personal in your interactions with others? How did it feel doing that? Did it have an effect on the nature of those interactions?

How are you going to apply what you learned in future interactions? (Be specific about *what* you might do with different individuals.)

4

HELPING OTHERS BE KNOWN

Ben and Liam—Buddies, Parts 1 and 2

You can't build an exceptional relationship all on your own. You can't grow closer with someone who never ventures beyond small talk. You can go 15 percent out of your comfort zone, as Elena did, but you can't force the other person to do the same. "Hey, I opened up to you, so now you have to open up to me, too!" might have worked during childhood games of truth or dare, but it's not exactly the stuff of exceptional relationships.

This chapter isn't about coercion or manipulation. Rather, it's about the process—which can sometimes be quite slow—of encouraging someone else to open up. Even if you can't control whether someone will self-disclose, you can smooth the runway. That involves knowing when to disclose more about yourself, when to step back to give the other space, and when to ask the right kinds of questions. It also requires supporting the other in achieving what *they* want, not what you want for them. Ben struggled to walk that narrow path with his buddy Liam.

Ben and Liam, Part 1

Ben and Liam, both grads of the University of Michigan, struck up a friendship at an alumni event in Chicago shortly after Ben moved there. They were both single and in their thirties, and hung out on a regular basis over the next year. They shared their love of biking and the White Sox, and their recent discovery of some reasonably good ski resorts not too far away. They saw each other on a regular basis and talked a lot about sports and work, even though their fields were quite different. Ben was manager of a Walmart, and Liam worked in finance for a large construction company.

Ben valued his friendship with Liam, and the more they hung out, the more he wanted to deepen it. In addition to their mutual interests, Ben enjoyed their contrasting styles. Ben was a gregarious big-picture thinker, while Liam was more reserved and, maybe because of his finance background, was drawn to facts and figures. Because they approached issues from these two different perspectives, their discussions were fun and interesting. However, one of the consequences of Liam's style was that he tended not to share much that was personal. Ben wondered what he might do to encourage Liam to share more.

One evening, at one of their favorite breweries, Liam told Ben he wanted his advice about something. "I have this co-worker, Randy, who's a problem."

"What's going on?"

"The main thing is that he takes credit for work he hasn't done." Liam went on to describe how they'd done a project together, but Randy had told their manager that he'd done almost all of the work. As he talked, he got more and more agitated.

"That sucks. You really sound worked up."

"Yes. He's driving me crazy. He's really slimy—I don't trust him at all." Liam went on to describe how upset he was, especially about Randy's going around him to talk to their manager.

"Did your manager believe him?"

"I think so. Randy always sounds so damn convincing. And that isn't the first time. Why are there people like that? It really pisses me off and I don't know what to do about it. I can't confront him because he'd spread rumors about me and ruin my reputation in the office. I've seen him do that."

Ben took it in, then asked, "What about going to your manager and telling him it was a joint project?"

"I'd sound like I was making a big deal out of nothing."

"Have you talked with some of your colleagues about it?"

"That's playing Randy's political game, and I don't want to do that."

Ben made a couple more suggestions, and Liam became visibly irritated.

"Look, I've thought about this stuff already—this isn't your usual organization, you know? It's a macho construction company, and you're supposed to take care of yourself." Liam then added, "My guess is this crap never happens to you."

"Huh? What do you mean?"

"Just that you seem good at all the 'people' stuff, you know?"

"Actually, I was just thinking about when I had a colleague like Randy."

Liam relaxed. "What happened there?"

"It was early in my career at Walmart, and this other manager constantly took credit for my ideas."

"So what did you do about it?"

"Actually, nothing. I really had no idea what to do. If I confronted this guy, he would just deny it. I knew that some other managers were aware of the situation, but they wouldn't stick their neck out and say anything. I didn't know if management knew, but I didn't want to go to them to complain and sound like I was whining. I felt caught in a no-win situation. I couldn't speak up and had no idea what would happen if I didn't."

"So what happened?"

"I was lucky. As it turned out, I got promoted and he didn't."

"You make it sound so easy."

"It wasn't. It drove me crazy. It was really stressful, and I felt pretty crappy about myself—I felt helpless. I hated that."

"Well, that won't work for me. I don't have your patience, and Randy bugs the hell out of me."

Ben was quiet for a minute, then said, "I get that you're annoyed, and it's a tough situation. But why is this bending you out of shape so much? In my case, a promotion hung on the outcome, but when you described this project last month, it didn't seem like a major one—not one that could really affect your career. What Randy's doing isn't fair, but what's so upsetting about it?"

"I'm not sure," Liam said. "I guess I just don't like messy interpersonal issues. I went into finance because numbers are objective. You might be able to handle those people problems, but they drive me crazy—I could never do your job. And I hate having to play office politics, which is what Randy does. I just hate it that people get ahead by doing that."

Ben's curiosity was piqued. "Yeah? Keep going."

Liam was quiet for a minute, shook his head ever so slightly, and then glanced up at the TV screen, saying, "Look, the White Sox are tied five-five. Let's grab another beer and watch the game."

Ben was once again taken aback by the abrupt change in the conversation but decided to let it go as they went up to the bar. He had noticed Liam do this at various times, but as he'd done before, Ben dropped it.

Encouraging Disclosure

Some of Ben's actions helped Liam share more, and others were less successful.

Ben's indication of interest in Liam's predicament and his empathy with Liam's frustration were both encouraging. Empathy is the act of conveying not only that you understand the other's feelings but also that you can identify with them: You can "walk in their shoes," as the phrase goes. It's important to note that you don't have to have been in the exact same situation as someone in order to feel empathy for them. For example, you can empathize with someone's feeling of sadness because you have felt sadness before, even if the situation they're describing would not necessarily make *you* sad. We often have students say, "I have no idea why he's so angry about this." To which we reply, "That's not the point. The point is that you know what anger feels like, so you can still empathize."

Empathy is different from sympathy, even though they're often used interchangeably. Sympathy involves acknowledging someone is in pain and providing comfort or support; it does not necessarily involve identifying with how they are feeling. Sympathy is also often linked with pity, which makes many people feel even smaller. Sympathy, unlike empathy, doesn't encourage more disclosure from the other. In fact, sometimes it can have the opposite effect, given that many people don't like it when someone else "feels sorry" for them.

While Ben initially did a nice job on the empathy front, he asked a series of questions that were not useful because they were actually advice. When he did so, Liam closed down. It was when Ben made himself somewhat vulnerable in disclosing his past feelings of helplessness that Liam opened up a bit more. But then Ben pressed for more disclosure, and that may have led to Liam's abruptly changing the subject.

You'll undoubtedly have interactions like this one, where you want to learn more, but the other is reticent. As important as showing interest and your self-disclosure are, that might only go so far. You have other options. At times like this, you first have to meet the other person where they are. Only then can both of you move into other, perhaps deeper, areas.

"Meeting someone where they are" has several dimensions. One is, *Are you speaking to what they want as opposed to what you want?* Another is, *Are you responding at the same emotional level?* Ben addressed these dimensions when empathizing about Randy's annoying behavior ("That sucks. You really sound upset"). Liam would not have met him if he'd made a flippant remark or gone deeper than Liam wanted, as he did later. A third dimension is, *Are you seeing the world as they see it?* Ben failed at that when he didn't take Liam's organizational culture into account and made suggestions that could work at Walmart but not in Liam's company. A fourth dimension is, *Are you not responding to what the other really wants?* Liam wanted to vent about Randy and his company's political climate, while Ben was curious about what personal issues were triggered for Liam.

For the other person to hear anything you have to say, much less tell you more about themselves, they have to know that you seek to understand them and their position. Once that connection is made, then it is possible to bring up other issues and delve into more questions. Ben realized that at the end of their conversation, before they went up to the bar. Even though he wanted to pursue the discussion further, he realized that wasn't where Liam was. Timing is yet another dimension of meeting somebody else where they are. Ben filed this incident away. Not everything has to be dealt with immediately.

Curiosity, Questions, and Advice

Being curious is a lot more complicated than it seems. At one end of the continuum, you truly don't understand something at all, and at the other end, you think you know all about it and are just asking questions to test your hypothesis. A problem with the latter is that you're probably not genuinely curious. You've largely made up your mind and are "leading the witness" to prove your case. That stance is unlikely to encourage the other to be more open and revealing.

The best way to make sure your curiosity is authentic is to hold the mindset that, in spite of how perceptive you think you might be and how well you think you know another person, you don't actually know what's going on for them. That keeps you naïve in the best sense of the word. And with this naïve curiosity, you are more likely to use questions that encourage disclosure.

Not all questions are created equal, and asking the right kind can help encourage someone to share. Open-ended questions widen the scope of the conversation by generating options, new perspectives, or new ways of thinking about a situation. Ben did that when he asked Liam to explain what was going on at work and what bothered him so much about the situation.

The most effective open-ended questions don't begin with the word "why." "Why" questions tend to drive people into their heads and out of their feelings. Such questions carry an implicit request that the other person justify themselves. For example, if Ben had asked, "Why are you so worked up?" Liam would have felt the need to come up with a logical explanation. If Ben had continued, "Why don't you just forget about Randy?" it's unlikely that Liam would have revealed his personal antipathy to office politics and desire for an objective world. Often there's more going on than can be revealed by a logical explanation.

Closed-ended questions, which usually can be answered with "yes" or "no," narrow the conversation and are more likely to be felt as intrusive and judgmental. An example is when Ben asked Liam, "Have you talked with some of your colleagues about it?" Equally unproductive are "pseudo-questions" that are really statements in question form. If Ben had asked, "Aren't you irritated with Randy because you envy his persuasive skills?" that would have been a pseudo-question. Both closed-ended questions and pseudo-questions sound a whole lot like advice or hypothesis testing in question form. Advice is rarely useful, as Ben found, even if the other person asks for it. Our eagerness to help often causes us to jump in with a solution that comes out of our own experience or doesn't fit the situation. Rarely do we come up with an option the other person hasn't already considered (and likely discarded). These were all traps that Ben fell into.

Giving advice can also increase the power discrepancy between two people. The person with an issue might feel one-down to start with, and if the other person acts as though they have the answer, that can exacerbate the gap. Another problem with advice-giving is that it's easy to misunderstand what the other really wants. Liam may have said he wanted Ben's advice, but did he really? People go to others for many reasons. Perhaps they want a chance to think out loud. Perhaps they simply want to vent and seek a sympathetic ear. Sometimes they just want support and empathy about an unfair situation, rather than help figuring out a solution. The listener needs to be clear about what the other person wants before they can fully understand how to be most helpful.

David experienced this some time ago when Jim, a colleague, walked into his office. "David, I don't know what to do with this problem and I'd like your advice." David eagerly gave Jim his full attention, because he really likes to help and he thought if his ideas were useful, they'd both feel good. Jim continued, "I see two alternatives and am not sure which one to take. I could do A, which has these advantages, but it has these problems. On the other hand, B is attractive for these reasons, but I have some concerns."

As Jim went on exploring both options in greater depth, David paid close attention, trying to figure out the right answer. As Jim continued his exploration, it seemed to David that option A would be the preferred outcome. He wanted to share his reasoning, believing it would help, but he bit his tongue and waited for Jim to finish. Then Jim got up and went to the door. "Yes, it's clear that B is the better alternative. Thanks a lot. This was very helpful." David felt let down and wanted to say, "Wait, you haven't heard my thoughts!" But he ruefully had to admit that his analysis wouldn't have helped. Instead, Jim just needed the space to figure it out himself.

This story speaks to another limitation of advice-giving. David's solution may actually have been right—for David. But it could have been wrong for Jim. Everyone has their own objectives and ways to achieve them. When people give advice, they tend to respond in terms of what *they* would do rather than fully taking into account how the other best operates.

Another knock on advice-giving: It can keep you from discovering what is really going on for the other person. In Liam's case, was it really Randy's taking credit for the project that made him so upset? Or was it that the office is highly political? Or was it Liam's (perhaps unrealistic) wish that the world be objective and rational? Our desire to help can lead us to prematurely jump in before we discover the real issue. There is wisdom to the adage "It's better to have the wrong solution to the right problem than the right solution to the wrong problem"—because you will discover it's the wrong solution much sooner.

If advice is so often useless, why do people continue offering it? Perhaps because another's issues seem so much easier to solve than our own. Perhaps because we want the chance to exhibit our analytical skills. Or perhaps we want to be the Lone Ranger who rides into the distressed town, resolves the issue to the townsfolk's adoration, and then rides away after leaving the silver bullet! Whatever the reason, ask yourself, "Am I giving advice to meet my needs or because I really want to help?"

In spite of all the reasons advice can be problematic, there are times when it works. But that requires certain conditions. If you are going to provide someone with advice, you have to understand the situation fully, really know what the other wants, and take their style and approach into account. Most important, you have to set aside what you would do. All of that is easier said than done. Furthermore, advice-giving doesn't necessarily contribute much to knowing the other person, other than learning their response to your suggestions.

In helping another be more known, you might want to look for opportunities to support them in more fully expressing their emotions. How do you know if they have understated their feelings? In a sense, you don't, but you can make a guess based on their tone, their nonverbal cues, and noticing when the intensity of the situation doesn't match the feelings being expressed. Ben picked up on Liam's agitation. Ben empathized by saying, "You really sound upset," which encouraged Liam to more fully express the depth of his anger.

Unfortunately, rather than continuing to listen for and reflect back Liam's feelings, which might have encouraged more self-disclosure, Ben did the opposite. He asked a series of logical questions that pulled Liam out of his feelings and into rational responses that he didn't find helpful.

There's a fine line between reflecting back unstated or understated emotions and asking leading questions. Case in point: "You say you are slightly bothered, but it doesn't sound like it. Are you more upset than that?" could be either. The difference is in the assumptions you make and your corresponding tone. If you accept that you never really know what is going on for another person, then you know you are making a guess. Your supposition is just that—a supposition. Not only is a question more accurate than a statement, but it creates less resistance than if you expressed the same idea as if you *know*. You can also make comments like, "That really sounds upsetting," or "I would certainly be really annoyed if that happened to me," because those reflect what is going on within you, which is what you do know. Those empathetic statements are likely to encourage the other to express their feelings more fully.

Ben and Liam, Part 2

A few weeks later, Liam and Ben met for dinner. Ben wanted to ask what had happened with Randy, but before he could say anything, Liam started with, "I've put the issue to rest with Randy—thanks for your help." He added, "Oh, and hey, I'm thinking of applying for a new opportunity in the finance department. It would come with a nice raise, but there are some personnel issues I want your reaction to since that's more your area." They got into a detailed conversation, with Ben asking exploratory questions and letting Liam take it in the direction he wanted. The issue was complex, and Ben was getting more and more intrigued. Liam appeared to be getting value from their discussion until, practically in the middle of a sentence, he abruptly changed the subject.

Wonder why he does that, Ben thought. *It's like a pattern with him. Should I ask him?* But he decided against it.

They continued eating, and their conversation turned to whether skiing was in the cards given the lack of snow. Ben was distracted and finding it hard to stay engaged. He was preoccupied by Liam's abrupt changing of topics and decided to go back to it.

Gingerly he asked, "Liam, I want to go back to something that happened a bit ago when we were talking about that new job and you changed the subject in the middle of the conversation. I'm puzzled. I've seen you do that a few times over multiple conversations and wonder what that's about."

"I was done talking about it," Liam responded rather curtly.

Ben, sensing that Liam didn't want to discuss it, just shrugged and said, "Okay."

Their conversation shifted to whether the new White Sox closing pitcher was going to make much of a difference to the abysmal season and whether they should bike a new route that weekend.

As their evening unfolded, Ben couldn't help but think, *I could be having this discussion with anyone. But Liam is so thoughtful and interesting. I wish I knew him a little better.* He decided to try again.

"Liam, I feel stuck. I wish we could talk about stuff beyond sports and superficial business things because I like friendships with a little more depth. But every time I try to find out more about what's going on, you close the conversation off. You did it when we were talking about Randy a few weeks ago, and you did it again earlier with the potential new job. What's up with that? It's kind of weird."

Liam's response took Ben aback. "Every time we get into a conversation that involves anything vaguely personal, you start with the questions—pushing for more and more. It's like I give an inch and you want a mile. I just don't like feeling forced."

"Why is it so hard for you to share more?" replied Ben. Then, "Oh damn, I think I just did it again! Never mind!"

"Nice catch," said Liam with a smile. "I don't feel like going into it."

"Fair enough. I know I can be pretty intense and push too hard too quickly. I've heard that before, so you're not alone."

"Thanks," said Liam. "Let's get back to planning a bike route."

Their conversation took on a lighter and easier tone and continued for a while longer.

As they pulled up their calendars to coordinate plans, Liam said, "I've been thinking more about what you asked me a while ago. I didn't mean to be rude; it's complicated. I've always been a pretty private person. The first time I ever really opened up, I was dating a girl in college who kept getting me to share more and then used it against me. It sucked."

"Ugh," responded Ben. "Sounds rough. Really helps me understand a little more. And look, I don't want to push for more than you want to share. I'll do my best not to bludgeon you with questions even when I want to know more. I'll let you take the lead."

Liam nodded appreciatively.

"But I also don't want to be constantly second-guessing myself. If you start to feel I'm asking too much, tell me and I'll back off."

"Will do," said Liam. Then he added, "And hey, I'll try to be a little more open."

IN THIS SECOND conversation, each took risks and those paid off, deepening the level of closeness in their friendship. If Ben had said nothing about Liam's switching subjects or had backed away (both common responses), the relationship would have remained at a more superficial level. Ben made himself vulnerable by telling Liam more about what he hoped for in their friendship. He also was vulnerable in acknowledging his tendency to push too hard and too fast. He paved the way for Liam to respond with his own disclosure.

The way in which Ben "caught" himself, followed by Liam's pledge to help him see when he was pushing too much, bodes well. They took some important steps, though they will need repeated iterations, with reciprocal risk-taking and vulnerability, for the relationship to continue to grow. But they learned *how* to disclose to each other and began to experience some of the benefits.

The difference between being curious and being intrusive can be a very fine line. If you believe someone really wants to get to know you and has told you why, you're likely to experience their questions as less invasive. If, on the other hand, you sense they see you as an interesting specimen to examine under a microscope, you'll be far less open. Even more so if you have no idea what they're going to do with what they learn.

Still, even if Ben had the best of intentions, they may have been lost on Liam. It is important to give the other person space, as Ben did in both conversations. He was careful to express genuine interest without being coercive, letting Liam take the lead. In being sensitive to Liam's needs without totally ignoring his own, Ben made it easier for Liam in walking that fine line and was successful, even if he did not do everything perfectly.

Self-Disclosure: Who Goes First?

Reciprocity is a crucial element in self-disclosure, but whose job is it to disclose first? Even though the more we disclose, the more control we have over how we are seen, we have to consider how much more difficult it is when issues of status or perceived status are in play. "Status" might be a level in the organization, degree of past achievement, or education. Unfortunately, gender, ethnicity, and socioeconomic background also create status distinctions. Expecting someone who might already feel one-down to initiate self-disclosure is a lot to ask. It's only logical that such disclosures come with a relatively higher feeling of risk. This is especially the case with people from marginalized groups, such as women in male-dominated fields and people of color.

Yet higher-status people are often unaware that their role makes it hard for people to disclose to them. Bosses frequently say to their direct reports, "I expect you to speak up," downplaying the risk of doing so. Those in a higher-power-and-status position need to not only be aware of this dynamic but also disclose to a greater degree than they would with someone of equal status.

When Carole started teaching at Stanford, for instance, she developed a friendly relationship with a senior professor in the organizational behavior department. Periodically they had lunch and found they very much enjoyed having intellectual debates as well as comparing notes about teaching MBAs. Though she enjoyed his company, he was not someone with whom she would have ordinarily been vulnerable, especially given the power differential between them—he was a full professor, while she was a lecturer.

One day, he invited her to lunch and told her he wanted her counsel because she had a reputation for engaging students deeply. What could he do to achieve similar results? To say she was flattered is an understatement, given his stature at the university. More important than the flattery, though, was the underlying vulnerability he demonstrated in asking for her input. Professors rarely admit that they do not have all the answers or that they need help, so this was a significant self-disclosure. Carole naturally offered all the ideas she could, many of which he implemented, and for which he always gave her credit.

While Carole was immensely flattered by his request, it also changed their relationship. His willingness to be vulnerable made her much more open to being vulnerable with him. In subsequent years, she asked him for advice, too. She also shared her professional challenges and deepest disappointments. They became and remain confidants and friends.

Although there was a significant status difference between Carole and her professor friend, she did not report to him. But could a boss be that open with their direct report? We saw that play itself out with a senior executive we worked with. John was a president of the Canadian division of a Fortune 500 company, in which he had built a culture where people could be open and direct with one another. One day, Darryl, his vice president for IT, walked into his office and said, "I just need to tell you that I'm having a hard time performing up to standard. I'm going through a very difficult divorce."

John had gone through a divorce himself and, sensing that Darryl might want to talk, said, "Let's get out of the office for a while. I have to buy new speakers and could use your expertise. We can get some lunch while we're at it." John used the time to let Darryl talk about the problems in his marriage and shared some of his own experience. Darryl later reported how much this meant to him, that he felt understood and supported and came to think of John as much more than just his boss.

Many managers would not have done what John did with Darryl out of concern that they would later have to excuse their employee's poor performance and the organization would suffer. That didn't occur in this case. In fact, Darryl felt more committed to both John and the organization, and when other members of the executive team learned of what John had done, they, too, felt more loyalty to their executive, and they pitched in to support Darryl through his transition. But if John hadn't initially built a culture of openness, he might never have known why Darryl's performance was slipping.

Do You Really Want *to Know the Other Fully?*

We've made a presumption here that people *want* to get to know others more deeply. Maybe you have some ambivalence. Do you really want to hear about all of someone's childhood traumas or the difficulties they're having with their partner? What about the obligations that come with more knowledge? Do you need to comply with their request or always agree with that person and take their side? Is their definition of an exceptional relationship that you're *always* available?

A good friend of ours, Annie, faced this issue with her friend Paula. The two had been friends for ages.

Then Paula developed an illness that required twice-weekly visits to the doctor. Her condition made it difficult for her to drive, so she asked Annie to take her. Annie was more than willing at first, but as the weeks went on, she started to grow resentful—not just of Paula but also of Paula's son and daughter-in-law. Even though they lived with Paula, the son and his wife begged off chauffeuring, claiming it was because of work and childcare demands.

Annie didn't know what to do. She was afraid that if she raised the issue directly with Paula, her resentment of the son and daughter-in-law (and growing resentment of Paula, for allowing them to beg off responsibility) would surface and damage the relationship. Instead, she found an excuse to cut down on her driving obligations. This did not hurt her relationship with Paula, but it did nothing to deepen it.

There can be other reasons why a person in Annie's position might not want to share her feelings. Perhaps she doesn't want to know more about what's going on between Paula and her son and daughter-in-law—what if there are real problems there and Paula decides to use their car rides as pseudo therapy sessions? At that point, it would be much more difficult for Annie to tell Paula that she didn't want that role.

We've spent most of these last two chapters telling you about the benefits of increased self-disclosure, but Annie's situation shows us that it can also lead to tricky or awkward situations. As relationships develop, people come to have growing expectations of each other. And while reaching out and responding to the other's needs is an essential part of building a stronger relationship, setting boundaries is also crucial. Different boundaries might be needed at different points in a developing relationship. You have to identify, surface, and successfully resolve these boundary concerns when they arise. Easy, right? Fear not, we'll get back to this in later chapters.

Deepen Your Learning

SELF-REFLECTION

1. Put yourself in Ben's position. *You would like to build a more personal relationship with Liam. You like him and value his analytical skills but wish he would be more self-revealing. You have an easy time with your own self-disclosure and wish that Liam would do more disclosing himself. What could you do to encourage that?*

    - Thinking of the various situations described in this chapter, what do you think you might have done? Any ways that you think you might have limited your effectiveness?
    - What does this say about your abilities (and style) in helping others become more self-disclosing?

2. Choose one of the key relationships you identified previously. Which of the following behaviors do you engage in that make it easier for the other to be more fully known?

    - Listening actively to try to fully understand them
    - Suspending judgment and not trying to quickly figure out what's going on with them
    - Being curious and inquiring about what is important to them
    - Using open-ended questions to encourage them to share more
    - Listening for emotions and helping their full expression (for instance, "You sound more than a little annoyed; what are you feeling?")
    - Empathizing—especially with feelings ("That really sounds upsetting")

- Showing acceptance ("I can really understand why you would react that way")

3. Conversely, do you have a tendency to do any of the following, which discourage the other to share and be more fully known?

    - Only half listen because you are thinking about (or have already decided) how to respond
    - Change the conversation rather quickly to talk about yourself or things that interest you
    - Think you have figured out what is really going on for them
    - Ask leading questions to make sure they accept your conclusions
    - Ignore their feelings and use logic to make your case
    - Make judgments about their comments or actions
    - Don't empathize with their situation

    Why do you tend to respond in these ways?

APPLICATION

The questions you answered in the previous section reflect how you perceive yourself. Does the other person in the relationship see you the same way? Go to them and ask what you do that supports or limits their willingness to self-disclose.

Remind them you're raising the issue because you want a more open relationship. You are leading with *your* self-disclosure to encourage theirs and, by doing so, deepening the relationship. That's what will make this a personal activity, not an academic one.

MAKING SENSE

If you completed the application exercise, you learned the extent to which the other's perception matched yours. But how easy was it to hear their view, especially if there was a mismatch with yours?

Think of the other key relationships you identified. What can you now do to encourage those people to be better known?

There's a dilemma inherent in this process. You're trying to learn new behaviors while building relationships—but you don't want the other person in the relationship to feel as if they are being used or serving as a subject in your experiment. What have you learned about how to walk that line? By the way, have you checked in with them about how they are feeling about this?

5

INFLUENCE IN BALANCE

Maddie and Adam—a Married Couple, Part 1

Most of us had relationships in high school—be they friendships or romantic relationships—where one person had much more influence than the other. The one with greater sway could decide the terms, timing, and circumstances of what to do at any given moment, while the one with less influence usually contributed an enthusiastic "Sure! Sounds great!" whether they liked the plan or not. For a while, this might have worked well enough. But sooner or later, the relationship faded or, more likely, because we're talking high school here, went up in flames. That's because for relationships to endure, influence must be balanced and matched.

The cycle of self-disclosure, support, trust, and then further disclosure is an important underpinning of balance. As each person gets to know the other better, they use that knowledge to further the process. We'd argue that there's always deeper ground to discover. For instance, the two of us have collectively been married for over ninety years (David for over fifty-five, Carole for over thirty-five), and we are still discovering new things about our respective spouses—and they about us. The objective in building strong and meaningful relationships is not to hurl pell-mell into self-disclosure or deepening for deepening's sake, but rather to take account of what each person needs so that these needs can be met in relative balance.

Reaching the point where each person is satisfied is not easy. As you'll see in this chapter, it requires understanding the calculus of give-and-take between the two and equalizing the influence each person has. What's more, relationships that are balanced at one point in time can be thrown off at others, as when one person's achievement comes at a significant expense to the other. That is certainly the case with Maddie and Adam.

Maddie and Adam, Part 1

Maddie and Adam had been married for eleven years and had a five-year-old daughter and a three-year-old son. When they met, Maddie worked as a sales representative for a pharmaceutical firm that developed cancer-fighting drugs. She loved her job, especially the travel (which sometimes took her to Hawaii), and gained satisfaction from the social value of her product.

Working full-time was quite consuming for both of them, but they had much to share in the evenings and on weekends. They enjoyed cooking together and entertaining. Their relationship felt equal to both of them; they made major decisions jointly, such as where to buy their first house and when to have a baby. Other responsibilities were shared; she was in charge of the kitchen remodel when they finally had enough money saved, and he handled all the logistics when they vacationed. They alternated with whom they celebrated winter holidays, spending one year with her family in town and the next visiting his in New York. Even with this division of labor, they each felt they could influence the other.

Maddie continued to work when her daughter was born but quit her job after her son came along. She and Adam had been able to juggle work and family demands with one child, but taking care of two young children and running the household became too much.

Thanks to a childcare swap she'd worked out with her neighbor, Maddie was able to volunteer a half day a week at the children's cancer center at the local hospital, providing her with some adult contact as well as a break from her all-consuming parenting and household activities.

Adam worked as a software engineer. He loved his job, which allowed him to constantly learn and stretch himself. The pay was good, but the hours could be long and often required working some evenings—and at least part of many weekends.

The relationship had some strains. Maddie was frustrated that even though they had a reasonable income, Adam tended to be tight with money. She thought it came from his upbringing, as his parents had had to watch every penny, but she was annoyed she had to defend each expense. She didn't consider herself extravagant. Rather, things wore out, and some purchases simply made life easier.

Their workweek was highly structured, and the couple didn't have much time together to talk without the kids present. Date nights rarely seemed to work out, and most evenings after dinner, both felt tired and tended to limit their conversation to what was going on with the kids and how their days had gone. Their intimacy suffered—in both the emotional and the physical sense—as they collapsed into bed without really having checked in with each other.

Maddie became increasingly dissatisfied. She missed the rewarding nature of her previous job and the intellectual stimulation of being with adults. She talked about her dissatisfaction with her mother, who just said, "This is the role of mothers. Look at the great rewards in raising two wonderful children." Maddie didn't find this answer satisfying but didn't know how to respond. *Even if that's the way society looks at the trade-off,* she thought, *that just doesn't work for me.*

When she raised her unhappiness with Adam, he was highly resistant. "Look, this is what we agreed to when we decided to have kids," he said. "And I'm stressed, too. This job has a lot of pressure."

Maddie thought, *Yes, but you have all that job satisfaction,* but didn't say anything. Adam continued, "Anyway, this is all going to get better when the kids start school full-time and are involved in clubs and stuff."

That was several years away, though, and the most Maddie could hope for, even then, would be a part-time job. It was hard to offset present dissatisfaction with a vague promise that things would get better in the future. *I certainly couldn't do the sort of work I did before,* she thought. *And by the time they're in college, my skills will be out of date.* She said nothing, not wanting to cause yet another argument. Instead, she left to do the laundry. For his part, Adam thought, *She has the most influence on the kids, and they will undoubtedly be closer to her than to me. What is she complaining about?*

THIS IS A tough situation without any easy answers. Some of the problem is a function of Maddie and Adam's stage of life—studies show that dissatisfaction with marriage increases once a couple has children and only decreases after those children have left home. But that doesn't mean Maddie and Adam are stuck. They can begin to rebalance. Before we explore how, we need to understand the issues that underlie their relationship. It turns out, these challenges look familiar to most of us.

Establishing What Feels Fair

All relationships have trade-offs, but for a relationship to be sustainable, each person has to have enough of their needs met, and each must give things up. Over time, the benefits have to exceed the costs. As relationships develop and each person allows themselves to be more fully known, the two of them can learn how to increase the benefits and reduce the costs.

We certainly see this calculus with Maddie and Adam. They value each other's intellectual company, they're financially well-off, they love each other, and they have the joy of children. In the early years of their marriage, the benefits far exceeded the costs. However, new costs and limitations arose—especially for Maddie—and those costs are growing.

At the core of functional relationships is a rough equity between two people, which produces a sense of what feels "fair." Eventually, you will feel exploited, even if your benefits exceed your costs, if you believe the other is getting an even *better* deal. You don't have to constantly run cost/benefit analyses, or be perfectly in balance at every moment. What matters is that, over time, both people see a rough equivalence.

Assessing the benefits and costs in a relationship isn't a rational tally of pluses and minuses, nor can it be. What each person values is highly subjective. For instance, Adam greatly values the challenge of his job and minimizes the cost of not having relaxed dinners with his wife and children. Another person might highly value dinnertime with family and be willing to pay the professional opportunity cost by leaving work at five-thirty.

Societal values, background, and personal history all influence the way someone assesses the costs and benefits in a relationship. For example, Adam may have been raised in a home that set more traditional gender expectations. He might also be influenced by the same social expectations conveyed by Maddie's mother when she said that Maddie *should* be satisfied with her present situation.

We are also influenced by comparison with others. Maddie might feel incredibly fortunate because a close friend, who also has two children, is divorced and struggling economically. However, she might feel differently if she compared herself to another friend who is happily married with children and holding down a full-time job.

It is crucial that each person be clear about what they want as well as knowing what the other wants. When Adam brushed off Maddie's dissatisfaction with "This is all going to get better when the kids start school full-time," he showed little empathy and was somewhat cavalier in ignoring the deep costs she was paying in the moment. So how are you supposed to know what you and the other want?

Rebalancing: Clarify Wants, Then Reassess

Again, emotions are great signposts. When we give credence to our feelings as an important indicator of what we really want, we have a good place to start. Maddie was feeling increasingly *constrained* by her role as a mother and the decreased intellectual and personal interactions with Adam. Her *frustrations* were not lessened when Adam correctly pointed out that this was the arrangement to which they had both agreed.

Unfortunately, we tend to judge the "appropriateness" of the needs and complaints raised by others from the perspective of our own needs and values. This is precisely what both Maddie's mother and Adam did with Maddie's concerns. This approach is distancing and decreases understanding. Maddie's needs had legitimacy as *her* needs, and she wanted to be heard and understood.

That doesn't mean that Adam's needs were irrelevant. In fact, his resistance to exploring Maddie's dissatisfaction might have come from a fear that if they made any changes to the status quo, his needs wouldn't be as well met. Voicing what he wants is as important. But each person in a relationship has a responsibility to ensure that not only their own costs and benefits are in balance but the other person's are as well. Unfortunately, Adam appeared not to be concerned with Maddie's relatively poorer set of trade-offs.

What might Adam have done to get them back in balance? He could have named his fear of losing an arrangement that was working well for him and then temporarily set that interest aside in order to help Maddie explore her frustration. His curiosity would have allowed him to understand his partner better and increase the chance that she would feel fully understood. Showing that you understand what the other is feeling is a form of giving someone what they need. (These are two of the components of "meeting someone emotionally," which is fully explained in chapter 9.) But we don't think Adam bears full responsibility for the couple's tension. Maddie is complicit, a point we'll come back to later.

When we can discuss our needs and dissatisfactions, we're more likely to develop a solution that works for everyone. Not always easy. Carole knows this all too well from her time as an at-home mom with an infant and a two-year-old. By the end of the day, she'd be desperate for adult interaction. Andy, her husband, would come home after a long day's work and sit on the couch to read the newspaper to unwind. She would fly around the corner from the kitchen and go into a long, uninterrupted diatribe about the new nursery school's not having any space or their son's having yet another ear infection. Andy, who is an introvert and needed some space and time to himself, would respond with little more than a polite "mmm-hmmm." This would infuriate Carole, since she is an off-the-charts extrovert. She wanted his full, undivided attention.

These interactions did not go well for either of them until Carole told Andy that she was not feeling heard, which left her feeling hurt. Andy then shared that he felt frustrated and pressured. Since those reactions were the last thing either of them wanted, the two of them were able to talk about the situation. They both realized that Carole had to give Andy some time to unwind. He wanted half an hour. "Half an hour!" she exclaimed. "I've been counting down the minutes until you got home. How about five minutes?" They settled on fifteen, which allowed them to change their dysfunctional pattern. Even though the solution didn't provide Carole with Andy's undivided attention the minute he got home, or provide Andy with as much time to decompress as he would have liked, they both got enough of what they wanted and, in the end, felt they were getting more than they were giving up.

The second step in rebalancing, once you've clarified wants, is to reassess whatever arrangements you've made in the past. Agreements that feel right at one point in time don't necessarily work as well later on. The decision that Adam and Maddie made when their second child was born worked when they made it and even for a couple of years afterward. But what was initially satisfying for Maddie grew less so, and what was missing grew in importance.

Conditions change in all relationships—new work opportunities arise, family members become sick, and people age. When individuals become locked into past agreements, they run the risk that their own growth, and the growth of their relationship, will stall. The best relationships continue to evolve as each person discovers new needs, seeks different benefits, and learns to deal with and let go of prior limitations. Problems arise, though, when people grow at different rates and in different directions, producing strain on the relationship. The danger is that one or both stop growing to avoid conflict. As we will see with Adam and Maddie, when this imbalance happens, the only productive way forward is to directly face these changes, understand their impact, and jointly explore how to address them.

Reassessing relationship agreements isn't simple. It's apt to result in change, and change often triggers resistance: *How is this going to turn out? Will I have to give up something that is really important to me or incur a cost I'm not prepared to pay?* It also brings unpredictability (*How are you going to respond?*) and perhaps guilt or recrimination (*Why did we not do this before?*). Be prepared for this not to be solved in one discussion and for it to feel bad and frustrating before it gets resolved. Reassessing relationships is crucial—just don't assume it will be a cinch.

Digging Deeper

What kept Adam and Maddie stuck in their past agreement? Was it just Adam's refusal to recognize it was no longer working? Was it Maddie's reluctance to push harder out of fear she would create conflict? While all of these played a part, a larger and more fundamental issue was their difficulty influencing each other in the face of contentious issues.

Note that Maddie's unhappiness with her home arrangement wasn't the only issue the two of them avoided. There was also what she saw as Adam's excessive frugality. Part of their difficulty was a result of status differences. When someone (generally a woman) quits their job to become a stay-at-home parent, the balance of power in the relationship shifts. The at-home parent often loses status with regard to decisions around money and how it's spent, which creates further tension.

Influence discrepancies exist in most relationships, though minor ones are rarely a barrier to talking honestly and coming to an effective solution. However, a significant difference in influence often results in a dysfunctional cycle.

Costs of Large Discrepancies

High-influence person

- Resists being influenced
- Believes they are always right
- Devalues what other has to say
- Tends to dominate

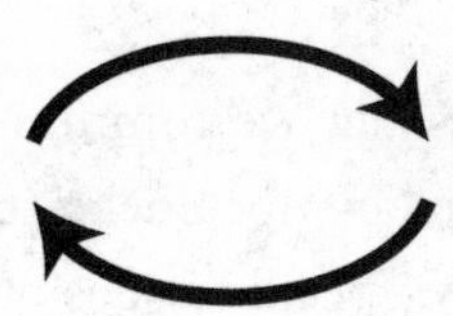

Low-influence person

- Becomes passive
- Emotionally withdraws
- Resists being influenced
- Withholds information about what is important to them

Alas, this dynamic sets up a self-fulfilling prophecy. Why should the high-influence person listen to the low-influence person if the former sees the latter as having little to offer? Since people resist being put in a dependent position (which the low-power person is in), they tend to withdraw. When they do, they contribute less, thereby reinforcing the perception that they have little to add.

Adam and Maddie colluded (unconsciously) in establishing a significant discrepancy between them. Adam didn't take Maddie's concerns seriously and offered a flip solution that left her feeling misunderstood, unappreciated, and powerless. Furthermore, he tried to hold her to their previous agreement, and in responding abruptly and without acknowledgment of what she'd said, he conveyed he was not very open to influence.

But Maddie added further to the discrepancy by not fully stating her unhappiness and backing down when she left to do the laundry. She also lost influence by letting Adam's logical arguments rule the day, superseding the value of her feelings, and by buying into his position that they'd made an agreement and that was that.

The couple needed a meta-level discussion. By that we mean, "Can we talk about why we can't talk?" They needed to temporarily set aside the content of their disagreement to discuss what was blocking their ability to communicate. To use an analogy, when you drive your car from home to work, your goal is to arrive at the office on time. But you also pay attention to how the car is operating. Do the brakes seem weak, the steering loose? Is the engine periodically sputtering? Ignoring those as you wobble down the road is not going to end well, as you might not make it to work at all. But such a meta-level discussion was unlikely if Adam felt satisfied and Maddie felt disempowered.

This ability to process *how* we communicate and problem-solve is one of the most crucial competencies in building deep relationships. It can help resolve specific issues at hand and make future problem-solving that much easier. We have already seen examples of this kind of processing in the two previous chapters. In chapter 3, Elena felt blocked about sharing personal issues with Sanjay and only overcame those after she shared the concerns that were holding her back. Likewise, in chapter 4, Liam abruptly changed topics when discussing work issues, and he and Ben only made headway when they explored what was behind this reaction.

While David and Carole were writing this book, they had multiple opportunities to practice what they preach. David would constantly come up with new content ideas that he wanted to discuss. Carole's first thought was usually, *Oh no, here he goes again—we're trying to take stuff out of the manuscript, and he keeps adding to it!* At these times she had three choices. The first was to say, "No, we're not doing that." The second was to say, "Okay, I'm too tired and have lost my patience, so you just do it." The third, which is what she most often chose, was to manage her irritation and consider his new ideas. Choosing to consider his ideas does not mean that Carole was not simultaneously open and direct with David about her feelings of irritation and the ways in which she had weighed her options in how to respond.

In other words, her choice was to double down on her commitment to David, the book, and their relationship. Regardless of how increasingly frustrated she felt about his seemingly never-ending suggestions (which she had to maddeningly admit were often good), what drove her decision was the belief that reaffirming her commitment to the book and the relationship was what mattered most. And as she did that, David also increased his commitment to her, the book, and the relationship.

If you don't double down on commitment when conflicts arise, you are less likely to have a good outcome, which then makes it harder to commit further. Suddenly, you are in a negatively reinforcing loop. On the other hand, the very act of demonstrating commitment can begin an important positively reinforcing loop. The more we commit and invest, the more rewarding the outcome is likely to be, and the better the outcome, the easier it is to commit more.

Breaking the Negative Cycle

Differences in influence occur at work, in sibling relationships, in friendships, and, of course, in marriages. Just because two people are trapped in a dysfunctional cycle doesn't mean that they're forever doomed to stay there. Either Maddie or Adam could break the cycle, although it's easier for the one with more influence to initiate the change. And, as challenging as it might be for the lower-influence person to take the initiative, it is possible. The first step is for Maddie to stop giving away the power that she has. People give influence away all the time, often without realizing they are doing so.

TEN WAYS YOU GIVE AWAY INFLUENCE

- Assuming that your needs are secondary to the other's
- Not listening to your feelings
- Letting yourself be interrupted
- Backing down when someone disagrees with you
- Avoiding conflict—not disagreeing with the other, keeping things nice
- Not giving feedback, assuming the problem is probably yours
- Being concerned about being liked/approved of and seeing that as most important
- Minimizing the importance of your comments
- Not taking credit for your accomplishments
- Not pointing out a problem unless you have a solution

Any of these beliefs or actions can make it hard for the lower-power person to raise the difficult issues and stick with it. However, the single most limiting one is the fear of conflict—believing that conflict is a sign of a flawed relationship and/or that once unleashed, disagreements will escalate and permanently damage or even destroy the relationship.

Some of these beliefs come from our upbringings and experience and are especially fraught for people who have been marginalized as a result of societal power differentials. (For example, girls are often raised to be "nice" and learn to defer, while black men often are taught never to show anger or pride.) While we are all impacted by the circumstances under which we were raised and the demographic groups we belong to, we have choices regarding the extent to which we allow ourselves to be controlled by them.

Even though arguments are rarely pleasant and can escalate to dangerous levels, sweeping problems under the rug can be just as perilous. Not only do the issues rarely go away, but they can fester and grow. For example, if Maddie stays silent, her resentment is likely to escalate into further negative thoughts: *Adam cares for himself more than he cares for me. All that's important to him is his career. He doesn't care about my growth and development. He just wants to use me as a housekeeper and babysitter. He is acting just like a typical self-centered man.* This would be an example of ways in which negative feelings grow when left unexpressed. She also knows how explosive expressing these thoughts could be—they could damage their marriage—and she worries that communicating her dissatisfaction could trigger these thoughts, which could slip out in a moment of anger.

Maddie's fears aren't entirely misplaced: These discussions *can* be damaging if handled poorly. Yet the solution isn't to avoid them. You need an important set of competencies to productively raise and resolve disagreements. Those are the subjects of the next chapters, so let's get into them!

Deepen Your Learning

SELF-REFLECTION

1. Put yourself in either Adam's or Maddie's position. If you are Adam: *You and Maddie made an agreement early in your marriage that you believed you could count on, that is working well for you, and that Maddie now wants to change.* If you are Maddie: *You made an agreement years ago under different circumstances, and that agreement no longer works for you.*

   - How would you be feeling?
   - How do you think you would respond? What would you be likely to do?

2. Discrepancies in Influence: Consider the dysfunctional trap that Adam and Maddie have fallen into as a result of the influence differential between them—Maddie has much less, while Adam has much more. How would you respond to this/what would you do if you were Maddie? If you were Adam?

3. Mutual Satisfaction: Select one of the important relationships that you identified in chapter 2 and write down:

    - What are the sources of satisfaction (benefits) you gain from this relationship?
    - What are the limitations (costs)?
    - What do you think the other person sees as the benefits they receive from the relationship?
    - What do you think might be some limitations (costs) that they experience?
    - How equitable/balanced does this relationship feel? To what extent are you both getting your needs met in rough balance with the other?

    Based on this assessment for you and this key relationship, is there a significant discrepancy between the two of you? If so, what do you think is the source of this discrepancy?

4. Mutual Influence: This chapter also stressed the importance of each person's ability to influence the other. For the same relationship you explored above:

    - How much do you believe you can influence this person?

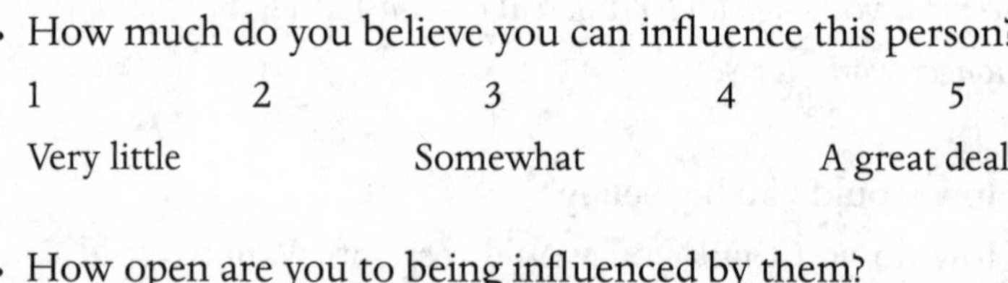

1	2	3	4	5
Very little		Somewhat		A great deal

    - How open are you to being influenced by them?

1	2	3	4	5
Very little		Somewhat		A great deal

- In general, what is the influence relationship between you?

1	2	3	4	5
I am much more influential		Roughly equal influence		Other is much more influential

If you chose 1 or 2 for this last question, what is it about how you act and/or how they act that results in your having more influence? If you chose 4 or 5, what is it about how you act and/or how they act that results in their having more influence?

What is the impact of the power difference, if there is one, on your relationship?

5. Giving Away Influence: On page 80 is a list of ten ways we give away influence. Do any of these apply to you? If so, explore why that is the case. What do you worry might happen to you if you do not engage in these behaviors?

APPLICATION

If you identified a discrepancy in mutual satisfaction or influence between you and the key relationship you chose, have a discussion with them. Do they see it the same way? Discuss what it would take to reduce the gap.

Note that in this discussion, you will be using what you learned in the previous four chapters. You need to disclose what you need, what your feelings are, and what you hope the conversation will do for your relationship.

Share the way(s) you tend to give away influence. Ask one of the key people in your life whether they see it the same way. If they do, how can they help?

MAKING SENSE

What was the impact of these discussions? What did you learn about yourself, and how did it affect your relationship? Did the discussion make it easier or more challenging to have similar discussions in the future?

Your discussion was not only *about* influence, but it was also about the two of you influencing each other. To what extent was each of you open to being influenced by the other? Given what you have learned, what will you do differently?

6

PINCHES AND CRUNCHES

Elena and Sanjay, Part 3

Jessica has a strong relationship with her brother Ryan. They're both single and live in the same city. They have busy, independent lives but have always enjoyed each other's company. Jessica has traditionally been the one more likely to initiate calls to catch up and suggest getting together after work for a drink or dinner. But in the last few months, she's begun to feel a tad resentful that she's the only one making these overtures; it used to feel more balanced. She knows Ryan is really busy with a new job and is at an age where he has a bachelor party or a wedding to attend on many weekends, so she doesn't say anything. He's always receptive when she reaches out, so she continues to do so, and she doesn't want to make a big deal out of it. Yet every time she calls him, she is a little more annoyed that she's the one who had to make the initial effort. Eventually, her annoyance grows into anger and hurt.

One Friday she calls him to suggest they catch a movie after work, and he says he's sorry, but he's just too busy with a report he has to finish up. Jessica explodes. "It's bad enough you're never the one to reach out to get together, but now, on top of that, you can't even make the time to grab a couple of hours with me. Obviously, you don't care much about our relationship anymore."

"I don't know why you're making such a big deal out of this,"

Ryan replies, surprised. "When did you become so needy? Our relationship used to be so easy. When you guilt-trip me, it makes me want to hang out even less."

Jessica concludes she would have been better off not raising any of this in the first place. However, had she raised it before her annoyance grew into anger, she might have been able to avoid a big blowup, saying something like "Hey, Ryan, it's starting to piss me off that I'm the one who always initiates getting together, and I want to raise that before it turns into a big deal. I know you're super busy. I want to respect that *and* also share that it doesn't feel good to be the one who always has to reach out first."

People often claim, as Jessica did, that they withhold critical feedback out of kindness, for the sake of the other person. But is it really for the other's sake or for our own? In this situation, Jessica was initially more annoyed than Ryan. How does keeping him in the dark help him or the relationship? And if not reciprocating is a pattern he exhibits with others, how does it help him for her not to raise the issue?

One of the ways that Jessica trapped herself was that she didn't pay enough attention to her growing frustration. Instead, she downplayed her emotions, something people do all the time. But there is truth in the adage "Own your feelings or they will own you."

In the language of Interpersonal Dynamics, we'd say that Jessica initially felt a "pinch"—a shorthand way of saying, "Hey, this isn't a capital offense, but it's bothering me." Pinches are inevitable in any relationship. For example, when someone makes a joke that you believe is slightly at your expense, do you raise the issue or, in the spirit of being a "good sport," laugh along with the others? Or say you've done a favor for another person and don't think that they've fully acknowledged your effort. Do you say something, or will they just see it as petty? Or perhaps you've shared something personal, but the other person didn't pick up on it, and you feel a bit let down. These aren't major conflicts; some of them pass, but others get under your skin and, if not dealt with, can grow into sizable problems—what we'd call a "crunch."

When a relationship first develops, both parties are on their best behavior. But as they get to know each other, one person inevitably does something that rubs the other the wrong way. Each of us has our own style of relating, of raising and resolving issues, and, in an organizational setting, of getting work done. These differences could be compatible. Or, well, not. It's a dilemma: You want to be more fully yourself, but what if being yourself causes problems with someone else?

Interpersonal issues are inevitable, a normal part of building and maintaining relationships. But as this chapter will show, it's easier to raise problems before they develop into major conflicts. For example, the two of us were working on a big project when David took some time to visit his grandchildren. Carole expressed frustration at having to wait for him to reply to some of her questions so that she could continue making progress while he was away. David felt a pinch, given the number of times he had patiently waited for Carole to carve out time for their project as she was launching her startup. It would have been easy for David to keep his annoyance buried, but he knew that the issue could fester. Instead, David told Carole that he felt a pinch from her comments. David's open communication helped raise the issue in a productive way: Carole acknowledged her own impatience, apologized, and expressed her appreciation for all the times David had picked up the slack. David told Carole she was a great partner, she reciprocated, and they got back to work.

When pinches are caught early, neither party is likely to be emotionally hooked. But when an annoyance is left to fester, once it's finally brought up, it's often grown bigger than the precipitating event and it can lead to multiple issues becoming intertwined. Let's say that your partner has been a bit forgetful of late, which you have found annoying. But each time, the pinch was minor, so you didn't say anything. Then they come home having forgotten the milk they said they'd buy, and you get into a fight, ostensibly over the milk. But the issue isn't the milk—it's a proxy for built-up annoyance.

Recently, David had a similar placeholder issue with his wife, Eva. He was in the kitchen making a cup of coffee and was about to leave when Eva said (with some heat), "Why did you leave the dirty spoon on the counter? Can't you put it away?" It would have been easy for him to say, "What's the big deal about one lousy spoon? And anyway, I clean up a lot of things."

Fortunately, he didn't, because the issue wasn't the dirty spoon. Rather, it was about what it stood for. Eva had just cleaned up the kitchen. Not only had David not expressed appreciation, but the cavalier way he had put a dirty spoon down had been taken by Eva as a sign that he was treating her like the scullery maid. It was only when they got to the real issue—how much each expressed (or didn't express) appreciation to the other—that they could have a productive discussion.

Elena and Sanjay, Part 3

Elena and Sanjay continued their lunches just about every week and got to know each other even better. Sometimes they talked about personal interests, but mostly they talked about work and changes in the company. These were affirming conversations for Elena, and her continued job success led to a significant increase in self-confidence. She didn't dwell on what happened at her old company anymore.

Sanjay was increasingly impressed with Elena's ability to see the larger picture instead of getting trapped in narrow departmental points of view. So, when Sanjay was promoted to take over the Latin America market, he asked Elena, who had grown up in Mexico, to come work for him. He not only valued her background and perspective but also didn't want Heather, who worked for him, to be the only woman on the seven-member team.

Elena found the new role exciting and the team meetings generally rewarding. The issues were important to her, and she joined in the conversations wholeheartedly. Sanjay had stressed from the start that he wanted all team members to "take the larger perspective" and "hold each other accountable to ensure the best results." Elena found taking this larger view easy to do, but other members had a harder time and frequently responded from their functional point of view.

Elena was perplexed that Sanjay didn't call them on this tendency. Having observed this repeatedly, she finally decided to comment after one of the members grew particularly protective of his area. "We need to take a bigger view and consider the larger purpose as opposed to being parochial," she said. The group went silent for a moment and the offending member nodded. When nobody else said anything, the conversation moved on. In spite of the silence that had followed her comment, Elena felt good about speaking up and noted that in subsequent discussions, more of the other members considered the broader perspective.

A week later, at one of their Thursday lunches, Sanjay said, "Now that you work for me, I'm concerned that the rest of the team might feel excluded by our lunch meetings and think that we're discussing the project and even making decisions. How about opening these lunches up to everybody?" Although Elena felt a twinge of loss, she appreciated his concern for how the team members might be feeling, so she agreed. Not all members joined them on Thursdays, but most of them did, and the camaraderie of the team increased.

Meanwhile, other dynamics of the team meetings began to bother Elena. Even though she liked the informal tone and friendly bantering, sometimes the humor had a bit of an edge to it. *I wish people would be more direct,* she thought, but decided to let it pass. What bothered her more was that, not infrequently, she would make a comment to which there was no response, yet five minutes later, one of the men would make the same point and others would pick up on it and run with it, with no acknowledgment that she had made it first. This was especially true with Steven, who seemed to have a hard time hearing her ideas but would nonetheless make the same suggestions shortly afterward. What especially galled Elena was that even Sanjay, from whom she would have expected more given his sensitivity, seemed to pay more attention when a male team member made a comment that she had previously made.

One day, walking out of a meeting with Heather where this had occurred yet again, she asked her if she'd noticed it. "Of course," Heather replied, and shrugged. In a somewhat resigned tone, she added, "But what do you expect? And the men interrupt us much more than they do each other. That's just the way the world is."

Elena wasn't satisfied with this conclusion, nor was she prepared to simply accept the status quo. Also, Sanjay's behavior particularly bothered her: Since he was their leader, she expected more from him. She'd thought he understood gender issues and anticipated that he would have pointed out this unhealthy pattern in the meeting. She was hesitant about raising her concerns with the group, lest they see her as "too sensitive." She was also concerned about talking to Sanjay about the problem for fear he would think she was using their friendship to ask for something special. *Oh well,* she thought, *it really isn't such a big deal. I'll just let it go.*

That didn't turn out to be so easy. When the pattern repeated itself in subsequent meetings, it bothered Elena more and more. Then the Latin America group gave a progress report to the executive committee, and one of the vice presidents was especially complimentary about an angle they'd taken. Sanjay said, "Yes, we feel very good about that recommendation." Elena thought, *That was primarily my idea and I had to push hard for it; it certainly would have been nice to have been acknowledged for it.* As they left the room, Elena walked next to Sanjay and quietly made her point. "We're a team," he replied, "and I need everybody to take a team perspective."

Why We Don't Raise Pinches

People are often hesitant to raise pinches out of concern that doing so might make them seem thin-skinned and petty. You probably know someone who can take affront at the smallest comment, and you don't want to be like them. Or you may think, *It's just not worth it.* Sometimes that's true, but sometimes if you dig deeper, you'll find it's more important to you than you initially realized. Try this: Change the first pronoun to "I" or "you," as in, *I'm just not worth it* or *You're just not worth it.* Do you still think the issue isn't worth raising? Sometimes you may, but often you realize there are more feelings there than you first recognized.

Many people are also hesitant to raise pinches out of concern that speaking up might make things worse. Will your complaint cause the other to retaliate? Will it trigger a bunch of other issues? Or do you hold back because you see the relationship—or the other person—as fragile? When this comes up in class, we ask the student, "If a friend of yours felt pinched by a comment you made, would you want them to tell you?" Almost universally, the student says yes. We add, "So, if you want that, wouldn't you want to do that for them when you're pinched?"

A final reason we resist raising pinches early on is that we assume the other meant no harm. We think, *If they didn't mean to bother me, why should I be bothered?* That rationalization may have worked the first time that Steven repeated Elena's unacknowledged point, but it was still a rationalization. As we will explore in the next chapter, there's a difference between another's *intent* and the *effect* of their behavior. That Elena was bothered was true in and of itself—her feeling didn't need a justification to exist.

The likelihood that Steven didn't mean anything by it could actually make it easier to raise the pinch. Let's say that in a meeting Steven twice picked up Elena's idea without acknowledging the source. Could she, as the two of them walked out afterward, lightly say, "Thanks for picking up my ideas that got ignored, Steven. But

I'd have liked if you'd acknowledged that I raised them first"? Steven would be likely to respond, "Sorry, didn't realize that I'd done that." And Elena could add, "I thought that might have been the case." The pinch is noted, acknowledged, and settled.

If Elena is only pinched, she can say this lightly. If she waited until she was more upset and expressed the same sentiment through clenched teeth, Steven would more likely hear it as an attack. But because she raised it early, Elena is likely to feel better, and Steven might be more aware of what he is doing that she finds problematic. If he continues to repeat her comments without acknowledgment, she now has a basis to bring it up again, but more strongly.

Many pinches do go away, but ask yourself, Will this pinch linger? Connect to other issues? Trigger a major fight about missing milk rather than what's really going on?

Once a pinch grows this way, it threatens to become a crunch. Crunches are much more problematic than pinches, because in addition to the likelihood that much stronger feelings now exist, you're also more likely to have developed a negative story about the other person. Elena wasn't there yet but was getting close, so it was wise that she raised her issue with Sanjay as they left the meeting, even though Sanjay didn't respond as she'd hoped.

As pinches grow into crunches, we begin to develop a story that is likely to include *negative assumptions* about the other person. Take Elena's pinch with Steven. She doesn't know him well, but his rather frequent tendency to "steal" her ideas (as Elena sees it) is likely to lead her to question his motives and character. It will become easy for her to construct narratives about him. *He has trouble with strong women. He likes to be the center of attention. He needs frequent affirmation from authority.* None of these theories—even if never stated—are likely to help her build a positive relationship with this key colleague.

Furthermore, once we have developed a negative story, we have a tendency to *selectively collect data,* or, as we like to think of it, "build a case that supports our view." The truth is, regardless of how objective you think you are, everyone is subject to confirmation bias. When you develop a belief, or even a hunch, you have a tendency to pay more attention to incidents that support it and discount any that are disconfirming. Elena will likely be especially aware of further cases where her ideas are ignored and then restated by others, especially Steven. Likewise, she will be cued to watch for times when she thinks that Sanjay is ignoring her or downplaying her contribution to the team. She will also be *less* likely to notice when she is being heard, acknowledged, or appreciated by either of them.

But Is It Funny? The Use of Humor in Raising Pinches

Let's imagine that Elena, rather than talking to Steven after the meeting, has had it with his "stealing" her ideas and in the meeting says, "Great point, Steven, and just what I said five minutes ago. I guess one needs a deep voice to be heard here." Even if it were said with a smile and light voice, how might that land? On the one hand, it could be a net positive. Everybody, including Steven, laughs, and he acknowledges her point. He (and others) stop doing it and Elena's contributions are heard.

Humor works in these situations precisely because of its power to help people connect. Victor Borge once said, "Laughter is the shortest distance between two people." Sharing a joke or a funny comment can bring us closer to one another. It can lighten the mood and lift our spirits. When we banter and kid around, we not only get to know one another better but also experience a special kind of freedom. As our colleagues Jennifer Aaker and Naomi Bagdonas's research suggests, "Laughter makes us more physically resilient to tensions and stressors . . . facilitates social bonding and increases trust. When people laugh together at work, relationships improve, and people feel more valued and trusted." In the best-case scenario, Elena's joke would improve her standing with her colleagues and increase her team's cohesion.

On the other hand, humor rarely works if the joke is at one person's expense or is an indirect way of saying something that isn't funny at all. And Elena doesn't know how her jab might land with Steven. It might be more than a pinch to him if he feels embarrassed at being put down in front of his colleagues. Even if he doesn't take exception, maybe he, and others, would hear it only as a joke, resulting in the message's getting lost. Even if the message got through, it could increase the distance between the two of them as he guards himself against possible future zingers and she guards against possible retaliation. It's unlikely to encourage him to be vulnerable. And it's possible this humorous comment would send a message that being indirect is how Elena and others want annoyances expressed—when, in fact, this tendency is something that Elena has found frustrating about the team.

Humor can also be a shield to hide behind if the other takes affront. What if Steven were to respond by saying, "That's snide; what's going on?" That *could* be an opening for an authentic conversation in which Elena directly states her feelings. But what if she says, "Oh, can't you take a joke?" Now she has put him down twice. Not only is the issue not dealt with, but whatever trust there was between them has been lost. Furthermore, this may not help Elena's reputation as a direct, trustworthy person with other colleagues.

The problem with using humor to convey a message is its inherent ambiguity. It's unclear exactly how upset Elena is at Steven's tendency to repeat her ideas. Is she really annoyed or only slightly pinched? And there is ambiguity in what Steven hears and how he takes it. It's better, especially if you're concerned about the relationship, to have the sort of direct conversation that Elena could have if she mentioned her concerns to Steven as they were leaving the meeting.

This is not to say that humor never works. But you have to be sensitive to the context. How large is your pinch? (Remember that there may be more to your reaction than you first thought.) What kind of sense of humor does the other person have? Some people enjoy a witty response, even if it's slightly at their expense, whereas others are likely to take it personally. You also have to consider the strength of your relationship. If the other person knows that you accept them, one kidding comment can go over well. And finally, consider the setting. When all of these factors are taken into account, humor can be used functionally.

For instance, David's friend Jane Anne likes to give small dinner parties. Although an excellent cook, she used to spend much of the meal apologizing by saying the food didn't turn out well; it was overdone or underspiced or a dozen other disparagements. This would continue in spite of strong denials from the guests, since her meals were always great. Those denials didn't seem to have an impact on Jane Anne, however, and she remained self-critical. Then, at one dinner, after the same routine occurred, her friend Peggy said, "Wonderful meal, Jane Anne, can I have the recipe? But the version without the self-flagellation." The roar of laughter seemed to sink in, because after that evening, Jane Anne's excuses noticeably diminished.

In this situation, Jane Anne and Peggy were good friends, and Jane Anne knew that Peggy both liked and respected her. She likely could sense that Peggy wasn't intending to put her down but instead didn't want Jane Anne to continue to put *herself* down. The other guests were also friends, so everyone understood the situation. In this case, the feedback worked and is a good example of how humor can be useful when used appropriately.

Humor is probably not an approach that Elena would want to use with either Steven or Sanjay. She tried to raise her concerns as a pinch as she and Sanjay left the executive committee meeting, but that had little impact, which caused her annoyance to rise further. This is now starting to move beyond a pinch, so she decides that she needs to have a direct talk with Sanjay. The challenge is how to have such a conversation in a way that can both resolve the issue and continue to build their relationship. That requires being able to give behaviorally specific feedback—a crucial competency that we turn to next.

Deepen Your Learning

SELF-REFLECTION

1. Imagine that you are Elena. *How would you respond to her situation in team meetings, during which your ideas tend to be ignored and then restated by others? Would you let it go or say something? And after the executive committee meeting when Sanjay brushed off your concern, what would you do? Think specifically about what you would do and say.*

2. Dealing with Pinches: Think about pinches you have felt in the past.

    - How do you tend to respond? Do you tend to just take it, brush it off, withdraw, look for an opportunity to pinch back, or get upset?

3. Key Relationship: Do you have a current pinch with a key relationship? What has stopped you from raising it?

4. Using Humor: How do you tend to use humor? What happens when you do? Are there any ways you use humor that are dysfunctional? Do you have a friend who uses humor well? What do they do that makes it work?

APPLICATION

If you identified a lingering pinch with a key relationship in question 3 above, raise it.

In the coming weeks, be aware of times when you feel pinched. Do you have a sense of which ones are worth letting go and which ones are worth raising? Do you recognize any patterns in your choices? What action are you prepared to take, having recognized these patterns?

Do you know somebody who doesn't respond well when you express a pinch with them? For example, do they brush it off, accuse you of being thin-skinned, or get combative? If these reactions inhibit you from sharing pinches, how could you raise this to improve the relationship?

If you tend to use humor a lot, go to a few people who know you well and ask whether what you say always lands as you intend. You might ask for specifics regarding when it works and when it doesn't.

Do you know someone who uses humor in a way that bothers you? It might have a put-down quality, or maybe they use it to convey a message indirectly. It's not a major issue, but a growing pinch leaves you feeling a tad uncertain and is keeping you from being as close as you want. Strategize about how to raise it to improve your relationship, and then follow through.

MAKING SENSE

In these discussions, you have begun the process of removing blocks to a deeper relationship. How did those go? What did you learn about yourself and about building relationships?

NOTE: Your application experiments might not initially turn out. What is most important is what you (and the other person) learn from them, including skills you develop in the process of repairing problems.

7

WHY FEEDBACK IS THE BREAKFAST OF CHAMPIONS

Elena and Sanjay, Part 4

Elena decided that she had to meet with Sanjay and give him feedback. The question was how to do it so that he would take her concerns more seriously than he had when they left the committee meeting. She didn't want him to feel attacked or put down. She also didn't want him to think that she was asking something special for herself or taking advantage of their friendship.

Elena can be direct without being abrasive by using *behaviorally specific feedback*. This is a crucial competence that allows you to raise difficulties in a way that minimizes defensiveness. It not only resolves interpersonal issues but also is key for personal learning and for building meaningful relationships.

This is especially important when you have feedback you don't think you can raise. The two of us disagree, and passionately believe that you can say (almost) anything to (almost) anybody if you stick with your reality. We put the "almost"s in parentheses because, having lived in academia, we are used to being cautious about sweeping statements. But after two glasses of wine, we drop the "almost." We agree with our Stanford colleague and JetBlue board chair Joel Peterson, who says, "Feedback is the breakfast of champions."

Sticking with your reality is more complicated than you might imagine, as there are actually three different areas of understanding, or realities, that exist when two people interact. Take the conversation between Sanjay and Elena as they walked out of the executive committee meeting, when Elena expressed feeling bothered that Sanjay didn't acknowledge her contribution to the group's report. The first reality is Sanjay's *intent,* which was that he wanted everybody to "take a team perspective." That first area is what only Sanjay knows. This includes his *needs, motives, emotions,* and *intentions*. The second reality is his *behavior,* and that is the area they both see. It consists of Sanjay's words, tone, gestures, facial expressions, and the like. The third reality is the *impact* of his behavior on Elena, and that's the area in which Elena is an expert; it comprises her reactions (emotions and responses). Note that initially, each person can only know two of the three realities. Sanjay doesn't know the impact of his behavior on Elena, and Elena doesn't know his motives or intentions.

If Elena sticks with her reality, she can raise issues in a direct, non-accusatory way that actually helps both of them understand what's going on. She can point to the behavior and share her reactions to it. She doesn't have to know Sanjay's intentions. It's when she moves beyond her reality and makes statements about Sanjay's motives that her feedback becomes accusatory. In describing this model, we tell our students to imagine a tennis net between the first and second "realities"—that is, between intent and behavior. In tennis, you can't play in the other's court, and the same is true with feedback. *You have to stay on your side of the net.*

Interpersonal Cycle: Three Realities

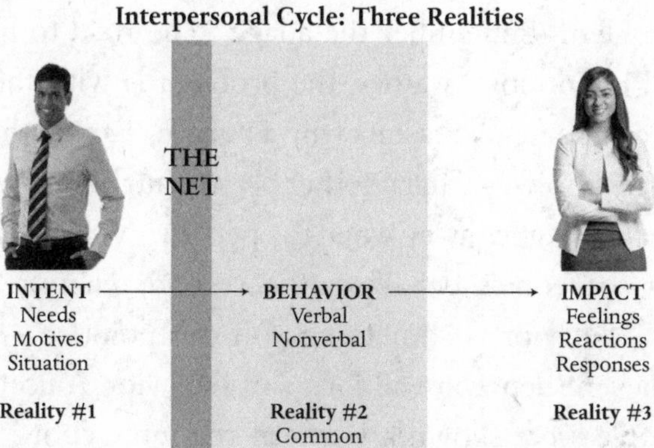

Why Most Feedback Doesn't Work

Generally, people don't use the feedback model. They don't stick with their reality but go over the net in making attributions about the other. People say, "You just don't want to cooperate," "You want to dominate this discussion!" "I feel that you only think about yourself," or "I feel like you don't care." (And you know our stance by now on feeling words. But in case you've forgotten, there are no feeling words in any of these statements!) No wonder so much feedback causes hurt and defensiveness, given the likelihood that the other person will feel misunderstood or, worse, attacked.

In an ironic twist, young kids are often better at staying on their side of the net than adults. When Carole's children were five and seven, she overheard the younger one say to the older one, "Nick, that's the third time you've picked the game and I don't like that. I pick the next game or I'm not playing." The younger one didn't know enough to impute a motive ("You want to control") or label him ("You're being a bully"). Instead, she was very specific about what Nick was doing that she didn't like and told him so. How simple. After that they took turns choosing what they played next, and . . . never, ever fought again. (Ha!)

Adults often fall into the trap of thinking that they know other people's motives and intentions. But unless they've explicitly told us, *what we surmise is only our hunch*. Their intentions are their reality, not ours. Furthermore, it's rare that the intentions themselves are the problem. Remember the adage "The road to hell is paved with good intentions." Rather, the problem is with their *behavior*, and there can be many reasons why a person, even with the best of intentions, acts in ways that another person might find problematic.

Feedback also goes awry when the person giving it thinks they're describing someone's behavior (the second reality), but they're really not. Behavior is something you can point to—words, gestures, and even silence are all forms of behavior. A useful test is to ask, If people were shown a video of the interaction, would they agree they saw the same behaviors? Conversely, saying, "You are dominating the discussion," is not an observable behavior; it is a judgment made based on a series of behaviors. What exactly did the other do that has led you to draw that conclusion? Did they interrupt and talk over others' comments? Or dismiss the value of another's contributions? Or keep on pushing their point until others gave way? The last three are behaviors.

This can seem like nitpicking, but insofar as the other has a tendency to deny your feedback, the more specificity you provide, the more difficult it is for them to do so. It is harder for them to dismiss the feedback when you point out the four times in which they didn't let others finish their point. It is those behaviors that led you to see them as dominating the discussion, but that is *your* conclusion.

Another common problem with feedback is that you're not always aware of all the ways you have been impacted by someone else's behavior. That's important because recognizing your reactions and, especially, your feelings is your area of "expertise" and forms the basis of your influence. How did Elena feel when Sanjay didn't acknowledge her contributions? Was she *slightly annoyed* or *very upset*? How did that, in turn, affect her attitude toward Sanjay? Did she feel less trusting? And last, did it impact her willingness to raise new ideas and lessen her commitment to the work? Sanjay is likely to pay the most attention to these reactions because they speak to his effectiveness, and sharing them will strengthen her feedback.

The Power of Behaviorally Specific Feedback

Behaviorally specific feedback is powerful for several reasons. If Elena sticks with her reality—Sanjay's observable behavior and her reactions to it—the feedback is indisputable. When she says, "I felt unappreciated when you didn't mention my role in that decision," Sanjay can't say, "No you didn't," because he would then be on her side of the net. But if she were to leave her reality and guess at his intentions by saying something like "The reason you didn't acknowledge me is that you don't think it's important to give credit even when credit is due," he could say, "No, that's not true," and they would reach an impasse.

There's another advantage if Elena gives feedback based on her reality: Sanjay is more likely to explain why he acted as he did. When Elena expressed her annoyance as they walked out of the executive committee meeting, Sanjay explained, "I want us to act as a team." Now she knows his intention. That's one reason the giver of feedback doesn't need to figure out the other's intentions: Sooner or later, the other person will tell you.

In raising her issue before she has written Sanjay off entirely, Elena has given him a gift. Remember, Sanjay knows only two of the three realities; he doesn't know the impact his behavior has had on Elena—only she does. To be an effective leader, he needs to know how his words and actions are coming across. As the saying goes, if you shoot in the dark, you are unlikely to hit the target. Elena's expression of her pinch was a cue to Sanjay that his actions might have had dysfunctional consequences. His immediate response was to brush her comment off, but if she had shared her reality, he would have been less likely to do so. As it is, this left her with a question about how much more to say.

The reason why we stress *behaviorally specific* feedback is that too much feedback isn't specific and therefore ends up being useless or even destructive. If Joe's manager tells him, "Joe, you have a poor attitude that interferes with your performance," it's bound to make Joe feel defensive and confused. It doesn't give him exact information on what he has done or how to improve. Which attitudes are the problem—all of them? What work is substandard—everything Joe does? No wonder people are hesitant to give feedback and think they have to "soften you up" with platitudes.

Focusing on behavior avoids these problems. Saying, "Joe, in the meeting today, I noticed that you were mainly talking about your area and not responding to others' concerns. If you want other people to take your issues seriously, you need to do that for them as well." That specific feedback is less likely to activate Joe's concerns about whether *all* of who he is and what he does is being questioned.

Many people are hesitant to give negative feedback for fear that it will be damaging and demotivating. The problem is with the term "negative feedback." The two of us intensely dislike the term because we believe all behavioral feedback is positive. Even feedback on problematic behavior is positive, because *behavior* is something we can change, and feedback on it is an opportunity to improve. We prefer the word "affirmative" to describe feedback on behaviors you appreciate and want to convey as strengths, and "developmental" for feedback on behaviors that you find problematic.

All feedback is data. The information may say something about the giver, and it may say something about the receiver (often both). But it is all data, and more data is better than less. Quite simply, you're better off knowing than not. Years ago, a student approached Carole after class and told her he'd felt disrespected when she looked at her watch while he was answering her question (there was no clock in the room, and she had material left to cover). Regardless of her reason, the student's feedback contained important information without which Carole would have been helpless to address the student's concern or be sensitive that others might feel the same way in the future. Feedback given with the intention of being helpful is always positive.

These guidelines are just as important when the feedback to be given is affirmative. If you say to me, "Nice job," it may make me feel warm and fuzzy in the moment, but it's somewhat meaningless. What exactly did I do that you appreciated? What was the impact on you? What might I learn from this so that I can leverage my strengths in the future?

We will return time and again in subsequent chapters to the behavioral feedback model because of its power in raising and resolving issues in a way that allows all parties to be more fully themselves.

This, in turn, not only keeps the relationship on track but also, as we will show in later chapters, improves and deepens it.

Elena and Sanjay, Part 4

Elena contacted Sanjay to "discuss an issue related to the Latin America team." He willingly agreed and told her to drop by his office that afternoon.

After greetings, Elena began, "Sanjay, I need to talk, because I'm getting increasingly frustrated by what's happening in the group. Some of it is with my peers, but some of it is with you, and I'd really like to work it out."

Sanjay looked surprised.

"Don't worry," Elena said, "it's not a capital crime, but I feel annoyed, and it's beginning to interfere with my enjoyment on the job."

"What's the matter?" Sanjay asked with concern.

"As I think you've seen, I'm really committed to this group and have worked hard to make suggestions that add to the discussion. But there have been many times when I make a point, nobody says anything, and then five minutes later, one of the men says the same thing and it gets a response. At those times I don't feel heard."

"Yes, I noticed that a couple of times," Sanjay responded. "And I'm sorry."

"You noticed it and didn't say anything? That's even more disappointing."

"Well, I'm not the schoolyard monitor," he said a little defensively.

"Sanjay, you're the leader, and so you're the role model. And when you don't say anything, you normalize it. But that's only part of the problem."

"There's more?"

"Yes. I can deal with my peers. But it's even harder and more disappointing that you tend to say little when I make a comment yet pick it up when a man makes the same comment a few minutes later."

"No, I don't do that."

"Well, in our last meeting, there were two occasions," Elena said, and identified specific incidents and the details.

Sanjay reflected for a minute. "Okay, I see that. And sorry—I'll watch for it. But you know that I really value what you contribute. Our report to the executive committee was much stronger because of the ideas you brought."

"Yes, Sanjay, I know you value my input and I don't think for a minute that you intend to ignore my comments. You might have been unaware of your actions—that's why I want to raise it." She paused for a minute and then continued, "As long as we're clearing the air, there's something else that I found demotivating."

"What's that?"

"It was the executive committee meeting yesterday. That idea that they most liked was one that I had to fight so hard for, and I got no acknowledgment from you."

"But as I said, it's important to be a team player. We're all in this together."

"I accept that. In my view, being a team player doesn't mean we lose our identity or that the different contributions that people make aren't acknowledged. I'm committed for a lot of reasons, and it would help if my contributions were recognized."

Sanjay thought for a moment and said, "I don't want to play favorites. I want everybody to feel valued."

"Sanjay, I want that, too, but I think we can be valued in different ways. It's not a zero-sum game. My being acknowledged doesn't mean that others can't be as well. I think all of us like to feel valued. Look, you do a great job managing meetings, keeping us on track, and focusing on our goals. But, as a leader, I think you also need to focus on the contributions each of us makes. I, for one, could use appreciation for the extra effort I'm putting in. I can't speak for others on the team, but I'd be surprised if I were the only one who felt this way. That's one reason I'm telling you this."

Sanjay was silent for a while and then quietly said, "I guess I know that, but . . . I think the reason I didn't mention your role at the executive committee meeting was a fear that, because of our friendship, people might think I was playing favorites."

"I get that." Elena nodded. "I'm not asking for favoritism. What I am asking is that you give each of us credit for what we bring. Giving me credit for what I've done doesn't preclude you from giving credit to Heather or Steven or anyone else on the team. I want to also be clear that my *intent* in giving you all of this feedback is to point out ways in which your behavior is affecting me negatively and to do that early enough for it not to turn into a big deal. It is precisely because I care as much as I do about our relationship that I feel compelled to have this conversation."

Sanjay nodded in agreement.

NOTE THAT FROM the beginning of the meeting in Sanjay's office, Elena stayed with her reality and didn't make any accusations or negative attributions of Sanjay's motives or intentions. (She did cross the net in making *positive* attributions when she said, "I *know* you value my input." People rarely become defensive when we attribute positive intent, and her objective in saying this was to separate intentions from behavioral outcomes.)

Elena talked about her feelings and what was happening to her. She also put the issue in perspective by saying, "It's not a capital crime," and acknowledging low-level emotions: *annoyed,* not *angry*. Then she talked about the impact Sanjay's behavior had on her involvement with the project, which was not only about her but spoke to what might also concern Sanjay. She clearly stated that her intent was to raise the issue because she cared about their relationship, which is also an important element of effective feedback. Furthermore, rather than taking an adversarial stance, she conveyed a common interest. She told Sanjay about specific behaviors that bothered her and was able to point to two recent examples. What is important about this last point is that those behaviors had recently occurred. Feedback that is close in time to an event is especially impactful because it is fresh in both people's minds. Commenting on somebody's behavior that occurred months before is much less useful since it has become but a dim and possibly distorted memory.

Because Elena spoke to what Sanjay cared about, she could be direct. Many people, especially in dealing with authority, believe that they have to beat around the bush. Elena didn't have to do that since she conveyed information that Sanjay needed to improve his leadership effectiveness.

Being clear about behavior is the starting point. But two people can draw different conclusions from the same action. Elena believes that Sanjay's not holding members accountable (an observable behavior) has the negative effect of decreasing his authority, but he might conclude that it gives space for others to take on that responsibility and not be dependent on him. What then? Neither of them knows how Sanjay's holding back is affecting the other team members, but now that they have identified the behavior in question, they can jointly work to find out its full impact.

Elena didn't make any inferences about Sanjay's intentions. In fact, it was Sanjay who shared why he acted as he did. Because she agreed with his goals, Elena could be an ally, not an adversary, and show him how his actions were interfering with achieving his objectives. She set up a win-win exchange. As we have mentioned in many cases, it isn't a person's objectives that are problematic but how they go about achieving them. That's why feedback is a gift.

Elena's statements (talking about herself, her feelings, and what she needed) were indisputable because they reflected her reality. Furthermore, by sticking with her reality without attacking Sanjay, Elena built conditions that made it easier for him to talk about his reality—his needs and his concerns. Note that her self-disclosure led to his self-disclosure, whereas if she'd asked accusatory questions, Sanjay would likely have closed down.

Beware the "Feedback Sandwich"

Too often, people use the "feedback sandwich," thinking it will make difficult feedback easier to hear. By "feedback sandwich," we mean starting with something positive (to soften up the other person), then saying something negative, and ending with something positive so they will feel good. "Joe, you really do a good job here. But there's an issue that we need to talk about. But you really are a valuable employee."

Unfortunately, this approach rarely works. As soon as you start with the positive, the other's defenses go up as they wait for the "but." They brush aside the good news and don't take it in.

The feedback sandwich is often utilized because you're concerned the recipient will feel totally rejected if you don't throw in some positive reinforcement. But that misidentifies the problem. The difficulty is not that the feedback is harsh or negative but that it's not behaviorally specific enough to be useful. It also contaminates affirmative feedback because it is seen as the ploy that it is—something intended not to provide a learning opportunity, but to manipulate.

But didn't Elena use the feedback sandwich when she told Sanjay the various things that he does well in leading the team? We'd argue she didn't, really. When she first walked into his office, she led with what was problematic for her and waited until she was well into the feedback process before noting what she appreciated. What she was trying to do was expand what Sanjay considered his areas of responsibility to include appropriately acknowledging each member's unique contribution.

Opening Pandora's Box

Sanjay and Elena's conversation can feel very tidy, but the world isn't always that simple. Let's now assume Sanjay responded to Elena's initial feedback by saying, "Well, I'm glad you're raising this, Elena, because I've been bothered as well. I want this group to get along, and you tend to be pretty judgmental."

Elena's first thought could be, *Why did I even raise this? Better to have let sleeping dogs lie.* But would that really be better? Many people fear giving feedback out of concern that the other person will turn the tables. However, if you're doing something that annoys someone, aren't you better off knowing? If you know, at least you have choices. Not knowing will leave you in the dark. We would argue that Sanjay is better off knowing about Elena's pinch and that Elena is better off knowing if she's pinching him, too. Depending on how she responds, this could be an opportunity rather than a problem.

Another reaction Elena might have is defensiveness, since she doesn't see herself as judgmental. Note that Sanjay is over the net here: He is labeling her instead of describing her behavior. This is an important choice point for Elena. She can either get into an argument ("No, I am not!") or she can manage her defensiveness and use the feedback model to gain a fuller understanding of his complaint. Doing that might sound something like this:

"Wow, Sanjay, I'm trying not to be defensive because I don't see myself as a judgmental person. But clearly, I'm doing something that's giving you that impression. What am I doing?"

"Well, you really came down hard on the guys about their not taking the larger viewpoint."

"Okay, I can see where you can get that impression, but that raises a couple of issues. You've said that you want members to hold each other accountable. Do you really want that? And if you do, is there a way that I could have done it that might have appeared less judgmental?"

This might lead to a rich discussion between the two of them.

Sanjay could acknowledge that he wants members to call each other out when they're going off course but has difficulty thinking of how else Elena could have done it. If Sanjay *could* suggest a more effective way for Elena to have raised that point, it would be a win-win outcome. She would increase her effectiveness and Sanjay would be less bothered. Multiple gifts all around.

Elena now has another choice. She has made her point and could end the conversation. However, she sees this as an opportunity to deepen their interaction and reiterate her intent, so she asks, "I don't know if this is right or not, but I was struck by the fact that you seemed hesitant to confront members when they only advocated for their area. I wonder how you feel about conflict, and again I want to say that even though this feels a bit risky to ask, my intention here is to be helpful to you."

"Yeah, that's an issue for me," Sanjay admits. "I'm more comfortable when things are calm and people get on well with one another."

"That confuses me, Sanjay. In our meetings, we've had some very intense debates, and you seem comfortable with that. Or am I reading that wrong?"

"No, you're right. But what we're talking about now is different. I don't want people attacking one another."

"I don't either," Elena says. "When I called those guys out on not taking the larger perspective, I didn't call them idiots or say they were incompetent. I was talking about their actions. If we can disagree on tasks, can't we disagree on people's behaviors, too? And, Sanjay, in this discussion, do you feel attacked by me? I'm asking because I'm frankly a little nervous about how you might be taking this. Should I have said nothing or been less direct?"

"No, no," Sanjay assures her. "While this hasn't been entirely comfortable, I don't feel attacked and I do appreciate your directness. In fact, the irony is not lost on me that this is probably a good example of team members holding each other accountable."

"Well, being direct is an important part of how I want to be seen.

So, if you can accept that, then I want you to be direct with me and call me out whenever you think I'm being judgmental or punitive. And I'm really glad we had this conversation. It not only cleared the air for me but also leaves me feeling better about the solid ground of our friendship."

"Yeah, me too."

IN THIS SCENARIO, Elena displayed some key competencies that enabled her to handle what could have been a challenging situation:

- She was able to control her initial defensiveness. It wasn't that Elena didn't *feel* defensive. Rather, she wasn't controlled by this reaction; she was able to acknowledge it and move on.
- Elena used the feedback model. She (a) described her own reality ("I don't see myself that way") without explaining or justifying herself; (b) acknowledged that Sanjay's reaction was his; and (c) asked for the behavior that gave him that impression.

Elena may have seemed to cross the net when she said, "I wonder how you feel about conflict." Isn't she talking about Sanjay's reality? Not really, because she raises this as a hunch, not a statement of fact, and encourages joint exploration. Furthermore, what's important beyond her words is her attitude. If she truly believes that she doesn't know, her tone and body language will convey that. These very words, with a different tone, could have been a leading question implying she knew the answer. That *would* have been crossing the net. This point is nuanced but important. It's less about getting the words just right and more about holding to the fundamental belief that you don't know what's going on with the other person. This is a great example of using a hunch productively. Elena wasn't sure but was making a guess. Staying curious about what was going on with Sanjay kept her from crossing the net.

Sanjay showed various competencies, too. As he shared more of his reality (fear that disagreements or holding people accountable would turn into personal attacks), Elena gained more insight about what was important to him. Sanjay listened as well. He heard Elena's feedback and agreed with the value of their directness with each other. This undoubtedly made Elena feel more heard and her feedback more valued. Finally, in this process, they got to know each other better, and it deepened the type of discussions they can have in the future. Not a bad outcome, Pandora!

"Hey, You're Over the Net"

When someone else's feedback is an attribution of your inner reality, as it was when Sanjay accused Elena of being judgmental, it's tough not to feel defensive. The first reaction is to rebut: "No, I'm not." A second tendency is to counterattack: "The reason that I do that is because you do X."

This is a normal response when we feel attacked, misunderstood, or placed in a one-down position. But defensiveness can lead to escalation and prevent both parties from learning. Accept you are feeling defensive, but don't act on it. Instead, use the feedback model to push the other person back to their side of the court. That's what Elena did when she said:

> "Wow, Sanjay, I'm trying not to be defensive because I don't see myself as a judgmental person [reality #1]. But clearly, I'm doing something [reality #2] that's giving you that impression [reality #3]. What am I doing?"

She's turned an accusation into a mutual learning experience. Although conceptually simple, it's not always easy to do. One of the most interesting and remarkable things that happens at the Stanford business school is the way in which the model of the net becomes more and more commonplace in everyday conversations as more of the students take Interpersonal Dynamics. We are also heartened about the extent to which it stays with alums for decades. "Over the net" has become a culturally defining term.

A great example of the utility of these concepts involved a young woman we knew who had learned about the net model from an older friend. Her high school tennis coach was very irritated with her and said, "Your problem is you're not committed." She calmly responded to him, "Can you tell me more about what you mean? I've never missed a practice or a game, and I happily play anywhere in the lineup you place me. That's what commitment means to me. But obviously I'm doing something that makes you think I'm not committed. What is it?"

The coach then raised his voice slightly and said, "You show up to practice without your uniform!" To which she responded, "Oh. . . . Okay, I'm glad I asked! I would have never known that was how you defined commitment. If you'd told me I was disorganized and forgetful, I'd have been the first person to agree. I get it now. I'll be back tomorrow for practice . . . with my uniform." Their relationship changed significantly once she learned the source of his irritation and was able to respond to it. Remember, sometimes feedback comes in very ugly wrapping—but that doesn't mean there's not a gift inside.

Since by yourself you can only know two of the three realities, receiving feedback is essential to being more effective. You need to know the third—the impact of your behavior. As we often say, "It takes two to know one." Sanjay now knows himself better as a leader as a result of Elena's feedback. But what doesn't work for Elena may work for other team members because our behavior impacts people differently.

For instance, David has a tendency to interrupt before the other person has finished talking. He does this with Carole; Carole interrupts him, too; and neither of us are triggered. In fact, we both find it energizing. But David was talking one day with Donald, another colleague, and noticed Donald frowning. "What's the matter?" David asked.

"You interrupted me," he replied.

David was puzzled. "So what's the problem?"

"That's inconsiderate," Donald said.

Is David's interrupting good or bad? That's actually a useless question. Interrupting is useful with Carole because she sees it as a sign of engagement, and it's dysfunctional with Donald because he experiences it as disrespectful. Donald's feedback made David more sensitive about differentiating how he dealt with other people, and it allowed him to work on the issue. In ensuing conversations, he told Donald that it had not been his intention to be disrespectful and he'd heard the impact it had on Donald. David said that he would really try not to interrupt but asked Donald for a little forgiveness when he forgot. On that basis, they were able to build a positive work relationship.

One final key point to consider is that feedback says as much about the giver as the receiver. When someone's feedback is about the other's motives or intentions—"The problem is that you want to win every argument"—the implication is that the problem is all about the other person. However, when the giver of feedback stays with their reality and on their side of the net—"I feel discouraged when I experience you frequently having the last word in our conversations"—it raises the possibility that the issue involves both parties.

In Interpersonal Dynamics, we repeatedly stress that *feedback starts a conversation. It doesn't end it.* Once you've shared your feelings, the work begins. You have to unravel all the issues and also ask how much of what's going on is about you. Think about it: Sanjay was upset when Elena confronted her team members—but that was partially due to his own difficulty with conflict. When you own your part in a disagreement, it often makes it easier for the other person to own theirs. Together, you can search for a solution that more closely fits each person's needs.

Building relationships where each person feels free to give and ask for feedback is key both to preventing pinches from becoming crunches and to helping each person develop in new and more effective ways. Truly, when people care for each other and their intent is to convey that, feedback is a gift. In sharing this concept with students, we often use a variation on the old Hallmark greeting card and say, "I care enough to say the very worst." Even if the person to whom you are giving feedback is momentarily taken aback, when done with genuine care and in service of the relationship, feedback is always a gift for which to be grateful.

Deepen Your Learning

SELF-REFLECTION

1. Put yourself in Elena's shoes. *Reflect on the sequence of events. You have a good relationship with Sanjay, but he is still your boss. How easy would it have been for you to do what she did? Would you have pushed as hard? What would have been easy and what more challenging? How would you have gone about raising those issues?*

2. Below are reasons you might have difficulty giving feedback. (Note that some of them overlap with ways we give away influence.) Which ones might be true of you?

    - Not staying on your side of the net; making attributions of the other's motives and intentions.
    - Not identifying what you are feeling (especially vulnerable emotions like hurt, rejection, and sadness).
    - Not conveying your intent in giving it.
    - Giving feedback in too-general terms. For example, being indirect, being nonspecific about the actual behavior, or sugarcoating the impact so the receiver misses your point.
    - Withholding/downplaying feedback out of a need to be well thought of or respected. Needing to be liked, seen as a "nice person." Wanting to please others.

- Worrying about being wrong or that the other will deny it. Thinking, *It's my problem, so I'm being selfish to impose it on someone else.*
- Worrying that the relationship might be harmed or permanently disrupted; believing that harmony in a relationship depends upon the absence of conflict.
- Fearing of conflict. Not feeling sure you have the skills to manage it.
- Feeling discomfort with challenging or confronting—especially figures of authority.
- Being concerned about whether the other will retaliate or give you feedback.

3. How hard is it for you to receive feedback, even if it's behaviorally specific? Do you . . .

   - become defensive, deny that it's true, offer excuses, justify your behavior?
   - jump to what the other does that causes the problem or retaliate by pointing out their faults?
   - become so upset that you can't take in the feedback, resulting in the other person's backing down or feeling guilty for raising the issue?
   - withdraw and distance yourself from the other person?
   - pay lip service to accepting the feedback but not take it in?

APPLICATION

Do you have difficulty in either giving or receiving feedback with one of the key people you previously identified? If not, pick someone else to engage with whom you find feedback conversations challenging. In preparation for that discussion, start with a diagnosis. Consider:

What exactly do you think is the problem?

How will you raise it so that they hear that it is in both of your best interests to discuss it?

What are the behaviors the other engages in, and how do they impact you?

Since you don't know the other's reality (i.e., what is going on for them, how they see the situation, and/or why they are behaving the way they are), what do you intend to do to find that out?

Now that you have done this diagnosis on your own, meet with the other to improve both of your abilities to give and receive feedback.

MAKING SENSE

What did you learn from this discussion about giving and receiving feedback? And what did you learn about yourself? Did you learn anything further about the challenges you identified in giving and hearing feedback? What do you want to do going forward based on what you're learning?

Several times, we have made the claim that successfully dealing with difficult issues can actually strengthen a relationship. In this and previous applications, did you find that to be the case? If not, what have you learned about conditions when that isn't true?

8

CHALLENGES IN USING FEEDBACK EFFECTIVELY

If only everyone responded to feedback like Sanjay did. Sure, some people work out difficulties smoothly, but life isn't always that easy. Disputes get messy as people react with defensiveness, denial, resistance, and retaliation. Even when things do work out, reaching a resolution can be difficult and painful.

Perhaps that's why instead of taking the direct road of the feedback model, people often veer off course toward avoidance or careen into heightened conflict. Instead of acknowledging our strong emotions, we ignore them and revert to logical arguments. Even the best-informed and most well-intentioned people can forget their reality and instead bludgeon the other with accusations. In this chapter, we look at why and what can be done to handle these pitfalls. In the process, we break down problem-solving into different stages to see where you might get stuck.

Although it may be uncomfortable, we encourage you to reflect on what stops *you* from effectively using feedback. Naturally, since relationships are co-determined, the responsibility isn't yours alone, but for now we want you to focus on you. This is not to make you the villain, but to emphasize that your actions and your responses are, in the end, the only ones you can control.

First, a disclaimer: The feedback model is not a magic wand.

Rarely does one piece of feedback, no matter how well crafted, resolve the issue. Say that you're upset with a family member because they always seem to find something to criticize. Just saying that you're upset is unlikely to solve the problem. There are probably many more issues, historic and contemporary, at play in their behavior and in your reactions to it. Most interpersonal issues are complex and layered. Remember, you only know *your* feelings and *your* needs. You have only part of the story. Feedback starts a conversation, but it's just the start.

Blocking Emotions

When feedback conversations don't go well, we conclude that we were right to see them as dangerous. What we don't see is that the problem was not in what we raised but in what we didn't. More often than not, the missing piece is emotions. Emotions are central to the feedback model, so it's crucial that we not only have access to them but actually express them instead of using one of the following justifications for staying silent.

"I SHOULDN'T FEEL [INSERT EMOTION]"

Are there certain feelings that, almost irrespective of the situation, you think you shouldn't have? "I shouldn't feel envious or jealous." "It's bad to be angry at somebody." "I'm really not hurt." Some of these thoughts may come from parental messages, the values you hold, or the image you want to portray. Or perhaps you're concerned that if you allow yourself to feel those emotions, they will overwhelm you or you will act on them.

Again, the important distinction is between how you feel and what actions you take. You have little choice about the former, since feelings come up whether you want them or not. But you have much more choice about the latter. If you're annoyed at your friend Sharon for telling you what to do, you're annoyed at Sharon. Recognizing that gives you options. You can reflect on *why* you're annoyed, and having that insight might be sufficient for the annoyance to significantly diminish. Or you can tell Sharon you're annoyed—simply stating it might also make the annoyance lessen. Or you might be so upset that you need to fully state the extent of your anger (though without attacking her) the next time she tells you what to do.

Feelings are never "wrong." What might be inappropriate is how you express them or what you attribute the cause to.

"I CAN'T JUSTIFY MY FEELINGS IN THIS CONTEXT"

Let's assume you're working on a project with a co-worker, and today he seems especially rigid and difficult to influence. You think, *I should give him a break since I know he has just been chewed out by his boss,* but you continue to feel annoyed—and now are annoyed at yourself because you can't let it pass.

Whether you understand why someone is behaving the way they are or has a logical explanation isn't relevant to the legitimacy of your feelings, though it may influence their intensity. You can choose to live with your annoyance or you could say, "I know you've had a run-in with your boss, but I am feeling annoyed at how you are responding. What can we do about this?" This is why feedback is usually only the start of a conversation.

"I'M SURE THIS FEELING WILL PASS"

Some feelings do pass, but others may linger. Even if you choose not to raise your annoyance and the feelings dissipate in the next hour, that doesn't mean they have entirely disappeared. Maybe they are "parked" somewhere and will come alive with even greater force the next time Sharon offers advice. An old TV car-repair ad said, "Pay me now or pay me later," with the latter being the more expensive repair. Don't you want to respond to Sharon now, before it gets worse?

"MY FEELINGS CONTRADICT EACH OTHER," OR [+5] + [−5] = 0

When it comes to emotions, this is poor math! We often have multiple feelings in a particular situation, and they can appear to be in conflict. (Remember, this is also a barrier to sharing feelings, which we talked about in chapter 3.) On the one hand, you're *annoyed* with your co-worker because of his controlling behavior, but on the other hand, you *appreciate* his willingness to work on this project even though he is extremely stressed. The danger is that allowing the positive emotion to cancel out the negative suppresses both feelings and results in your saying nothing or watering down your feedback.

But both feelings are true, so emotional math says [+5] and [−5] do not equal zero; they just equal [+5] and [−5]. Instead of withholding your feelings, express both of them. Doing so results in being better known—through both the emotions themselves and their intensity, because both say something important about you. It might also be that until both emotions are fully expressed, they won't go away.

"I'M SO MAD I DON'T TRUST MYSELF TO SPEAK"

What happens when the other person does something that just makes you furious? You're so angry that any concern for them has just flown out the window. You think, *I am so upset, I don't give a damn why they did that. I don't trust myself in what I might say.* Could you just say that last sentence and ask for twenty minutes to cool down and then talk about it? That lets the other person know what is going on for you. It might be that just expressing this is enough to lower your temperature. But if not, twenty minutes should be enough. You want the emotion to be manageable—you don't want it to evaporate or to fester further. This type of emotional regulation and appropriate emotional expression are important elements of emotional intelligence. As Daniel Goleman notes, emotional intelligence begins with self-awareness and the ability to recognize our feelings as they arise. The capacity to manage (not suppress!) our emotions comes next.

One emotion that is especially difficult to manage well is anger. Most people don't realize that anger is a secondary emotion. When someone feels too exposed to express certain emotions, such as hurt, rejection, or envy, it often feels safer to express anger. This is especially true of men, who have been socialized not to express vulnerability. The transfer from a more basic, vulnerable feeling to anger can be so automatic that the person who is upset is unaware of the underlying feelings. But expressing anger can lock both parties into rigid, defensive positions.

We're not suggesting that expressing anger is never appropriate. And we do think it is important to allow ourselves to feel it. In fact, it can be very useful to recognize anger if you can resist moving to blame and accusations and explore what lies underneath it. Your emotions are your emotions, and if you're feeling angry, you're feeling angry. It's what you do with that anger that can be problematic.

Making Up Stories

We have noted our tendencies to make up stories about why someone else is behaving the way they are. As human beings we have a strong need to make sense of our experiences. But when it comes to feedback, few things get us in more trouble than making up stories, especially when we don't even realize that's what we're doing.

When you move from a guess, to a strong hunch, to certainty, you create a story that guarantees curiosity will disappear. That happens whether the story you have made up is a classic example of being over the net ("He just wants to have the last word") or data selected to fit a negative narrative ("He doesn't respect me; he's always looking at his phone when I'm trying to talk to him"). Even if you ask something at that point, it is likely to be a pseudo-question, such as, "Isn't the reason you always have the last word that . . . ," which won't encourage an open discussion.

Once we make up a story, an attribution is an easy leap. "He just wants to have the last word" quickly turns into "He's insecure." "She only likes to talk about herself" becomes "She is self-centered." Once attributions are made (for which we select confirming data, as previously noted), we often jump to labels. "Self-centered" becomes "narcissistic." Attributions and labels oversimplify and are dangerously reductionistic, as they create a very specific lens through which we see someone else.

So what to do with this almost automatic inclination? You have several options. One is to reflect on what it is about your friend Susie's tendency to talk about herself and her latest accomplishments that bothers you. Could it be that you are envious that she does something that is difficult for you to do? Or are you waiting for her to ask you about what is going on in your life? Noticing your thought process is an important place to start (a reminder that much of becoming more interpersonally competent requires mindfulness).

Another option is to leverage our storytelling tendencies to develop a positive explanation. For example, if your initial story about why Susie talks about herself contains a negative motive, you could instead come up with a story that her intent is positive, and that what she is actually trying to do is build a relationship in which you both feel free to share and celebrate your accomplishments. Creating an alternative story might introduce enough uncertainty to drive you back to curiosity.

A third option is to simply name what you're doing. "Susie, I'm noticing that you often talk a lot about what you do and how well it's all going. That bothers me and I'm sorry to say that leads me to making up a story about you that you self-promote because you are insecure, which I don't want to do. It is *my* story and unfair to you. What is your intent when you tell me about your achievements?" You are acknowledging these are *your stories* and not an unequivocal truth. But this only works if you can allow for the possibility that your story is wrong.

The Problem-Solving Stages

Let's presume that you haven't fallen into any of the traps outlined above but you want to address a troubling, complex problem with many layers. You've mentioned it lightly before, but it didn't appear to have an impact, and the problematic behavior has continued. It's now starting to become entangled with other issues, and you're afraid that it could lead to a major conflict. You've decided to take the bull by the horns and fully deal with it. How to do this without the exchange getting out of hand?

There are four critical stages when it comes to addressing complex issues. First is getting the other person to *take the issue seriously*. Second, they have to be willing to *fully share what's going on for them*. Third, you want to arrive at a *mutually satisfying solution*, not just settle for the minimum that will end the discussion. Finally, you need to determine if the relationship is *in need of some repair work*, because when the discussion has been contentious, it is easy for each person to feel bruised and the relationship to suffer.

Each stage is helped by following the feedback model, and each stage can be sabotaged by violating it. Fortunately, perfection is not required; even temporarily getting off course need not be a disaster if you can catch yourself. Remember, *the only mistake is refusing to learn from your mistakes.*

STAGE 1: GETTING THE OTHER PERSON TO TAKE THE FEEDBACK SERIOUSLY

People will usually consider your concerns if they see that your intent in doing so is in their best interests. There are a few ways to do this, none of which are mutually exclusive:

- *"This is how your behavior is affecting me."* This basic approach works when the other person cares about you. For example, "I'm bothered because three times in the meeting you changed the subject while I was still talking." However, it's less effective if the other isn't concerned about your well-being. They might brush you off or, even worse, respond with, "Well, I guess that's your problem!"
- *"Your behavior is not meeting your goals."* This assumes that the other has stated their goals: "Hans, you said that you wanted others to speak up, but the way you shut down Simon makes me hesitant to disagree and is likely to get people to hold back." The other person's goals could also be self-evident: "When I don't experience you considering my ideas, I am less open to yours and you lose influence with me." Even if you don't have much of a relationship, you get their attention by pointing out how their actions aren't achieving their objectives.
- *"You might be meeting your goals, but you're paying some unnecessary costs."* When another person's behavior bothers you, ask yourself, "Are they paying a cost as well?" "Leah, I also want efficient meetings, but when we're rushed, the ideas we come up with aren't as good." You are supporting Leah on the primary goal but getting her attention by pointing out these undesirable consequences.
- *"Am I doing anything that is causing your behavior?"* Most *inter*personal issues have an *inter*personal cause. Acknowledging your part can make it easier for the other to accept theirs. "Kyle, does

my tendency to jump in with solutions decrease your willingness to initiate?"

NOTE: These four variation on the feedback model apply to all relationships as will occur with Maddie and her husband in chapter 12.

STAGE 2: SHARING *ALL* THE ISSUES

Let's presume you're both at the proverbial table, ready and invested in talking. The task now is to explore the issues. "Issues" is plural because frequently the first point raised isn't the only, or necessarily the most important, area of contention. In the previous chapter, Elena started by sharing one issue: her frustration that her comments in team meetings were not acknowledged. Then as the discussion unfolded, this expanded to also include the fact that Sanjay not only participated in that behavior himself but also didn't give Elena credit in the executive committee meeting.

Not only can the person initiating the feedback have several issues, but raising them may trigger the other person's concerns. That's what happened when Sanjay responded to Elena's initial feedback by saying, "Well, I'm glad you're raising this, Elena, because I've been bothered as well. I want this group to get along, and you tend to be pretty judgmental." What started off in Elena's mind as rather simple grew much more complicated.

Their conversation could have turned into a real mess. Not only were there more issues on the table, but Sanjay's accusation might have caused Elena to become defensive, leading her to retort, "Well, the reason I had to speak up was because you didn't do your job." Sanjay could then respond defensively with a counter-accusation, and they'd be well into the blame game. Neither would be curious, because the objective would be to win. They'd have forgotten behavioral feedback entirely.

When problems are complex and intertwined, things can feel messy. Imagine there's a muddy swamp, and you need to cross it to get to the high ground on the other side. At first, you carefully look for rocks to step on so as not to get mud on your shoes. But halfway across, the rocks end. You have a choice: "Do I go on and wade through the swamp, or should I turn around?" Turning around ends the discussion, with one person stalking out of the room or, just as dysfunctional, saying, "Let's just agree to disagree." The latter might make sense when it comes to politics or large ideological differences, but not in the context of building robust relationships.

It's tricky, but it *is* possible to press on when each side is locked into a defensive position. It can still feel messy, but you can stop the escalation in order to separate out the intertwined issues. If that doesn't work, you can temporarily set aside the content of the argument to ask, "What's going on—why are we stuck?" This allows you to process how you got into the swamp in the first place and how you can productively move forward to the dry ground. This won't work, of course, if it just becomes another arena for mutual blame. Instead, both parties need to look at the specific behaviors that led the discussion off course and then share what feelings came up. This is also a good time to reiterate that your intent in giving the feedback is to help both the other and the relationship. Then you can get back to problem-solving.

STAGE 3: RESOLUTION

Rather than searching for "an answer," it is important to recognize that there are multiple desired outcomes. First, you want to ensure the discussion has *solved the initial problems in a way that satisfies both people.* These sorts of problems usually have more than one viable solution. The temptation is to grab the first one that appears out of relief, just to end this difficult conversation. Instead, continue to explore options until you discover a solution that meets the needs of both. This might take time and require multiple conversations.

Second, you want the discussion to *improve your problem-solving ability.* This may include understanding how you got into this problem in the first place, but it also should examine how you went about resolving it. Were there places you got stuck, or was it more tortuous than necessary? The objective is to *increase,* not decrease, each person's willingness to raise difficult issues in the future.

The third and fourth objectives deal with aspects of the relationship itself. Do *you know each other better* because in the discussion you've shared relevant parts of yourself? Again, that was true with Elena and Sanjay, as Elena talked about her style of interacting and Sanjay admitted his difficulty with conflict. And finally, has *your relationship improved as a result* of the effort? In Sanjay and Elena's case, they came to an agreement that both wanted to be as direct as possible with each other going forward.

STAGE 4: REPAIR

Let's say you've achieved those objectives. Well done. Now take stock: You may need to do some repair work on the relationship. The process may not have been an easy one; things might have been said that caused hurt or regret. Has the importance of the relationship to both of you been lost in this process? Has one or both of you felt devalued?

Saying "I'm sorry" is often a critical component of repair, but many people can't bring themselves to say the phrase. Some see it as "losing face," while others fear being misinterpreted. For example, the words can be heard as you taking full responsibility for any harm, even when you're just sorry the two of you are in this situation. Yet saying "I'm sorry" is very powerful. It extends an olive branch that can stop an adversarial exchange in its tracks, help people reconnect after a disagreement, and serve as a form of disclosure that makes you vulnerable and increases the chance of a reciprocal response. A good apology conveys that you truly are sorry (e.g., not "I'm sorry you feel that way," which can be taken as just a pro forma response). That requires you to actually feel sorry, since most people can fairly easily pick up whether you genuinely mean it.

Beyond apologies, affirming the other, and the relationship, matters: "Even though we find ourselves in this pickle, I want to be sure you know how much I value you and our relationship." A genuine expression of empathy is also important to repair: "I'm hearing how hard this conversation has been for you, and I really appreciate your hanging in there."

And last, check back the next day to see if any of these stages need revisiting. With time for the issue to settle, does it feel as complete as you thought? Are there any lingering issues that got pushed under the rug in the haste to reach resolution? If nothing else, checking in signals concern for the other and the relationship, and that, in itself, is a form of repair.

Dealing with Defensiveness

One of the great benefits of the feedback model is that it can minimize feelings of defensiveness. If the other has stayed on their side of the net, they're sharing their reaction to your *behavior*. It is not a judgment of your character. You still can feel somewhat defensive, but you don't have to see it as a total rejection of who you are.

This speaks to the difference between *being defensive* and having to *defend oneself*. If somebody makes an accusation that you think is inaccurate, is it being defensive to correct them? If somebody misunderstands you, is it defensive to explain yourself more accurately? If you are attacked, isn't it appropriate to defend yourself?

The problem might not be defensiveness but rather its side effects. It can block your ability to hear feedback, or you might too quickly dismiss that feedback with explanations, even if you heard it. When you think the feedback is exaggerated, defensiveness can keep you from exploring what aspects might have some validity. Dismissing feedback as completely wrong results in defensiveness that blocks you from wanting to explore why the other person feels the way they do. So how can you accept your feelings of defensiveness without these limiting consequences?

Imagine defensiveness as a continuum. At the extreme end, you're so overwhelmed with emotion that you can no longer hear anything the other person says. (Haven't we all, at one time or another, experienced that?) In such a flooded state, it may be best to halt the feedback. "Sorry, but I'm so upset, I can't take any more of this in. I need some time to absorb it, and then we can come back to it."

But more times than not, when you feel defensive, it's not that extreme; you can still hear and deal with what someone is telling you. Acknowledge the feeling, and hold back your tendency to rebut. Instead, try to understand what the other is saying. Set aside the need to "be right." The most important issue at that moment is the feedback that the other is giving—not defending your identity or ego.

What if you give feedback and the *other* person appears defensive? The same conditions apply. If you see that the other is totally emotionally flooded, you can say, "I'm concerned. If I were in your shoes, I might feel overwhelmed. Is that going on for you? Would it help to take a break and come back to this later?" Again, do come back to it. If it's having that much impact on the other, it must be important.

More frequently, people respond to feedback in ways that sound defensive. They say, "Wait, I don't do that all the time," or "The reason that I do it is because of X and Y." At that point, the feedback giver's tendency is to back down ("Oh, it really isn't such a big deal") because they assume that the other person is closed to learning. Not only does backing down not solve anything, but the assumption might be wrong. Why not assume their comments are a sign that they're trying to make sense of the information? They may be struggling to reconcile the feedback with their view of themselves, but they still hear.

Consider what would happen if they didn't push back at *all*. Say you gave a colleague an important piece of feedback and they responded in a very calm and rational voice: "Thank you very much. I've never heard that before. I will take that in and change immediately." Would you really believe them? Wouldn't it be likely that your feedback went in one ear and out the other?

Try to see the value in their struggle, and don't back off, but join them. If they say, "Wait a minute, I don't do that all the time," you might respond by saying, "That's right, you don't, but you did it here and there [naming specific behavioral incidents], and it bothers me / is not meeting your goals / is costly to you." If it's an important relationship and the behavior is getting in the way, reiterate that and then be persistent for both your sakes!

Whether you are giving or receiving feedback, defensiveness is often a sign that there is a kernel of truth in the feedback, and therefore something valuable to explore. A therapist friend of ours once said, "Sh*t sticks only if there's something for it to stick to." We find that often to be true. If somebody attacks you—even in harsh terms—with something that doesn't resonate, any defensiveness is short-lived. But if your defensiveness lingers, there's usually some part of the accusation that is hitting home. It may be something that you don't like admitting, or you may be concerned it's blown out of proportion, but it does stick, nonetheless. Recognizing that gives you choices in how to respond. Can you acknowledge the part that feels at least partially true? If you do, you lower your resistance to hearing more of the other's feedback, and, possibly, to learning something from it.

The Ability to Learn

As mentioned in the beginning of this book, our extensive teaching, coaching, and consulting has shown us that the key determining factor for both relationship development and individual growth is an ability to learn. It's also instrumental to success at work, regardless of your position. We have seen time and again that not only does a reluctance to learn block success, but the failure to address interpersonal deficiencies (rather than a lack of technical expertise) is career limiting.

Individual and relational learning are often interlaced, as Sanjay and Elena found. When Elena gave Sanjay feedback about needing to be acknowledged for her contributions to the team, he learned about the negative effect of some of his individual actions. But they also discussed how they wanted to relate to *each other*. Elena asked whether the way she was giving Sanjay feedback felt like an attack and whether she should not be as direct. Sanjay's saying that was not the case freed up their interactions.

Receiving feedback from another, as Sanjay did, furthers your development, since you learn what you do well and what you can do better. So why would anyone resist hearing it? Some of that is because of mental models, like the belief that the giver's intention isn't to help but to put you down (and make themselves look better). Maybe the person who gave the feedback did it in such a disconfirming way that it was difficult to hear. Perhaps it was over the net or judgmental. You still may learn, but it may not make you eager to solicit feedback from them in the future.

Consider, too, whether there's something in *you* that blocks your learning. Do you need to hold on to a certain image, and does accepting feedback threaten that image? Or does accepting feedback mean admitting failure or inadequacy? We sometimes hear, "I love to learn; I just don't want anybody to know that I'm learning." It's tempting, we know, to hold on to an image of infallibility, but that can be quite costly.

Accepting the validity of someone's feedback also doesn't mean you must act on it. Feedback is information for you to decide what to do with. It's data with which to expand your choices. As a colleague of ours says, "It's like clothes—try it on and see if it fits." It might be that someone suggests you change some significant assumptions and behaviors, like your tendency to avoid conflict. But you're afraid that if you really take that in, you'll say things that you later regret.

One option is to start off small and consider experimenting with people and in settings where you feel relatively safe. So, for example, if you are working on being more direct and less conflict avoidant, you might want to try applying this with a close friend. Your friend has a tendency to cancel plans at the last minute, and that bugs you. When raising this with him, you might include telling him that you are working on being more direct. That is likely to be within the 15 percent outside your comfort zone and therefore a good place to start. In stark contrast would be going to your boss and telling her that the way she keeps changing priorities is driving you nuts.

We have repeatedly said feedback is a gift—but just because someone gives you a gift, it doesn't mean you're required to use it. This may not be the best time to take action. Seeing feedback as data that informs and expands our choices—not a requirement for change—makes it easier to hear and consider.

Deepen Your Learning

SELF-REFLECTION

1. Discounting Feelings: Do you have a tendency to discount your emotions in any of these ways?

    - "I shouldn't feel certain emotions."
    - "I can't justify my feelings in this context."
    - "I'm sure this feeling will pass."
    - "My feelings contradict each other." ([+5] + [−5] = 0)
    - "I'm so mad that I don't trust myself to speak."

    Are there other ways you block recognizing and/or expressing feelings? If so, where do these tendencies come from?

2. Making Up Stories: Do you have a tendency to make up stories about others' reality? Or to move from a hunch to certainty? Under what circumstances is that more likely to occur?

3. Four Stages of Problem-Solving: What might you do at these four stages that hinders effective problem resolution?

    - Getting the other person to take the feedback seriously
    - Sharing all the issues
    - Resolution
    - Repair

4. Defensiveness:

    - Your defensiveness: How frequently do you get defensive? What situations tend to trigger that? And how do you handle it when you feel that way?
    - Other's defensiveness: How do you respond when the other person gets defensive?

APPLICATION

In the self-reflection section, you indicated how you see yourself behaving. But how might another see you? Go to one of your key relationships and check some of your perceptions out with them.

Hopefully, the self-reflection section and/or discussions with others have generated several development areas for you to explore. For example, "I want to be more open to feedback and less defensive."

Select one or two areas that you would like to work on and set some change goals. Change is easier and more likely if you have somebody supporting you. Go to one of your relationships and ask them to help you reach your learning goals.

MAKING SENSE

On the basis of what you read, reflected on, and tried out, what did you learn about challenges in using feedback effectively? And what did you learn about yourself?

What do you want to do going forward based on what you're learning? Note that by now you are building a toolkit that can come in handy anytime with any relationship, not only with the key people you identified at the start. The more you practice with others and then extract lessons from that "doing," the more you will learn.

9

CAN PEOPLE REALLY CHANGE?

Phil and Rachel—a Father and Daughter, Parts 1, 2, and 3

Over the past several chapters, we've seen our characters face some problematic behaviors and learn to do things differently. Elena learned that being vulnerable requires strength. Sanjay learned there was a cost to avoiding conflict. Liam learned that abruptly changing topics was distancing. These are all important lessons, but what about behaviors that are more fundamental and that have been reinforced for years? Will feedback, no matter how direct and well delivered, really change these long-standing patterns?

We believe that people can change. It can be difficult and requires persistence, but we couldn't have stayed in the business we're in for this many decades if we hadn't seen it happen repeatedly. People might find it challenging and may not want to change at a particular moment in time, but that's different from not being capable of it.

The famous organizational theorist and MIT professor Richard Beckhard explained with an interesting formula the conditions under which people are more likely to change: $R < D \times V \times F$. The R is for "resistance to change." In order for change to happen, the product of the other three variables has to be larger than the resistance. The D stands for "dissatisfaction," meaning you need to be aware of the cost of your present behavior. The V stands for "vision," meaning you need to see the benefit of new behavior and believe that the result will be worth the effort, and the F stands for "first steps," meaning you believe you can acquire new skills that make change easier.

The story of Phil and Rachel explores just how tricky this formula—and changing long-standing patterns—can be.

Phil and Rachel, Part 1

Phil and his daughter Rachel were both physicians working at the same hospital, although Rachel was also building a small private practice on her own. They'd always been close, bonding over basketball (both played varsity in college) and the practice of medicine.

Rachel recognized that their relationship hadn't changed much since she was a teenager. Her dad had always been very invested in her success—he was her biggest advocate and cheerleader as well as her chief professional counselor. When Rachel's young daughter Emma expressed an interest in basketball, Phil renewed his passion for informally coaching the sport. Unfortunately, most of what Phil tended to give was advice—to both Emma and Rachel. This had been useful when Rachel was playing college ball and when she navigated medical school, but she found it less and less helpful as time went on.

They didn't have all that much to talk about beyond sports and medicine, and Rachel wished she had more of a sense of her father's internal world. When her mother was alive, Rachel would find out how he was feeling from her but almost never directly from him. When Rachel told her dad what was going on in *her* life, he tended to respond with parental advice rather than his own disclosure.

Since her mom had died the previous year, Rachel made it a point to have Phil over for dinner with her husband and kids at least every other week, or to go on a weekend outing together. She also tried to grab breakfast or lunch with him at the hospital when their schedules coincided.

On one such day in the hospital cafeteria, Phil and Rachel bantered as usual about the dismal lunch offerings, talked hospital politics, and mentioned some interesting cases they each had. Then Phil launched into his usual pattern of questions.

"What did you decide about expanding your practice and taking on that friend of yours as a partner?"

Rachel felt the familiar clench in her stomach. *Here we go again,* she thought. She'd been trying to decide for months whether it was time to expand her one-person private practice and invite her longtime friend and colleague Nadya to join her.

"I'm still thinking about it," she said. "Like I've said, there are lots of pros and a few cons that I'm evaluating."

"Well," said Phil, "I think you're crazy if you don't seize the opportunity to snag Nadya right now. She's a really great doctor and you've been friends since medical school, so you clearly get along. People like her don't grow on trees, you know."

"The question has nothing to do with whether she's a good doctor or we get along, Dad. It's more complicated than that."

"What's so complicated?"

Rachel thought about once again explaining that the decision was fraught with financial and logistical complications but decided not to go there. Phil continued sipping his Coke and eating his lunch in silence, waiting for her response.

After a minute, Rachel finally said, "Dad, we've talked about all of this before, multiple times, and I really don't want to go over it all again."

"No-brainer. You should just do it and stop overthinking it."

Rachel felt her anger rise. She was irritated by her father's advice and felt her concerns were being dismissed. She was also frustrated with herself: She had once again let the conversation move to something happening in her professional life about which Phil had opinions—and strong ones at that. Given how many times they'd had a similar interaction, Rachel felt more than a pinch; she was downright pissed.

She was also annoyed that Phil hadn't gotten the message that his advice was unwelcome. Even though she'd raised it very gently several times before, he was back at it again. *I don't want to beat him over the head, because he takes things so personally,* she thought, *but this has got to stop. I'm forty-three years old, for goodness' sake. This conversation is no different from when I was eighteen. There has to be some way to change that. I'm not sure how much longer I can bite my tongue when he oversimplifies an issue I'm struggling with, flippantly telling me what I ought to do.*

It was near the end of the lunch hour and they both had patients to see, so she decided to let it go. "Dad, this is not useful, so let's drop it."

Phil looked hurt and said, "Geez, I was only trying to help."

"Well, it wasn't helpful," Rachel snapped. Then, catching herself, she said, "Emma is practicing with her team and the new coach this Saturday afternoon. Why don't you come over for lunch, and then we can go over and watch them practice?"

Phil looked relieved and nodded. "That would be good. See you Saturday at noon."

They both picked up their dishes and headed back to their respective clinics.

Even though Rachel had a full schedule with patients that afternoon, she found her mind wandering back to the lunch conversation. *It is so annoying that he doesn't get it,* she thought. *But maybe it's too much to expect. He's been this way all his life. Maybe there is something to the saying that you can't teach old dogs new tricks.*

She also thought of a recent conversation that she'd had with her friend Tomiko, who'd said, "I have the same issues with my dad. Look, Phil's sixty-eight years old. What do you expect? And he's always been a little tin eared. Once I started just accepting my dad the way he was, things got much better between us. Personally, I think you're better off dropping it and living with the advice-giving behavior." Rachel wondered if Tomiko might be right and she should give up trying to get Phil to take this issue seriously. But this didn't feel fully settled for her.

At lunch on Saturday, Emma was full of energy and chattered about her middle school team and the new coach.

"How is he?" asked Phil.

"*He* is a *she,* Grandpa," Emma said. "I think she's good. But a lot of the other girls don't take it very seriously, and Coach has a hard time managing them, so we haven't played much yet."

Phil frowned. "The season will be over before you know it. You really need to work hard, Emma."

Rachel felt her stomach tighten again. "She does work hard, Dad! Now, Emma, go suit up, we need to leave in a few minutes."

As Emma left the room, Phil turned to Rachel and said, "You should just march yourself in there and let that coach know that unless she rights that ship pretty quickly, she's sunk."

"Dad, for God's sake. She's just getting started."

"I'm telling you," said Phil, "the sooner you address this, the better. I can tell you from all those years watching you play. Emma's love of the sport is on the line here."

"Stop it! You're just making me feel like an inadequate mother. And earlier this week you made me feel like an inadequate professional, incapable of making a good decision about taking on a partner. I'm getting more and more irritated."

Phil was taken aback. He looked down at the floor and initially said nothing. He then responded defensively. "Look, all I'm trying to do here is help. I only have your best interests at heart. And I certainly don't want to frustrate or irritate you. If you want, I'll just stay out of your business entirely."

"Dad, that's not the solution. No, I don't want you to stay out of my business. But there's a way that we talk about my business that just doesn't work for me anymore. We've got to leave for practice, but we need to find some time to talk more about this. What's going on isn't helping either of us."

As they all got in the car, Emma chatted with excitement, but both Rachel and Phil were silent. *What can I do so that he will respond differently?* Rachel wondered. *Can he really change?*

RACHEL'S PREDICAMENT IS not unusual. You've probably told someone that a behavior of theirs bothers you, only for them to repeat their actions time and time again without seeming to learn. Observers might shrug and say, "That's the way he is; that's his personality." But we would argue that's just not the case. There's a big difference between personality and behavior. Personality is extremely difficult to change—if you're an extrovert, you're unlikely to become introverted no matter how hard you try. That doesn't mean you can't work on leaving more space for others to speak, which is a behavior. No one's born with genes for being inconsiderate or self-centered. Is it really in Phil's DNA that he so often defaults to giving advice? Um, we don't think so.

This isn't to suggest that it's easy to modify long-held habits. But it's worth exploring why a behavior is so central to someone that they don't seem able to change it. In Phil's case, he's given advice for decades, and it's been very useful to Rachel in the past, reinforcing its value. Additionally, he's a doctor, an occupation where giving advice is not only routine but historically expected. The medical setting also stresses rationality, which requires keeping emotions in check. So it's not all that surprising that he doesn't disclose a lot of his feelings to his daughter.

When someone engages in habitual behaviors, as Phil did, others learn to adapt, thereby reinforcing them. It is doubtful that patients, nurses, or interns complained about Phil's advice-giving habits or asked that he interact in a more self-disclosing manner. Also, probably out of a sense of kindness, his wife perpetuated his reticence to disclose feelings to his children by being the interpreter between them. And while giving advice has been one of Phil's strengths as a physician, when overdone, as with Rachel, it becomes a weakness. Given this is a learned behavior, can't it be modified?

Carole's own family had a similar pattern. Her father was a man of few words, a prototypical strong, silent type of his generation. In many ways Carole was the son her dad never had, and they had much in common—both were competitive, pragmatic, and driven. Carole always felt very close to her dad and fondly remembers numerous conversations where he was quite vulnerable, particularly when he talked about his war experience. Even though she always sensed that there was so much more to know, she never pushed. So it came with some sadness when Carole's stepmother (the woman her dad married late in life, after he was widowed) recently told her that one of his biggest regrets was that he was not more involved in raising Carole and her sister. Carole had never imagined he'd have this thought, because she'd never probed. Now she wonders what might have happened had she pushed herself outside her comfort zone and asked for more closeness. How much more would she have known about him? How much more known would she have felt by him? And how much deeper might the relationship have been?

When you conclude too quickly that a certain set of behaviors is "the way that person is and will always be," you might be doing them an injustice. Instead, try to understand all the factors that perpetuate that pattern of behavior. Asking Phil to be emotionally self-disclosing is no small request—his patterns have been heavily reinforced and changing them will be clumsy—but that doesn't mean Rachel shouldn't ask or should assume change is impossible. Phil's behavior might simply be deeply reinforced.

Think of a sport where you've developed "wrong habits." For example, let's say you started off in tennis with a weak backhand and compensated by switching hands so that you could always play your forehand. When the coach demands that you play backhand, your initial shots are inferior. *Why switch when I was doing okay?* Phil may have a similar feeling.

Even understanding that her dad has some deeply ingrained patterns, it would still be easy for Rachel to put all the blame on Phil. *Why doesn't he get it? Is he that tone-deaf?* she thinks. But wasn't she partially responsible for their impasse? Yes, she expressed her feelings (in words, tone, and nonverbal signals) and pointed out the problematic behaviors, but she did it by snapping at Phil rather than showing empathy and by providing detailed feedback that fully described the situation. Her shorthand might have been attributable to lack of time (both at the hospital lunch and before the basketball practice), but it might also be a reflection of her internal conflict.

On the one hand, she was growing increasingly frustrated with Phil's repeated advice-giving, but on the other hand, the last thing she wanted to do was hurt his feelings. She was sensitive to how difficult his life must be now that his wife was gone, and she didn't want to make it even more difficult. *I love him so much,* she often thought, *and he drives me* so *crazy*. Because she felt internally blocked, her feelings came out muddled and unclear.

Another problem is that Phil heard her request about advice-giving as if he had to stop it completely. Often when you want somebody to modify a behavior, you don't have something that extreme in mind. As one of our colleagues often points out, it might be easier to think of this as a dial to be turned down a bit as opposed to a switch to be turned off. Might there be times when providing advice would be useful? Also, might it be useful to recognize that what Phil really needs and wants is to be helpful and show him other ways he could get that need met? The point is, Rachel could make change easier for Phil.

Phil and Rachel, Part 2

After the basketball practice, Rachel reflected about her recent unsatisfying lunch conversations with Phil and realized that avoiding a full discussion could jeopardize the future of their relationship. She saw that she hadn't been as open as she could have been and decided to double down on letting Phil know specifically how his behavior impacted her and their relationship.

She suggested they take a hike the next weekend to talk things through, and while he wasn't sure what the problem was, Phil agreed. That Saturday, they met at the start of the trail. As they set off, she said, "Thanks for agreeing to walk and talk, Dad. I know you aren't big on this kind of stuff, so I appreciate it." Phil just shrugged, so Rachel added, "This is really hard for me."

"What's so hard? Just spit it out."

"I'm afraid what I want to say to you is going to hurt your feelings, and I don't want to do that," she said. "I'm also afraid that if I don't say this to you, it's going to hurt our relationship."

"When did you become so melodramatic? What are you getting at?"

Rachel decided to let the first comment slide. "What I'm getting at is that when you give me advice, I find myself more and more irritated. It doesn't seem to matter how many times I tell you that it irritates me; you keep doing it. I'm kind of at a loss as to what to do about it and worry that if we don't address it, the problem is just going to get bigger."

"What problem?" said Phil, stopping on the trail.

Rachel looked incredulous. "*Really?* Did you just say that? The problem is that it drives me nuts when every interaction we have eventually ends up with your giving me advice. And when I tell you that the advice isn't helpful, you ignore me and plow ahead. And then the bigger problem is that you don't seem to be hearing that it's a problem no matter how often I raise it!"

Phil looked really hurt. "You're telling me I have to stop giving advice? You're asking me to be someone I'm not, and unless I become that person, then our relationship is going to hell in a handbasket. I guess I'm a bad father."

Rachel felt tears in her eyes as they continued walking. Phil didn't say anything else. *Maybe Tomiko was right,* she thought. Then she stopped walking, as did he. She decided to try again.

"No, Dad, you are not a bad father. But when you respond the way you just did, it drives me crazy. Going into this self-flagellating mode keeps us from dealing with the problem. It's become a much bigger deal than the advice-giving behavior itself."

They walked in uncomfortable silence for a while, until Rachel finally broke it. "Look, Dad, we have to talk about how we can work this out. Just to be clear, I am not asking you to change your personality. It is your actions, your behaviors, that are the issue. And those you can control."

When Giving Feedback Hits a Wall

Rachel had two objectives. The first was not to back down. And the second was to do a better job giving Phil feedback on his advice-giving and responses to her attempts to talk about it. This is not as easy as it sounds. Even though she was more direct on their hike than she'd been before, it didn't really seem to be working, and Phil's reaction only increased her frustration. She could have easily given up or blown up.

With Ben and Liam, and again with Elena and Sanjay, feedback worked because both giver and receiver shared the same sense of joint responsibility to move into a problem-solving conversation. Although Rachel provided feedback that also stayed on her side of the net, Phil wasn't willing to play ball. Instead, he acted in ways that made it hard for Rachel to continue.

He showed hurt feelings, inducing guilt. He withdrew and said little, and he shifted the focus of the conversation back to advice-giving and away from their inability to talk things through. The barriers Phil put up are not uncommon. There are others, too, that Phil didn't use but that we see all the time. (Some of these were mentioned in the prior chapter in which we discussed dealing with defensiveness.)

- Denial
  "No, I don't do that. I think you're imagining that."

- Defensiveness
  "I don't do that very much. This was just an exception, and anyway, others do it as well."

- Explanations / excuses
  "The reason that I did it was because . . ." "This is what you do that makes me do that: . . ."

- Retaliating
  "Well, you do things that are a problem. This is what you do."

- Blaming
  "You raised the issue in the wrong way." "It's because you didn't handle it properly."

- Putting the other down
  "I'm disappointed in you." "I had hoped that you would have done better."

- Questioning motives
  "Aren't you raising this issue so that you can dominate?"

When someone puts up these barriers, they're not really hearing the message. The feedback giver will often back away (as Rachel considered doing) or refrain from offering feedback in the future.

There are some circumstances in which responding with resistance makes sense. What becomes a problem is when the receiver consistently relies on these responses in a way that prevents them from taking in the feedback.

Rather than giving up or pounding the other harder, it might be necessary to temporarily shift the focus of the feedback. Let's imagine that you want to give an employee—let's call him Sam—feedback on a certain behavior: He has a tendency to say he'll do something and then doesn't follow through. But just about every time you bring it up, he has an excuse. The pattern blocks Sam's ability to hear feedback and your desire to give it.

The feedback can now shift to his pattern of excuses. "Sam, you have a tendency to have an excuse each time I raise the issue of your not coming through, and it really bothers me." But what if when you do that, he has another excuse? What seems like an infuriating loop is actually an opportunity: You can point it out right as it's happening. "Sam, this is what I am talking about."

This is similar to what Rachel faces. There is not just one single time that Phil didn't get the message about his advice-giving. Time after time, she raises it, only to have him brush it aside. There's an underlying problem in their ability to problem-solve together, and *that's* what she needs to address.

Phil and Rachel, Part 3

"Dad," Rachel pleaded, "say something."

"I have nothing to say."

Rachel cried softly. "Dad, that can't be true. You must be feeling a lot, and I want to hear it—as I want to feel free to share how I am feeling."

There was a long pause while Phil seemed to take it in but remained silent.

Rachel continued, "I'm going to give this one more try. And I am desperate to have you hear me. I wouldn't be doing this if I didn't love you as much as I do and I didn't care as much as I do about our relationship. Can we sit down over there on that flat rock and try again?"

Phil stopped walking and looked at her. He nodded and followed her to a large flat boulder overlooking the valley. The afternoon sun streamed through the trees.

"Please, Dad. This is so important to me, and, I really believe, to both of us."

"Okay. Tell me again what's so irritating about my advice."

"Dad, your advice-giving is not the big issue."

"I'm so confused. I'm offering to talk about my tendency to give you advice, and now you don't want to talk about that. What is it that you want from me, for God's sake?"

Rachel hesitated, unsure about whether to press on. Ordinarily she would have responded with a "Never mind" and they would have resumed their walk. But she realized this was part of the problem. *If I don't say this now, I'm never going to say it,* she thought.

"The bigger and deeper issue is that I often don't feel heard or acknowledged when I give you feedback or talk to you about something that's a problem for me."

Phil was quiet as he looked out at the valley floor beneath them.

"Dad, this is really hard for me, and your nonresponse is just making it harder."

"I'm doing my best. When you have a problem, I offer solutions. I hear you don't like that, even though I don't know when that became the wrong thing to do."

"Dad, it's happening again, right now, between us."

Phil, somewhat irritated, said, "What the heck are you talking about?"

"I appreciate your wanting to talk about your advice-giving tendencies, I really do. And that is certainly something I want to talk about more as well. But I just told you there is something bigger to this for me, which you did not acknowledge. The very exchange we are having right now is the pattern I want to talk about. I again don't feel heard, and what's more, I feel dismissed." She put her arm around him and continued, "Please, Dad. I love you and this is so important to me."

Phil softened, though it was clear he was uncomfortable. "Okay, I'm starting to get that you want me to listen to you more. Even though I think I am listening."

"Yes, Dad, but the issue is not whether you are listening to me, it's whether I'm feeling heard. Those are actually different."

"Hmmm, I never even thought about that. So should I just tell you that I hear you? I can do that."

"That would help, but I mean something more. By 'being heard,' I mean are you really trying to understand me? Several times in the last week, I said that I was irritated. Not only did you not acknowledge that you heard that, but I didn't hear that you were concerned about it or wanted to find out what was going on with me. We can't work out our issues if we don't try to understand each other."

"But that's why I offer solutions. It's my way of showing you I understand and care."

"Dad, I don't need your solutions. If you work to understand me and I try to understand you, the solutions will come out."

"That's hard for me," said Phil. "I'm used to giving answers, not asking questions. Questions are what Mom was so good at." There was a long moment of silence, and then he continued, "But I think maybe I'm starting to see what you're getting at."

Rachel smiled. "And this moment is the first time I have felt heard by you in a long time."

As they resumed their walk, they went back to the advice-giving conversation, and Rachel sensed Phil's effort to hold back on giving answers. Instead, he seemed to really try to understand why she was so bothered by their previous interactions.

Going back to the Beckhard formula of R (resistance) $<$ D $\times$ V $\times$ F, Rachel increased her father's understanding of the cost he was paying by causing her unhappiness (the D for his dissatisfaction), helped him understand what could be better (showed him a vision—the V—for how it could be), and showed him more about how to get there (the F for "first steps").

Meeting Someone Emotionally

Rachel wanted Phil to see how problematic his advice-giving was to her, as well as to respond differently when she talked about what was important to her—she didn't want him to shut down. She also wanted something we call "feeling emotionally met." Being able to connect in this way with another is especially important when you're at an impasse, where conflict and emotions are high and each person is having difficulty understanding the other.

There are two ways to think about meeting others emotionally. One is what they need to feel, and the other is what you need to do.

When people feel emotionally met, they feel fully heard, understood, seen, accepted, and not judged. That requires hearing beyond the words and listening for underlying meaning. This is not how Rachel felt from most of Phil's responses until the very end. It was not necessary that Phil agree with Rachel or think her requests were "right" or "correct" for her to feel met. What he had to do (and finally did) was to convey that he understood what she was feeling and why she was feeling it from *her* perspective.

There are a variety of behaviors that help someone else feel emotionally met (this is the *doing* part). They include:

- Active listening that assures the speaker that you understand them. Some of this is conveyed nonverbally, with eye contact and head nodding. Listening slows the conversation down in an important way. Giving someone plenty of space to stay in their feelings as opposed to talking them out of them or countering with your own is the key.
- Paraphrasing/acknowledging feelings. Repeating what you've heard someone else say is a powerful way to convey you have heard them, and to find out in the moment whether you heard them correctly.
- Active empathy—for example, saying things like "That sounds really crummy," or simply being with the other person and lis-

tening actively while they stay in their feelings. That may require that you temporarily set aside your feelings, if yours are different.

- Conveying care. Again, this can be done with words, but it can also be nonverbal, as when Rachel put her arm around her father.
- Suspending judgment and engaging in curiosity and inquiry. This means asking open-ended questions and really trying to understand what is going on for the other person.

Obviously, one rarely uses all of these behaviors at one time. However, meeting someone emotionally is likely to require a number of them. When fully present with the other, you can usually sense what's appropriate. Sometimes just saying, with feeling, "That's really horrible," is sufficient. Rachel felt emotionally met when her father stopped to take in what she was saying and simply responded, "But I think maybe I'm starting to see what you're getting at."

When we are highly emotional, being able to set our own feelings temporarily aside so that we can fully hear the other person might be too big a request. I might have to first acknowledge that it is too hard for me to be fully present to your feelings in this moment. And if I do, it is important to then come back and re-engage when I am feeling less emotionally triggered. We are not suggesting that meeting someone emotionally is a way to avoid disagreement or conflict. It is simply *a* way of responding to someone else when they are in a heightened emotional state. And it is a way to connect at a very personal level.

One Conversation at a Time

It took a great deal of persistence, but Rachel made significant progress. It would have been easy for her to give up on her father and conclude that he just couldn't hear her in the way she wanted.

Maybe his admission "That's hard for me" helped her realize that what she was asking was a major change in behavior for him. However, it is rare that one conversation, even as successful as this one appears, can fully change such deeply rooted habitual behavior. But at least it's a start; Phil now understands what is happening for Rachel and has learned some new ways of interacting. It is almost certain that he will regress and fall back on familiar patterns. What is crucial is that Rachel not give up. It's a process of "two steps forward and one back," and it's important that she continue to acknowledge his progress, as she did when she told him she finally felt heard. Too often, we focus on what a person does wrong, forgetting how impactful positive reinforcement can be.

Remember that sometimes a straight line is the longest distance between two points. A discussion starts on one topic, and it becomes apparent that there are other, more important issues to deal with. When this happens, take a pause. Step back. Is there a barrier that needs to be confronted? As Rachel did on the hike with her father, put the first topic aside and *look at how you are talking.* Notice how you are feeling. Speak to that! Resolving that deeper issue will help not only with the issue at hand but also with future problem-solving, resulting in a far deeper and more robust relationship.

Deepen Your Learning

SELF-REFLECTION

1. Put yourself first in Rachel's shoes. *Even though you are frustrated with your father, you don't want to hurt him. How do you think you would handle this situation? Would you give up? Which of the various approaches that she used would you have tried? Not tried?*

   Now put yourself in Phil's shoes. *You really value the relationship that you have with your daughter and don't want to lose the closeness you have. But you are comfortable with the way you presently interact and would find it difficult to do what Rachel wants. How would you handle that situation? What would you have done and said?*

2. Outdated Agreements: Are you in a relationship (key or other) that you care about, but in which some of the ways you relate seem stuck in the past?

3. Your Contribution: Could you, like Rachel, be doing something that is making change unlikely in this relationship? For instance:

    - Assuming "That's the way they are; that's their personality"
    - Lacking clarity in your feedback (about specific behavior and impact on you or on what you need)
    - Assuming change is easier than it is
    - Lacking persistence and patience
    - Neglecting to use D × V × F (dissatisfaction × vision × first steps)
    - Wanting the change for your sake and not taking into account what the other wants

APPLICATION

Based on the reflection above, have a conversation with the other person to see if you can redefine the relationship so that both of you benefit.

MAKING SENSE

How did it go? What did you learn (about yourself and about influencing another)?

In retrospect, is there anything you would have done or said differently?

10

OWN YOUR EMOTIONS OR THEY WILL OWN YOU

Mia and Aniyah—Longtime Friends, Part 1

See if this sounds familiar: You're having what starts out as a perfectly lovely dinner—with your parent or your partner, your friend or your child—when seemingly for no reason, the conversation takes a nosedive. Some innocuous comment leads to a retort, which leads to an accusation, and things only get worse from there. Suddenly, allegations fly, old injuries are raised, and for the life of you, you can't figure out why. It's like steam you didn't even realize had been building up is now out of control, and something has finally blown up.

While there's no one-size-fits-all diagnosis, chances are excellent that the mismanagement of emotions played a role. "Mismanagement" can mean many things. It can mean that suppressed feelings have built up to the point of this explosion. It can also mean you've been numbing emotions—that you're scarcely aware that they've been there all along.

Previous chapters covered the many reasons you might push emotions away. This chapter shows the price you pay for doing this and how it can not only build explosive conditions but also cause each party to get locked into a rigid position. The more you know your emotions, the less likely you are to be controlled by them, and the greater the number of choices you'll have in how to express them productively.

Mia and Aniyah, Part 1

Aniyah and Mia have been friends since they were college roommates and confidantes around boyfriends, career choices, and the transition to adulthood. This close, trusting relationship continued after graduation, even though they lived far apart. They regularly talked on the phone and visited each other when they could. They attended each other's weddings and shared the ups and downs as children came into their lives.

Then Mia and her husband, Jake, moved their family to Philadelphia, where Aniyah and her husband, Christopher, lived. Mia and Aniyah hoped this would allow the four of them to get together, but their husbands never quite gelled. The two women instead tried to regularly meet up for dinner, but what with children and full-time jobs, these dinners were less frequent than they'd hoped.

They loved seeing each other, but they found their previous intimacy had diminished. They didn't talk about it, but they shared less with each other than they used to. *Maybe it's because I have Jake and other friends,* Mia mused. *That closeness might have been something I needed earlier in my life but don't need as much now. Not to mention that the kids take up all my time. Or maybe it's because Jake and I are better off than Aniyah and Christopher, and it's weird for them.* She decided to put those thoughts aside and looked forward to an upcoming date with Aniyah.

They met at one of their favorite French bistros and spent the first part of dinner catching up on life, as was their custom. Toward the end of the meal, Aniyah lamented, "I'm so tired all the time. I'm always behind on everything and no matter how much I cut back on my sleep and exercise, I can't seem to make much headway."

Mia nodded. "I know just what you mean. I'm juggling a lot, too, between the promotion, the kids, and the new house construction. What I'd give for five more hours in every day!"

Aniyah felt a tiny bit of resentment, though she knew Mia meant well. So she responded, "Yeah, I know you have a lot going on, too. But at least you're tired as a result of all kinds of good stuff. I'm stuck in the same rut at work, and half the time I feel like a bad mother for all the time I could be with the kids."

"What are you talking about? You're a great mother!"

"Nice of you to say, but I don't think so. Just last week I was supposed to chaperone Evan's field trip but had to cancel. My boss asked for yet another last-minute change to the report we've been working on. Evan was so disappointed." Aniyah's eyes started to water. "I'm sorry, I don't know what I'm getting all worked up about; I guess I'm just tired. Or maybe I hadn't realized how much it was all getting to me."

"Maybe it's time for you to finally find a new job."

"What's that supposed to mean?" Aniyah asked.

"Just that I've heard you complain about it for quite a while now," said Mia, "so it seems like it's time to look for something else."

Aniyah felt disappointed and irritated. "Easy for you to say, Mia. Everything is just great in your life. Plus, we need my income and my job pays well."

Both of them lapsed into silence, which broke only when the waiter came to offer them dessert and they declined.

"I'm only trying to help, Aniyah, but I feel like anything I say gets your back up. Why are you so sensitive?"

"Sometimes being sensitive about what's going on for someone else is a good thing," Aniyah replied.

"What does that mean?"

Aniyah sighed deeply. "Look, I'm really tired. I shared something personal, and all I got from you was telling me to find a new job. I know you mean well, Mia, but it feels like you are not hearing how hard this all is for me." Aniyah thought about all the times she'd left their conversations feeling more and more insecure. Mia always seemed to have all the answers. *Doesn't Mia ever struggle with anything?* she wondered.

"How can you say that? Of course I know how hard this is for you!" Mia fired back. "How could you possibly think I don't?"

"I just don't," answered Aniyah. "Plus, hearing about your promotion and the new house you're building makes it all worse. I know I shouldn't say that because I wish nothing but the best for you."

"So I shouldn't share what's going on in my life but just listen to your issues? Geez, it's like a minefield with you. I don't know what to say that won't make things worse." *As usual,* Mia thought, *Aniyah is oversensitive. Talking with her feels like walking on eggshells.* "Maybe we should call it a night."

Aniyah paid for her half of the meal and with a resigned tone said, "Agreed."

"Well, that was a great use of an evening away from Jake and the kids," said Mia sarcastically as they walked toward their cars.

"Now it's gotten late," said Aniyah, "and I'm even more exhausted than when I arrived. I just need to get home. Sorry."

"Me too," said Mia.

They got in their respective cars feeling angry and resentful toward each other.

Releasing Steam: What Happened?

In a nutshell, Mia and Aniyah violated everything covered in prior chapters.

1. They let pinches build up: Each of them had a number of issues. Aniyah was bothered that Mia rarely raised any personal problems of her own. Aniyah didn't find her especially empathetic when Aniyah shared her struggle. Instead, Mia gave advice, which Aniyah saw as an indication of how little Mia really under-

stood her. Aniyah also felt envious of Mia's greater job satisfaction and affluence.

Mia also had pent-up pinches. She was tired of Aniyah's continued complaints about her job and her (perceived) unwillingness to do anything about it and sounding like a victim. She wanted to help Aniyah but was frustrated by what she thought was Aniyah's hypersensitivity. Mia wanted to share more about her job and the new house but felt inhibited because she sensed Aniyah's envy.

Any one of these issues wasn't such a big deal, which is probably why Mia and Aniyah hadn't previously raised them—even though, if brought up earlier, they might have been more easily resolved. But the buildup over time made them destructive.

2. <u>They didn't state their feelings:</u> Even though there were "I feel" statements, they began "I feel *like*," which expressed a thought, not an emotion. At the same time, their tone and choice of words conveyed some strong unexpressed feelings.

3. <u>They played the blame game:</u> If Aniyah and Mia's respective husbands asked them, "How'd it go?" as they walked in the door, each would have talked about all the reasonable things they tried to communicate and how inappropriate the other person was. When Aniyah told Mia, "It feels like you are not hearing how hard this all is for me," and "Everything is just great in your life," a number of unexpressed emotions morphed into an attack. This allowed each to feel self-righteous and blame the other. When Mia asked, "Why are you so sensitive?" she wasn't really asking a question, she was making an accusation.

The blame game is rarely productive. It doesn't lead to self-reflection and inhibits openness to discovering the underlying problems, let alone wanting to solve them. It closes down the other person, creates defensiveness, and usually leads to reciprocal blame.

4. They didn't attempt to understand each other: Since each of them believed she was right and that the other was behaving poorly, and each assumed she knew the other's motives, there was little incentive to move into inquiry. The time when this might have been most fruitful was when Aniyah started to tear up after talking about missing her son's field trip. If Mia had responded at a feeling level and with empathy said, "Aniyah, I'm worried. What's going on?" it might have shifted the entire conversation.

Instead, Mia chose to make a logical recommendation ("Maybe it's time for you to finally find a new job") that closed Aniyah down and left her feeling even more vulnerable. It was a missed opportunity on Mia's part, but her pent-up annoyance blocked the empathy she might have normally felt for one of her best friends.

As the conversation went on, each of them became more self-righteous and defensive, making it harder to be curious about what was really going on with the other. At one point in the conversation Aniyah asked, "What's that supposed to mean?" And later Mia said, "What does that mean?" However, in both cases, their tone was more defensive/attacking than an expression of real interest.

It was fortuitous that the evening ended when it did. The two friends were not in a space where they were managing their emotions particularly well, and their feelings could easily have escalated into a level of damage from which the relationship might never have recovered. This is why we feel so strongly that you must own your emotions or they will own you. By "owning," we're not suggesting suppressing, which is what each of them did. Rather, owning and managing emotions is about *expressing* them, but doing so in productive ways.

Recognizing and Owning Emotions

When David first started conducting T-groups at Stanford almost fifty years ago, students often responded, "I don't know," when asked what they were feeling. In the ensuing years, research on emotional intelligence and other factors have made emotional expression more acceptable in society, and total unawareness is far less common. But most people have a tendency to first go to their head, to try to understand what's going on logically, before paying attention to their own or someone else's feelings. It's a hard habit to break. The two of us have worked in this field for decades, but at times even we need to pause and ask ourselves, "What exactly am I feeling?"

In Carole's case, pushing down feelings—numbing them—started early. Her mother had a terrible temper, and Carole's earliest memories are of cowering somewhere in the house where she could remain under the radar while her mother ranted, screamed, and slammed doors. Carole became deeply afraid of anger, seeing it as a bad emotion that was best not to feel. She had to work hard to become aware of when she was angry and learn to express it appropriately. As Brené Brown points out, we can't selectively numb emotions, for "when we numb anger, sadness, and fear, we also numb gratitude, love, and joy."

The workplace hasn't exactly been an ally in the cause of emotional expression. For decades, organizations stressed the importance of keeping feelings out of the workplace. In 1975, Carole was hired at a Fortune 500 company, the first woman to be hired in a nonclerical role. The first thing she learned was that if she was going to succeed in business, especially as a woman in that era, she had to act like the men—meaning be aggressive, strong, bold, and above all, calm, rational, and unemotional. Feelings had no place. She became very good at this, and it served her well. However, as she rose up the ranks, moved to another company, and became a high-level manager, her rational model became limiting.

At one point she was running a $50 million sales and marketing business when, at a management offsite with her team, she got choked up as she passionately spoke about what they could achieve if they all pulled together. She was met by stunned silence. One of her managers (a man, by the way; they were all men) said, "Wow, looks like you're human after all." And then Carole really did burst out crying. "You don't think I'm human?"

She tore up the day's agenda and declared there was nothing more important to talk about than this. What followed was one of the most genuine, authentic, and rewarding business conversations of her career. A conversation about who she really was and what she deeply cared about, followed by each of the managers sharing who they were and what mattered most to them. Feelings of hope, sadness, pride, disappointment, frustration, and caring poured out of everyone. They all came to realize that they had been leaving half of themselves, perhaps the most important half, in the parking lot. The more they talked, the more fully they became known to one another.

After that offsite, they built themselves into an unstoppable team. To this day, Carole knows those seven men would follow her anywhere. Had this happened during her first year on the job, when she had less credibility and confidence, it is unlikely the outcome would have been as good.

Emotions are delegitimized beyond workplaces, too. Most of our education system stresses logic and reason, as do early socialization experiences: "You shouldn't be angry." "You shouldn't be hurt by negative feedback since the other said they were just trying to help." "You shouldn't be mad at your baby brother" (even though he is now taking all the attention that you used to get!). Our shouldn'ts often prevent us from recognizing what we *are* feeling.

Parents with the best of intentions still send signals that negate feelings. When David's son, Jeffrey, was four, David took him to the neighborhood park to play. In going down the slide, Jeffrey hit the back of his head on the bottom edge and started to cry. David rushed over, picked him up, and said, "Jeffrey, you're not hurt." But he got his comeuppance. Still with tears streaming down his face, Jeffrey retorted, "How do you know how I feel? Only I know how I feel."

David wasn't consciously trying to deny Jeffrey's feelings. He just wasn't being honest about his own. The more accurate (and supportive) thing to say would have been, "I'm feeling bad that you're hurting."

Even when people do express feelings, they tend to downplay their intensity. We conceptualize emotions on a ten-point scale, from very mild to extreme. Not infrequently, it's only when an emotion passes a threshold of seven that people notice or report it. While low-level feelings might not be worth expressing, what about those in the midrange? Sometimes in a T-group, a participant will say, "I was a *little* annoyed at that comment." We then hold our hand sideways with a quarter-inch gap between thumb and forefinger and say humorously, "Just a little?" The student often laughs and says, "Actually not," leading to a more accurate and fruitful conversation.

Somatic responses (such as a flutter in our stomach, a slight change in our heartbeat, tingling in our neck, tightness in our throat, or damp palms) offer important clues about our emotions. These responses can wake us up out of our numbness and help us recognize the severity of what's going on. More often than not, though, we ignore them—even when research suggests that doing so can adversely affect our health, our happiness, and the quality of our relationships. We also "leak" emotions, through sharpness of tone or facial expressions of disdain, which results in even more dysfunctional exchanges, like the one between Mia and Aniyah. But it's likely that in the heat of their argument, neither of them were fully aware of all they were feeling.

What Could Mia and Aniyah Have Done?

The two friends were in a tough spot. They were both exhausted, in a public place, and sitting on pent-up feelings. Perhaps the best thing they did was call it a night and minimize the damage. That said, as mentioned, they would have had more options if they had chosen to go down a different path earlier in the conversation.

Let's pick up the story where Mia said, "I'm only trying to help, Aniyah, but I feel like anything I say gets your back up. Why are you so sensitive?" There are at least three good options here. At the heart of all of them is the interpersonal cycle from chapter 7 and the concept of staying with your reality and on your side of the net.

OPTION 1: STICKING WITH FEELINGS

Let's suppose Aniyah responded by disclosing: "Mia, I'm really feeling hurt, partially by that comment, but also by this conversation." Even though we have argued that a willingness to be vulnerable can break down barriers, it might be too much to expect Aniyah to be that vulnerable since she was already feeling one-down and she'd just been accused of being overly sensitive. But if she could have expressed her pain, it might have led Mia to do the same and respond with empathy and an apology: "I'm sorry. I don't want to hurt you. What can I do?"

Perhaps Mia could be the one who sticks with her feelings to break the logjam. She might catch herself by saying something like, "Oh, that was a horrible thing to say. I'm sorry." Or "I feel bad about how I've been responding to you this evening. It's just been so hard for me to hear your unhappiness. Everything is not always so rosy for me either."

That would be great, but let's do another plausibility test. How likely is it that, just after her accusation, Mia would pivot 180 degrees, especially given her growing irritation with Aniyah's complaints? Is it reasonable to expect that she would disclose those feelings? Probably not.

However, there is a way for Mia and Aniyah to share their feelings without having to abruptly shift from anger to compassion. We previously noted that anger is a second-order emotion and there are usually more vulnerable feelings beneath it. If either Mia or Aniyah were aware of this, could they have stopped to ask themselves, "What *am* I so upset about? What is making me so angry?" Then it might have been possible to follow up with, "I realize that the reason that I am so upset and angry is that I am also feeling [hurt/discounted/helpless, etc.]."

Such emotional openness on either of their parts would likely be the quickest way to stop this growing escalation. But that's difficult to do in the heat of the conflict, so while option 1 exists, it's hard to access.

OPTION 2: RECOGNIZING AND OVERCOMING EGO TRAPS

There are a series of ego traps that Mia and Aniyah could have avoided during their contentious situation, such as refusing to apologize until the other did first, thinking that admitting hurt was a sign of weakness, or needing to make the other out to be the bad person in order to feel better about themselves.

False pride locks you into a rigid stance and often leads to giving up control of what will happen. Often just catching yourself by recognizing that it is your ego at play is enough. Admitting that false pride is at work can be easier than the first option. Could either have recognized any of these traps or other ways they were being self-righteous and admitted that?

OPTION 3: PROCESSING WHAT'S GOING ON AND FOCUSING ON THE FUTURE

As we have discussed before, when two people are stuck, it is sometimes important to step back and ask, "What's going on? Can we get out of this?" Either Mia or Aniyah could have said that, being mindful that it not turn into a blame game.

One of the ways they could have prevented the blame from escalating was to talk about what they wanted from the relationship. Mia and Aniyah were not as intimate as they'd once been. Each of them missed their more personal, caring interactions and past closeness. Either could have said, "This evening's conversation isn't like the ones we used to have. In the past, I felt a real caring and closeness that I'm missing. I'd like to have that again. What about you?"

If either of them could have received that offer openly, and if they could each have avoided the trap of accusing the other of sabotaging their former intimacy, there's a chance they could have identified what they each wanted. At that point, it might have been possible to work on some of the built-up pinches.

Note that these three options aren't mutually exclusive but could, in the best of all possible worlds, build on each other. Stepping back to look at what is going on and reminding themselves of the relationship they want and miss could have led them into inquiry and disclosure of their feelings. The greatest takeaway is that when you're aware of feelings in real time, you have more choices on how to proceed.

All three options require vulnerability, which is challenging when you're feeling hurt and misunderstood. But as they say, no risk, no reward.

Clearly, Aniyah and Mia did not choose any of these options during the heat of their dinner. That doesn't mean it's too late for them. They'd reached an impasse, a logjam, but logjams can be broken. The next chapter explores how.

Deepen Your Learning

SELF-REFLECTION

1. Put yourself first in Aniyah's situation. *How would you have likely responded at different junctures?* Then put yourself in Mia's position and do the same thing. Don't answer with how you think you should have responded but how you likely would have.

2. Getting Stuck: Think back to various times when you have gotten "stuck" in arguments with others. Do you see a pattern in ways that your ego got in the way? Consider which of these following statements ring true:

   - I have a hard time apologizing until the other person does first.
   - I have a difficult time saying that I am sorry.
   - It is hard for me to admit that I was wrong.
   - I tend to think my position is usually right; it's hard for me to understand the other's position.
   - I need to show that the other is more responsible for the problem than I am.
   - I try to find reasons for finding the other person at fault.
   - I find it hard to say that I am feeling hurt.
   - When I have been hurt by another, I find it hard to let go of my resentment.
   - I tend to see any negative feedback or criticism as a personal attack and get very defensive.
   - I am self-righteous when I think the other person is wrong.

   These tend to be ways that we protect ourselves. For the item(s) you selected, what are you concerned might occur if you didn't do this?

3. Logjams: Mia and Aniyah got into their logjam for four major reasons. For the situations you identified above, do any of these tend to occur?

    - Letting pinches build up
    - Not stating your feelings (but getting into logical arguments or making accusations)
    - Playing the blame game
    - Not trying to understand the other

APPLICATION

Take one of your key relationships in which, at one time or another, you have gotten stuck. Based on the list under the second self-reflection question above, which ones tended to occur for you or the other person? Discuss this with them and see if you can work out a way to prevent it from happening again.

Do you have a disagreement (with a key relationship or anyone else) that is unresolved? Decide how you will break that logjam and give it a shot.

MAKING SENSE

How did your conversations go? What did you learn about yourself and about these types of discussions? What are you committed to doing the next time you are in a conversation that is stuck? What especially do you want to use from what you have learned?

11

BREAKING THE LOGJAM

Mia and Aniyah, Parts 2 and 3

Let's go back briefly to the metaphor in chapter 2 about hiking Mount Washington. Mia and Aniyah had anticipated an easy climb up to the headwall. Then the weather changed, storm clouds came, and they got soaked. They are now at the foot of the most difficult part of the climb. Should they try the ascent? It will be hard, and the rocks are slippery. Should they turn back? If they keep going, they could get hurt, but if they make it to the meadow, the hardship will make their accomplishment all the more meaningful and the view all the more satisfying.

That said, maybe it's not worth it. Maybe they should just retreat. They're at a key decision point, and how they move forward has everything to do with their commitment to each other, their ability to handle this difficult situation, and whether their relationship is worth possibly more conflict.

Although Aniyah might feel stuck, she actually has a range of options. She could give up on the long-term relationship. She could wait to see if Mia makes the first move; however, that would entail giving up control of what happens next. She could take the initiative and reach out to Mia. But if she does that, what should she say? If she shares her feelings, would Mia label her again as being too sensitive? What if Aniyah expresses her opinion that the fight was all Mia's fault? Wouldn't that make it even worse? She has numerous choices, but each has potential costs.

Mia and Aniyah, Part 2

As Aniyah drove home that night and thought about the dinner conversation, she got more and more upset. By the time she pulled into her driveway, she was in tears. Her husband, Christopher, met her at the door. The more she described what happened, the worse she felt. She concluded, "Maybe it's time to let that friendship go. It's more trouble than it's worth."

"Do you really want to give up on a twenty-five-plus-year friendship?" Christopher asked. "You two have been through a lot together."

"Well, if the relationship is important to her, and since the disaster this evening turned into is mostly her fault, she'll have to take the first step," said Aniyah.

Christopher was quiet for a moment, then said, "Do you want to give up that much control and leave the outcome entirely in her hands?"

"I don't know," Aniyah responded. "All I know is that I'm exhausted, and I desperately need to go to bed and get a good night's sleep."

The next day as she drove to work, Aniyah reflected on Christopher's comments. She and Mia *had* been through a lot together, and Aniyah missed their prior closeness. In fact, that loss was what upset her the most. She felt both sad and empty. She wondered whether Mia felt the same way. *Relationships do end,* she mused. *Is that what Mia wants?*

She considered reaching out to Mia but didn't know how to frame a follow-up conversation. She still felt burned by the "Why are you so sensitive?" comment and didn't want to raise the issue in a way that would perpetuate Mia's view of her. She thought of calling but decided not to. *I'm not sure I can control what I say,* she thought, *especially if she puts me down again. . . .* Instead, she decided to drop Mia an email so that she could be more thoughtful.

That evening, Aniyah wrote Mia: "I don't know about you, but I'm still feeling bad about how dinner went last night. We've had a long-standing friendship and we've been important to each other for many years. I don't know how you feel, but I'd like to meet again to see what we can do. But let's not meet for dinner. I think we need a more private place and a little more time than a hurried meal."

The next day Mia responded: "Glad to get your email; how about meeting at noon a week from Saturday at the community gardens gazebo, which is always empty? Will that work?"

Aniyah felt relieved that Mia had responded so quickly, but there was little in her reply that indicated she was as upset as Aniyah. *Am I going to come across as the needy one again?* she thought. But she'd made the overture, so she responded, "Yeah, that sounds good. See you then."

The community gardens were close to Aniyah's house, and as she walked there the following Saturday, she was grateful that Mia had chosen a spot that would be easier for her. But she also felt nervous and worried the meeting wasn't a good idea. *What's going to come of this?* she wondered. *Are we going to get anywhere or just make things worse?*

Mia was already at the gazebo, and as she had predicted, no one else had claimed the space. It was a beautiful day, the temperature was perfect, and the small gazebo was cozy and inviting. Mia greeted Aniyah with a hug, sat down, and gestured for Aniyah to do so as well. "So," Mia said, "what's on your mind?"

"I was hoping that what's on my mind is on yours as well."

Mia sighed. "What *is* it with you?"

Aniyah felt her defenses go up immediately. "What is it with me? What is it with *you*? How can you be so insensitive? I feel like you don't care about our relationship."

Mia said, "Just because I don't get all worked up about every little thing and don't react the way you do doesn't mean I'm insensitive or I don't care!"

"Wait," Aniyah said. "Let's not do this again."

"No," Mia agreed. "Let's not."

They sat in silence for a moment and then Mia asked, "What's going on, Aniyah?"

"That's the issue," Aniyah said. "Why is this all on me? Aren't you concerned about our relationship, too?"

"I never said it was all on you!" Mia said a bit defensively. Then she softened her tone. "I'm just worried. I care so much about our friendship and I feel helpless."

"It really helps me to hear that," said Aniyah. "But that's the first I've heard that any of this is bothering you. I really don't know how much you care about our friendship. Do you miss the intimacy and closeness we had as much as I do?"

"Of course I do. Isn't it obvious? What do I have to do to make it clear?"

"Actually, it's not obvious," Aniyah said. "Take the email that I sent suggesting we meet. I took the risk of saying I felt bad about how dinner went and what it might mean for our relationship, and your response was 'Glad to get your email.' I had no idea if you felt like I did."

"But I don't understand—why do I have to say it?"

"Because it would help," Aniyah said. "I'm not a mind reader. Look, you label me as needy and just said that I worry about every little thing. That puts me in a one-down position, as if I'm the problem person, and that label makes me feel insecure. Yes, of course I have needs, but don't you have needs, too? Isn't this an equal relationship?"

Mia paused for a minute to take that in, then, in a soft tone said, "Okay . . . I'm starting to see that now, and I'm sorry. Yes, I was upset, too, and wish I had been more explicit about it."

After a moment of mutual silence, they both started to physically relax a bit. Then Mia added in an even softer tone, "Am I doing anything else that's pushing you away?"

"Well, actually, yes," said Aniyah. "For a while now, things have been falling into place perfectly for you while I've been struggling, and it makes it really hard for me to be with you."

"So I should just not talk about what's going on for me because it's good? Is that the only way we can be in a relationship? Do you want me to hold back big parts of my life and myself? That feels kind of one-sided to me."

"No, of course not," said Aniyah. "If we're going to have a close relationship, we need to feel free to talk about all aspects of our life. Look, you accuse me of being too sensitive. On the other hand, I don't hear you acknowledge how I might be feeling when you talk about all the expensive details of your new house—isn't that being a bit insensitive?"

Mia started to tear up. "I'm sorry, but you're the only person that I can fully share my success with."

"And I want to be there for you," Aniyah responded softly. She paused. "What's going on? What are the tears about?"

At that, Mia let her tears flow uninhibited. "You know my background, growing up where all the other kids were from rich families. We weren't poor, but I always had less than the others. It feels so good to be successful, and I don't want to brag, but who else can I share this with?"

"Oh, Mia, I *do* want to celebrate with you." Aniyah reached for Mia's hand. "And believe me, I'm happy for you and want to be the person you can fully let it all hang out with." Aniyah let that statement sit for a few minutes as she allowed Mia the space to cry.

"Still," Aniyah said after Mia had stopped crying, "I have to admit that sometimes when we talk, it leaves me feeling even worse about the stuff that isn't working that well in my life. I feel inadequate so often, and it's really painful to feel that way even when I'm with one of my best friends."

"But what can I do?" asked Mia.

"I know you're trying to help," said Aniyah. "But when I share what's going on, you give me casual advice like 'Maybe it's time to find a new job.' Then when I don't respond positively to that, you call me too sensitive. In fact, I'm sitting here worried that's what you'll say next, or worse, that you're thinking that even if you don't say it."

"That's hard to hear," Mia said, "but I also get it. That's not how I want to be with you. I had no idea how hard all this was on you. I'm so sorry I said you were too sensitive. And you're right—I wasn't sensitive enough."

"Thanks so much for saying that," said Aniyah. "That really helps. I'm feeling better understood than at dinner. If you were a casual acquaintance, this would be hard enough, but I hate the fact that I'm envious of you and I don't know quite how to handle it."

"I don't know quite how to handle it either," admitted Mia, "but I'm glad we're talking about it openly. I feel hopeful we'll figure it out."

A Close Call

Mia and Aniyah broke the logjam, but it was a close call. The dinner itself could have been the last straw for either of them. Or Aniyah could have waited for Mia to take the first step in its aftermath, as she thought of doing initially. Mia also might not have responded to Aniyah's email right away, which could have resulted in Aniyah's giving up. Finally, the friendship could have fallen apart during the gazebo conversation, beginning as it did with accusations of insensitivity and oversensitivity.

In contentious situations like these, it's common to get stuck because you're afraid that opening issues up will worsen the argument. Another tendency is to oversimplify the conflict to right and wrong, believing the other person is totally at fault and that you bear no responsibility. Such oversimplification narrows the options for reconciliation, making either or both parties hesitant to move. In that state, you stop hearing each other, which makes it more difficult to move toward a productive resolution.

When you feel hurt and distanced from someone you care about deeply, what you most need is to feel heard and fully understood—as previously noted, two key aspects of "feeling emotionally met." In order for this to happen, though, you have to understand your own needs and feelings, and then speak those needs and feelings aloud. No one is a mind reader. Then and only then can you move into mutual problem-solving and repair.

Both Mia and Aniyah faced a series of major choice points. At each juncture they could decide to turn toward the issue, and each other, or they could turn away. They were at one such point immediately after their disastrous dinner. Fortunately, Aniyah turned toward Mia. Even though she was feeling hurt, she was willing to take the risk and increase her level of vulnerability by reaching out and writing that she was feeling bad about the dinner and that the relationship was important to her. Such vulnerability tends to result in reciprocal vulnerability, as emphasized throughout the book. However, Mia did not respond in kind in her email, which was a lost opportunity for further connection.

As they started to talk in the gazebo, they were at another choice point. They had just engaged in mutual blame, as Aniyah called Mia insensitive and Mia retaliated by claiming that at least *she* didn't "get all worked up about every little thing." This was a potentially explosive point in the conversation and the reason so many people don't surface difficult interpersonal issues in the first place. The fear is that the charges and countercharges will escalate into increasingly damaging accusations, and then neither party will have any idea how to recover. It's perfectly plausible that Aniyah could have gotten up and said, "I've had it—one hell of a friend you are," only to have Mia respond in kind.

The key point here is that either Aniyah or Mia could have

stopped the exchange from escalating. That's indeed what happened when Aniyah said, "Wait. Let's not do this again."

Fortunately, Mia responded positively. But they weren't out of the woods yet. Especially contentious situations usually indicate multiple issues are at play, which you may not initially realize. When strong emotions such as anger get out of control, it is like throwing gasoline on a fire and leads to a major conflagration. But, if managed and understood, these strong feelings can help us see that *the more emotions we feel, the more likely it is that there is something deeper going on.*

Aniyah's question "Aren't you concerned about our relationship, too?" started to break the logjam, as Mia was able to finally disclose her feelings. "I'm just *worried*. I *care* so much about our friendship and I feel *helpless*." By being somewhat vulnerable, Mia made it easier for Aniyah to share more of the issues that were bothering her. This allowed them to move into curiosity and, in doing so, to begin to understand what was behind the other's actions and reactions. They were also more ready to name the core issues in their relationship, such as envy, and the type of support that each needed from the other.

Aniyah did something else that led to a successful turn in the conversation. In addition to sticking to her feelings, she focused on Mia's behavior and what she found troubling. Rather than continuing the personal attacks about Mia's insensitivity, Aniyah pointed out that Mia's response to her email, her tendency to give advice, and her reluctance to disclose her own feelings caused problems. Remember, feedback is both more accurate and easier to hear if it is behaviorally specific, when the giver sticks with her reality.

Aniyah and Mia didn't break the logjam perfectly, and that's okay. Handling difficult interpersonal issues doesn't require using exactly the right words at exactly the right time. Both Aniyah and Mia could have shared their feelings earlier (and heard the underlying feelings of the other better). They could have noticed when they were over the net. They stumbled but then caught themselves.

The most valuable lesson in this exchange is the importance of persistence. At any point, they could have turned away from each other, potentially damaging the relationship further. Hanging in there and turning toward each other took patience, self-management, and a willingness to go a few rounds. But, as Mia and Aniyah found, it's well worth the effort.

Mia and Aniyah, Part 3

Aniyah thought about Mia's comment about her childhood. "I knew a little about your upbringing," Aniyah said, "but even in college we didn't talk about it that much. Sounds like there's a lot more to it than I realized."

Mia then really opened up. "Yeah, it was a pretty gross culture, when I think about it. All the kids wore designer clothes, vacationed in Cannes, and lived in mansions. People constantly tried to one-up each other about status. I wasn't even in their league. I wore clothes I bought in consignment stores, I had never even been west of the Mississippi, and we lived in a tiny apartment. I'd never have other kids over, and I spent all this energy trying to hide that I really didn't fit in."

"Mia, I had no idea it was that tough for you," replied Aniyah. "I can't believe we've been friends for as long as we have and this was something I knew so little about. Ugh, I'm so sorry."

Mia nodded in appreciation and continued, "When I went back to my twenty-fifth high school reunion last year, I felt equal to everyone else for the first time, like I'd finally arrived. By and large, my jobs have been better than theirs, and that felt very validating. Yet as I heard them all going on and on about their houses in the Hamptons and apartments overlooking Central Park, one-upping each other just like they used to, the last thing I felt like doing was telling them about the good things in my life. I hate that kind of bragging. I find it really distasteful and can't stand the idea of wealth being a metric for who to befriend." Mia paused. "And since I don't want to brag like they do and don't want anyone to feel belittled the way I once did, I don't talk about all the great stuff that is going on in my life to anybody but you and Jake." Mia started to cry.

Aniyah felt her heart soften as she began to more fully understand Mia. She shook her head slightly and said, "How ironic that I was feeling about you the way you felt with your friends in high school. I'm so glad we're talking about this!"

"That's painful to hear, but it's true," Mia said quietly. "How ironic. I'm sorry that I did that to you."

They both felt more relaxed and continued to chat about other childhood memories for a while. Then Aniyah suggested they might walk around the park. As they walked, Aniyah talked more about how stuck she felt at work and why hope about an impending shift in management kept her from leaving. This time, Mia nodded supportively and gave her the space to just vent.

As they continued their walk, Mia and Aniyah talked more about what they needed from each other and, in the process, reaffirmed their commitment to their friendship. Aniyah assured Mia that she really did want to give her the chance to revel in her success, and Mia promised to respond with fewer knee-jerk solutions and just listen.

Taking Responsibility

This chapter—in fact, the entire book—deals with two related statements: *In almost every case, we have choices,* and *How the other person responds makes some choices easier and others more difficult.*

Mia and Aniyah each could have prevented this conflict or more quickly moved out of it, independent of the other. Time and again, the two of us have seen students, colleagues, clients, and friends give up this freedom to act. At the same time, people do influence each other, and if we want deep relationships, we need to be aware of how we might be freeing or constraining the other as well as how their actions affect us. Remember, others can *influence* us, but they need not *control* us.

Where these two concepts come together is around the issue of taking appropriate responsibility, not too much and not too little. In that disastrous dinner, neither Mia nor Aniyah took responsibility for what was happening—it was all the other person's fault. Then in the process of disclosing their feelings and concerns in their subsequent meeting, they each began to take ownership for their actions as well as point out how the other's actions made it easy or hard for them to act as their best self.

There can be danger in taking no responsibility for the other's reaction. If Mia had said, "You're your own person and shouldn't have been affected by my disparaging comments," she would not have been owning the fact that they're in a relationship with each other. Conversely, there can be danger in taking too much responsibility, which would have happened if Mia had said, "Oh, it's all my fault." That would have made Aniyah out to be a helpless victim. What the two of them finally did was hold both statements as equally valid: *I have a choice* and *I am affected by you*.

It is also worth noting that sometimes it is easier to share problems than successes we want to celebrate. The latter can make us feel vulnerable, given our fear that the other person will see us as "too full of ourselves." But part of being a good friend is being willing to be an appreciative audience and happy for you when things are going well, rather than labeling you a braggart. That is what Mia expected from Aniyah.

Once the logjam broke, Aniyah and Mia's exchange moved them further into problem-solving and repair. They shared their backstories—the reasons why they had certain reactions or certain needs. In doing so, they surfaced multiple issues in their friendship. Initially, many people only share emotions that feel safer and are usually more superficial. That often prevents the most important issues from emerging. Instead, you have to patiently surface what's really going on with each party. Mia and Aniyah were only able to do this once they worked out a series of agreements that allowed each to be more fully herself and fully supported by the other.

IT'S POSSIBLE THAT Mia and Aniyah could have had a pleasant dinner without this conflict if Mia had said with compassion, "You seem so down. What's going on?" Or if Aniyah had said, "You know, Mia, I don't find your suggestion helpful," Mia would probably have said, "Sorry," and changed the subject. This would have been a way of handling the pinch in real time and avoided their kerfuffle. It might have made for a nicer evening . . . but they would not have had the conflict that surfaced so many issues that ultimately brought them closer.

Even though conflict can feel stressful and even dangerous, it can actually be helpful. Conflict can surface issues in a very direct way. It can bring out emotions, indicating what's really going on so you know where others stand. In Mia and Aniyah's situation, where several incidents had built up, the conflict brought them all to light, where they could be dealt with. Their disagreement, as painful as it was, forced them to identify what really mattered most to each of them. Their ability to deal with the issues not only led to a productive resolution but also reaffirmed their commitment to each other and to their friendship. They were able to turn an initially negative interaction into a positive outcome. Being able to use conflict productively is a complex issue that we will explore in greater detail in the next chapter.

Deepen Your Learning

SELF-REFLECTION

1. Put yourself first in Aniyah's and then in Mia's shoes. *Look over what they shared: How easy/challenging would it be for you to disclose*

all they did? Are there ways in which you might have gotten stuck? Then reflect further on how you might have handled the situation.

2. Being One-Down: It is challenging to take the initiative when you feel in a one-down position. Putting yourself in Aniyah's place once again, how hard would it have been for you to be vulnerable? Have there been times in a conflict situation where you have felt one-down and waited for the other person to make the first move? What did you do? What insights do you have about yourself from your answer to these questions?

3. Key Relationships: Think of specific incidents when one of your key relationships did something where you felt one-down. What was the incident and how did you respond?

4. Being One-Up: Do you think you might be doing something that makes one of your key relationships feel one-down or causes them to have a difficult time being vulnerable with you?

APPLICATION

In the third and fourth questions above, you may have identified relationships where you or the other may have felt one-down. Discuss this with them and what you can both do to change that.

MAKING SENSE

What did you learn from these discussions on vulnerability? Did they increase the extent to which you were each willing to be vulnerable with the other? What did you learn about what you need to do to make it easier for the other person to be vulnerable? How easy was it for you to be vulnerable?

12

USING CONFLICT PRODUCTIVELY

Maddie and Adam, Parts 2, 3, and 4

Mia and Aniyah's argument surfaced some core issues—Aniyah's feeling unheard, Mia's feeling censored, and both not feeling as close as they once were. When they realized the root of what was going on for them, they willingly made adjustments to their approach with each other. Their problem wasn't simple, but it did contain an easy solution.

But many conflicts don't have easy solutions. Let's say you rely on your parents for childcare, which they're happy to provide, but they are much firmer disciplinarians than you are. It upsets you, but you're afraid if you call them on it, they'll back away from giving the childcare that you desperately need. It seems like your needs are mutually exclusive: You want the free childcare, done with a softer hand, and they want to be firm. Also, what if they accuse you of taking advantage of their generosity? Or what if it brings up unresolved feelings about how strict they were with you when you were a kid? There's a whole wasp's nest of issues in danger of being disturbed.

For these types of conflicts, everyone needs to bring their A game, because it's likely to get harder before it gets easier. That is especially the case with the contentious issues around work and childcare facing Maddie and Adam from chapter 5.

Maddie and Adam, Part 2

A few weeks after Adam and Maddie discussed their disagreements—to no satisfying end—Maddie had lunch with her friend Teresa. Teresa had finally sorted out her family's childcare issues and had been able to go back to her full-time job. "It can be done," she said. "It's just not cheap." Maddie asked how she was able to work it out with her husband. "It wasn't easy," Teresa said, "and it took some negotiating, including his agreeing to step up and do more housework, but we reached an agreement."

That evening, Adam came home after Maddie had put the kids to bed. He'd called earlier to tell her he had good news, so she waited to eat so they could talk over dinner. She felt hungry, tired, and grumpy. She also kept replaying her conversation with Teresa in her head.

Adam walked in the door with a big smile and said, "I have something wonderful to tell you—can't wait to talk about it over dinner." As they sat down, he proudly announced that he'd been offered a new assignment, which signified a big opportunity. He'd learn a lot and be better positioned for a coveted promotion. Maddie listened but didn't say much. Adam described the additional responsibilities the assignment required, saying that one of the costs would be "cutting more into evenings and weekends for a while, but it will be worth it."

Maddie sighed and offered a quiet "Good for you."

"That's it?" Adam said.

"Well, Adam," she said, "this just makes what we've been trying to talk about for months even worse. I'm already unhappy with how much more responsibility for the kids and the household I have, and now you're telling me you're going to be around even *less*. It's hard for me to get really excited about what that means, no matter how great it is for you."

"This again?"

"Yes, this again!" Maddie said. "And it's not going away."

They stared at each other for a minute, and then she continued, "I had lunch with Teresa today and she told me about a great day care she found so that she could go back to work full-time. Maybe if we could look into that and free up more of my time, that would help, especially if you're going to spend even more evenings and weekends away from home."

"But we can't afford that," Adam said. "The cost of childcare is exorbitant. We can't spend that kind of money right now, when the kitchen remodel substantially depleted our savings."

"Well, then maybe you should consider turning down the assignment."

"That doesn't make any sense," said Adam. "This opportunity sets us up for a lot more success in the future."

Maddie considered picking up the dishes and silently carrying them to the kitchen but stopped herself. Instead, she said, "Adam, I can't be excited for you because I feel resentful more than anything else. I am not going to quietly retreat this time. I've had it! Things have to change, and we need to talk about it. Your career decisions are costing me, personally, and they're hurting our relationship."

"What do you mean?"

"Look, you have everything. You have an exciting job that's interesting, challenging, and meaningful, and all the adult interaction anyone could want. I'm stuck at home with a three- and five-year-old."

"Isn't that meaningful?"

"Sure, in a certain sense," Maddie said. "But do you want to trade places? How would you feel if your whole day was spent grocery shopping, cleaning the kitchen, and playing with little children, as adorable as they are, devoid of adult conversations and intellectual challenge? Would you want that?"

"Wait just a minute," Adam said. "Don't make me out to be the bad guy here. We *agreed* to this arrangement—that I'd be the breadwinner for a while, and you'd take care of the kids and house. Two working parents just brings too much stress—we decided that together."

"I know, and I'm sorry," Maddie said, "but I can't buy into that decision anymore. When we made it, I didn't realize the extent of the downside."

"I don't know what to do for you, hon. I love you."

"I know you love me—that's not the point. The point is that I'm starting to think we show love differently. Look, I want to support you and cheer for your work successes. I am and want to stay committed to your development. *And* I need you to be just as committed to mine. I'm not feeling that; I worry that you'll be happy if I just take care of the kids and the house. That's not contributing to my happiness and growth. And I spend a lot of time feeling unhappy."

"So you want me to give up this new assignment?"

"No, of course not. I want to support you and give you the full appreciation you deserve, but I need you to support me too."

"I guess I don't know how to do that. You usually just walk away when we get into this. It leaves me feeling kind of helpless."

"Really? That surprises me," said Maddie. "It never occurred to me that you felt helpless. I thought you didn't care about my feelings or just wanted to be right."

"Well, you're right that I cared about being right." He smiled sheepishly. "But I also really care about you. You're my wife and life partner."

"And you're right that I have been walking away from these conversations, but not because there was nothing you could do. I walked away because I was afraid of the conflict and scared about what it meant for us. I guess now I'm more afraid of what will happen if I just keep walking away."

"What are you afraid of?" Adam asked softly.

"When we first got married, we had an equal relationship. We made key decisions together, and we helped each other grow. I'm afraid we've lost that. I fear you'll brush me off or respond with something that will leave me feeling worse, like reminding me of the rewards of motherhood or how the kids will grow up feeling so close to me. I'm also realizing that by my not saying much about my growing resentment, I'm at fault, too. As hard as this feels right now, I think the first step in addressing what's going on between us is for me to stop running away."

How Maddie Regained Her Power

When two people avoid dealing with important issues, as Maddie and Adam did, they often get stuck and can't move into productive problem-solving. Maddie faced two issues with Adam: The first was their differences regarding childcare, but the second, which blocked them from dealing with the first, was the power imbalance that caused Maddie to believe she couldn't influence him.

Maddie began to narrow the power discrepancy by first ceasing to be controlled by her fear of the conflict that might result if she expressed her feelings and concerns more strongly. She questioned the legitimacy of the socially defined gender roles that her mother praised, and she questioned the previous agreement she and Adam had made on the grounds that she hadn't understood the full consequences. She took a stand and didn't run away as she had in the past. Maddie also used all four of the variations on the basic feedback model:

This is how your behavior is affecting me. She talked about her feelings of unhappiness and resentment.

Your behavior is not meeting your goals. She talked about not being as supportive and excited about Adam's possible new assignment as he would have liked.

Your behavior may be meeting your goals, but it is costly to you. She acknowledged that he was meeting his goal of occupational advancement but at great cost to their relationship and to their joint goal of an equitable, fair marriage.

Am I doing anything that is causing that behavior? She owned her part of the problem in her past behavior of running away and avoiding conflict.

The conversation would have unfolded very differently if Maddie had been over-the-net accusatory. Imagine if she'd said: "I feel that you only care about yourself." "I feel that you put your success before my happiness and our marriage." "You just want to use me to bear your children and clean your house." "You are just a typical self-centered, exploitative man." Adam would be unlikely to own any of these accusations, and they'd make him defensive. Accusations may make the giver feel good by releasing pent-up anger, but they drive the other away.

As we have stressed, a major source of power comes from being aware of your emotions. Maddie's resentment over Adam's new opportunity helped her realize just how bad the situation between them had become. Awareness of your feelings allows you to make more informed choices. If she had once again reasoned herself out of her feelings (*I should be happy taking care of the kids—they'll only be this age once—and it makes sense, for the whole family, for Adam to maximize his earning potential now, so I should just be happy for him*), she wouldn't have raised what were really important issues in their marriage or gotten Adam's full attention.

The objective at this point is not to get Adam to accept her solution of paying for day care. That would be premature. Instead, it's to get him to the table to seriously discuss the issues. After all, Maddie had only her point of view and needed Adam's to engage in joint problem-solving. But they had more work to do first.

In order to surface the problems in their marriage, each had to be willing to hang in there even if doing so initially resulted in more conflict. Intense disagreements produce strong emotions, which can make it difficult to hear the other person's concerns and lead to more deeply entrenched positions and greater risk of escalation. However, as we saw with Mia and Aniyah, the same intensity of emotion can also signal the importance of an issue, leading to more willingness to roll up your sleeves and get to work.

Maddie and Adam have made progress, but they aren't yet at the point where they can problem-solve. That doesn't mean they're in deep trouble. The issues are out on the table, and Maddie is clearly not retreating.

Maddie and Adam, Part 3

Adam took everything in. "This is hard to hear," he said, "but I'm glad we are talking about it."

Maddie's body relaxed. "Thanks, that really helps."

They sat in silence for a minute, appreciating where they were. Then she added, "We need to go back to making the most important decisions in our life together and redefine how to support each other."

"Yup," said Adam. "So . . . how?"

"I suggested something that I think would really help—some additional childcare. But you immediately shot that down as too expensive."

"Well it *is*!"

"Wait a minute! Yes, it's expensive, but who are you to say it's *too* expensive? Are you the ultimate authority of what is *too expensive*?"

"I'm the one who agonizes over the finances every month," said Adam. "I don't see you doing that."

"That just makes me angry," Maddie said, her voice rising. "This is usually the point where I walk away from our conversations, but I'm not going to do that again. Adam, I'm speechless. How can you imply I don't care about how much money we spend? You know damn well that I'm frugal. I'm the one who went searching for cheaper options on the kitchen remodel. I really feel hurt by that comment!"

"I'm sorry," Adam said defensively, "but I worry about money *a lot*."

"For goodness' sake, don't you think that I do, too? All I'm asking for is some childcare so that I can do something beyond taking care of the kids and the household day in and day out."

Adam crossed his arms. "Well, putting them in day care isn't the answer. You know what all our friends say—kids in day care get sick all the time. You'd have to miss work anyway to pick them up, only we'd still be paying for someone else to take care of them, and we'd both be stressed. It just makes no sense. What else do you have in mind?"

"I don't like what's happening, again! I bring up ideas, and you veto them. If you don't like my suggestion, then you come up with a solution. Kids and family are both of our responsibilities. These are your kids, too. This is *our* problem, not just *my* problem."

Adam didn't respond.

Maddie asked, "What are you thinking?"

"Nothing."

"How could you be thinking nothing? You must be thinking *something*."

"Well, I suppose if this is really important to you, then you'll have to earn enough to cover childcare after taxes."

"Wait a minute, Adam. That hardly feels like a fair solution. What happens if I can't initially cover it all? This makes childcare sound as though it is my sole responsibility, not *ours*. And it is *ours*. What happened to that part of you that was once concerned about me? You're making this sound like what I'm asking for is some sort of luxury."

Adam took this in and finally said, "This just upsets all that we'd agreed to. It throws everything up in the air, and I don't know what to do."

"What I'm asking you to do is think of options and not just immediately reject mine. What do you think we should do?"

Once again Adam was quiet. Then he said, "I don't want to have this conversation anymore."

"It's not like I'm loving this. But I'm pretty sure nothing is going to get better if you refuse to talk about it, and I care too much about us to let it go."

"We've talked it to death and we're not getting anywhere." His arms remained crossed. He looked down and said nothing more.

"I don't think it's going to do any good to run away from it," Maddie said. "Let's both try to hang in there until we get somewhere. We've stopped short of resolving this too many times before and I'm afraid of what will happen if we do that again."

They sat in silence across the table from each other, neither quite knowing what to say next.

Why Conflict Is So Scary

At first blush, it looked like Maddie and Adam's encounter was going downhill. This is what many fear about conflict—heated emotional back-and-forth arguments, accusations, escalation, and further entrenched positions. There is no question that conflict is uncomfortable and messy at best, and sometimes even frightening. At the height of an interpersonal conflict, we fear irreparable damage or the end of the relationship. But ending the conversation at this point only increases the likelihood that what we fear most will occur: permanent deadlock. Furthermore, it results in little to no learning.

Even though it's easy for one or both parties to take things very personally, this kind of escalation need not get out of hand. Look at what happened when Adam suggested Maddie was flip about money: Maddie could have tried to suppress her feelings (as she had done in the past) or gone to the other extreme and blown up with retaliatory attacks. Instead, she raised her voice and reported feeling angry. She was clear. Her words and tone were congruent with the situation. It worked, though it's worth noting that no one alternative is always the "right" way. In spite of her anger at Adam's accusation that she was not as concerned about their expenses, she responded with the *facts:* "You know damn well that I'm frugal. I'm the one who went searching for cheaper options on the kitchen remodel." She then shared her feelings rather than attacking Adam. ("I really feel hurt by that comment!") In all of these statements, she demonstrated the importance of sticking with her feelings and the facts regarding what she did and said.

When Maddie responded to Adam by saying she was angry and hurt, as opposed to, say, labeling Adam a tightwad, she stayed on her side of the net. This choice was more likely to avoid escalation and move the conversation toward problem-solving.

At one point, Adam started to stonewall Maddie when he said, "We've talked it to death and we're not getting anywhere," crossed his arms, looked down, and went silent. As psychologist John Gottman notes in his research, stonewalling is infuriating. Adam's initial move toward stonewalling was blocked when Maddie said, "I don't think it's going to do any good to run away from it. Let's both try to hang in there until we get somewhere." Note that while Maddie didn't back down, she also didn't push by saying something like, "Damn it, I'm not going to let you just go silent," which would have made Adam feel cornered. Instead, she reiterated her intent, indicating how much she cared about the relationship. She stayed at a similar emotional level as Adam and remained factual.

Maddie and Adam, Part 4

After a protracted period, Maddie broke the silence and asked, in a genuinely curious way, "What is it about this whole money-and-childcare thing that's so difficult for you?"

Adam was quiet a little longer, struggling with where to begin. "I guess I think a lot about Reed," he said, referencing his best friend from college. "After we graduated, he took a better-paying job than I did. But money just burned a hole in his pocket. He always had to have the newest and fanciest cars, and he went deeply into debt to buy a large house when we were still renting. His wife also liked to spend money, and they went on fancy vacations—remember how they were always going to Fiji and Singapore? It's why we never joined them. But then he went bankrupt, and not only did he lose everything, but their marriage broke up, too. That has so stayed with me—and scared me—that I don't want anything like that to happen to us."

Maddie felt tears welling up. "I knew about their divorce, but I don't think I ever knew the whole story or the impact it had on you. This is clearly important stuff for you, Adam, and I so appreciate that you shared it. I think understanding this piece of the puzzle may help us get somewhere. I can understand your concern with money, and I support that. But we are nothing like Reed, and child-care won't bankrupt us. As much as I want to support you, I also need you to support me."

Adam nodded, and they both lapsed back into reflective silence but maintained eye contact this time.

Maddie broke the silence again. "You know I wouldn't be having this conversation with you, as tired as I am, if I didn't love you. I am still committed to you and to our marriage."

"Me too. I've been so nose-to-the-grindstone that I haven't picked up on what was going on. You sounded angrier and more resentful before. But what I'm hearing this time is your disappointment, sadness, and fear."

"We're both exhausted," Maddie said, "and maybe it's better if we sleep on it, as long as we both agree to come back to the subject tomorrow. Since it's Saturday, maybe it will be easier to carve out time. My mom already has plans to take the kids to the zoo for the day."

"Yeah, that's probably a good idea."

* * *

IT'S FORTUNATE THAT Maddie responded to Adam's stonewalling with empathy and curiosity ("What is it about this whole money-and-childcare thing that's so difficult for you?") instead of pushing harder. She broadened the scope of the conversation without running away from the original issue. She invited Adam to share more and gave him plenty of space to do so. Adam and Maddie's conversations highlight how the problem-solving stages we described earlier in the book are neither linear nor distinct. Particularly when a problem is complex or thorny, it's important to take steps toward repairing the relationship even while issues remain unresolved. Maddie's curiosity was authentic in conveying her care and worry. She was able to be direct about her needs and concerns while still connecting with Adam, all of which made it easier to get the issues on the table and begin that process of repair.

The earlier repair attempts begin, the more productive the likely outcome. Had Maddie escalated with contempt or walked away during this conversation, or had Adam closed down, there would have been much more damage to the relationship. Instead, they continued to engage with each other until they both felt at least somewhat heard, emotionally met, and able to express their commitment.

It was also important that they took a *break*. When you're exhausted or so emotionally flooded that you can't take in much more, a temporary hiatus makes sense. There's an important distinction, though, between refusal to deal with a situation and taking some time and space to let thoughts and feelings settle. Such self-reflection is almost impossible when you are highly emotionally triggered. Critically, Adam and Maddie set a specific time to come back to the issue. This kept them from avoiding the problem until the next time it reared its head, when it likely would have had even more anger attached.

An adage from the 1960s personal growth movement was "Never let the sun set on a dispute." We strongly disagree. A break can provide needed perspective, whereas the desire to "get this over with" can lead to hasty agreements that don't feel good after we've slept on them.

Also useful was their taking shorter breaks during the discussion. A problem with conflict is that the back-and-forth can be so rapid that there isn't time to consider whether other approaches might work. Even though the silence between Maddie and Adam might have initially felt like an impasse, it was only after they were quiet that Maddie was able to move from argument to curiosity. Short breaks don't have to be a form of avoidance. They can be opportunities to assess feelings and whether those emotions are clues to deeper issues.

The times when the couple sat in silence could easily have felt frustrating and led them to want to *do something*. But there's a saying for this that we do like: "Don't just do something; sit there." In the Interpersonal Dynamics course, we say, "Trust the process." That means, "At this moment, I may not know what's really going on or what the solution is, but if we can hang in there in expressing our feelings, then it will become clearer and eventually work out." That's the stance Maddie took when she said, "Nothing is going to get better if you refuse to talk about it," and "Let's both try to hang in there until we get somewhere."

In this process, Maddie and Adam began to redefine the rules of the game:

1. No running away—we are sticking with this until we resolve it.

2. Both of us have a responsibility to come up with possible solutions.

3. Costs have to be incurred and accepted by both of us.

Even though they made these agreements, Adam and Maddie had not yet fully moved into problem-solving territory. They progressed from trying to prove each other wrong to beginning to understand what was important to each of them and the other. They began to see that the issues were about more than just childcare. Though there was still much ground to cover, they turned a significant corner toward resolution. They are not yet at exceptional, but they have laid the groundwork for getting there.

Deepen Your Learning

SELF-REFLECTION

1. Put yourself in Maddie's shoes. *She is in a difficult spot given her strong needs to both rectify what is going on and not damage her marriage. In reviewing what she said and tried to do, how would you have handled those situations? Which ones might have been especially challenging for you?*

2. Effective Approaches: After Maddie got over her fear of conflict, she was able to use it productively. She:

   - hung in there and didn't back down
   - didn't escalate by name-calling
   - owned her part in the problem and didn't put all the fault on Adam
   - used the feedback model and its variations without making accusations
   - was in touch with her emotions and used them effectively
   - didn't get defensive when Adam made a negative attribution about her approach to their finances and instead used facts to rebut
   - broadened the scope of solutions they considered
   - made sure both stayed with the topic and didn't run away
   - was able to be curious and inquire about what was going on with Adam

- agreed with his goals and was explicit about disagreeing on ways to accomplish them

When you are in conflict situations around important issues and have strong feelings, how many of these approaches do you tend to use? Which ones are easier? Which are more challenging?

3. Key Relationship: Does one of the people in your key relationships use conflict well? What specifically do they do? Conversely, is there someone with whom conflict is problematic? What do they do?

APPLICATION

If you identified a person who handles conflict well, ask them how they are able to do that when upset or attacked.

If you have a relationship with someone in which conflict resolution is problematic, discuss how to improve that.

MAKING SENSE

What did you learn about conflict management and about your strengths and limitations? What steps are you going to take for your further development?

If you had a discussion with someone with whom conflict resolution is problematic, how did that discussion affect your relationship? What did you learn about raising a potentially difficult situation that you are going to use in other discussions and with other people?

PART II

TACKLING THE SUMMIT

IN THE MEADOW

YOU AND YOUR companion have just made it over the headwall. It's been a good climb, but it's taken a lot of energy, and you decide to sit down in a welcoming meadow for a rest. The summit of the mountain looms ahead, but the view around you is quite lovely, the grass soft.

Now, in the meadow, you have more choices. Stay where you are and appreciate what you've achieved? Hike along the meadow, skirting the side of the mountain and stopping at one of the warming huts? Go on to the top? Dark clouds are forming on the summit of Mount Washington, but you have climbed through them before and like the challenge. The view up there is spectacular once the clouds have cleared, and you also feel equipped to handle any bad weather.

But you don't have to make those decisions yet. . . .

In the previous chapters, you acquired an invaluable set of competencies—especially if you have used the Deepen Your Learning suggestions and applied the material. You have learned how to build good relationships and then develop them into ones that are strong, robust, and mutually rewarding. You have learned that you can make it from an easy path to the most challenging climbs. (If you're interested in reviewing the competencies from part I, they can be found in appendix B on page 285.)

These competencies are relevant for all relationships, be they with casual acquaintances or much closer friends. They're applicable not only with family and friends but also at work with colleagues, direct reports, and even your boss. It is not accidental that the Interpersonal Dynamics course has been taught at Stanford and other leading business schools for more than five decades. People do business with people, so getting these competencies right at work is a key determinant of professional success.

Even if you read no further, you will have gained a great deal. In these final chapters, though, we will see how the five featured relationships of the book move along the continuum toward exceptional. Some make it, and some don't. The people in each relationship face a crucial dilemma and using (or not using) these competencies impacts their ability to transition their relationship from strong and functional to exceptional, something so deep that it feels almost magical.

All five relationships have developed significantly. The players have grown to know each other better, established some norms that legitimize raising issues, learned how to express their needs with minimal blame, and, to varying degrees, worked on effective problem-solving. What will it now take to transition to exceptional, and how will they know if they've achieved it? How does anyone?

There is no one precise point at which this happens, and to some extent it's in the eye of the beholder. But you'll know you've reached exceptional when you don't have to hold back significant parts of yourself that are relevant to the relationship—nor does the other person. It's when you can easily say that you're feeling uncertain or confused about what is going on with the other person and with you, so that you can talk about it. It's when you can deal with major issues, even though it feels scary.

Even then, exceptional isn't an end state but rather has its own continuum. Each person can always disclose more, support and challenge more, and move into new areas of growth. You come to understand the nuances of the deepening connection, and your "antennae" become even more finely tuned.

Many times, relationships transition to exceptional organically, in an iterative, ever-deepening cycle. These may be long-term family, friend, or work connections in which differences and disagreements are resolved and don't get in the way of increasing closeness. There are no big, difficult conflicts or thorny issues. Neither person minces words when one of them feels a pinch, and more important, they both know how to resolve those while they are relatively small. Each is committed to the other's learning and unafraid to shine a light on whatever they think will benefit the other. Truth telling and loving confrontation are norms established early and upheld throughout the relationship. An accumulation of *quantitative* steps becomes an unquestionable *qualitative* shift over time.

In other cases, relationships become exceptional as a result of critical choice points, as we'll see in the next three chapters. In chapter 13, we return to Maddie and Adam to examine what it takes to resolve contentious issues. Chapter 14 describes a crucible moment for Elena and Sanjay during which setting boundaries strengthens rather than hurts their relationship. And in chapter 15, we explore Mia and Aniyah's dilemma of how to handle a situation in which one person desperately needs something important that triggers a painful issue for the other.

Not all deep relationships make it to exceptional. In chapter 16, we look at various examples where that is the case and explore why. We also examine the tricky issue of exceptional relationships at work. The bottom line: They're possible but require some extra considerations.

Finally, relationship development is not a straight line. In the final chapter, we will look at what happened between the two of us that temporarily destroyed our exceptional relationship. We focus on how we went awry, how we recovered, and how it helped us grow even closer.

So, while not all exceptional relationships are born of a crisis, that is the focus of four of the final five chapters, because shying away from crises out of fear is often what stops us from getting to exceptional. To return to our mountain-climbing analogy, let's assume this is the first time that you and your companion have made this climb. Even though the two of you want to reach the summit, the top is shrouded in dark clouds and the wind is picking up. It would be easy to just stay in the meadow and not make the final extra effort. Moving to exceptional can, with many relationships, be just a steady climb, but some relationships require facing major challenges. We hope these final chapters will encourage you to take them on.

13

RESOLVING CONTENTIOUS ISSUES

Maddie and Adam, Parts 5 and 6

When two people sit down and collaboratively solve problems, the solution is usually far superior to what either could have come up with alone. They will consider a wider range of options, catch flaws in each other's thinking, and benefit from each other's style. One might be more comfortable with risk while the other might be more cautious. Or one might focus on successes achieved, whereas the other might see problems still to be dealt with. Each needs the other for balance, but the balance only works if they each learn how to use their tendencies productively.

Maddie and Adam, Part 5

The morning after Adam and Maddie surfaced their issues, Maddie's mom collected the kids for an outing, and Adam and Maddie sat down at the kitchen table together over coffee.

"I've been thinking a lot about our conversation last night," Adam said. "And I want you to know I heard you. You're right that I've been pretty focused on my career and what I want, and not as focused on what's going on with you. I'm sorry for that."

Maddie's eyes welled up. "Thank you for saying that."

"Okay, so let's recap where we are," said Adam, and he went through the issues he understood to be on Maddie's mind. She did the same for him. "So what do we do now?" Adam said.

"I was thinking about it while falling asleep, and I have a couple of ideas," Maddie said. "The Winnikers have Janie's mother live with them, but even though you get along with my mom, I'm not sure either of us want that." Adam nodded in agreement. "We could look into an au pair, but our house isn't really that large and we like our privacy."

"I thought of that, too, but rejected it for the same reason."

Maddie continued, "A third option is to take a really close look at the monthly expenses together and see how much money we might be able to spare toward some childcare. With that in mind, I could then start exploring some of my options for perhaps a part-time job or more volunteering."

"But all the money we have to spare goes toward our savings cushion. I'd feel more comfortable if we keep that safety reserve."

"I would, too, but we can't have everything. You said that this new assignment comes with a pay raise and puts you in a better position for a promotion that would also come with another raise. Aren't both of us investing in the present for payoffs in the future?"

Adam thought it over. "Okay," he said at last. "I see your point."

"But?" said Maddie. "I know you too well. What are you worried about?"

Adam laughed. "Yeah, you do know me too well. But I'm not sure I can answer that. Logically, I agree with the investing-in-the-future approach, but it's still unsettling for me. I don't fully know why." After a little reflection, he said, "I think one of the things that's bothering me so much is that I thought we'd made an agreement after Derek was born that you would stay home with the kids. And now you want to break it."

"Really?" Maddie asked. She felt defensive but resisted escalating the discussion. "It hadn't even occurred to me that this was part of the problem. Yes, we made an agreement, and I hear that my wanting to change it is really upsetting. But things change all the time. What is it about this change that's so hard?"

"I know that things change, but that's the issue. There are so many damn moving parts, I want some things to be stable, like us and our agreements. I have a really hard time having set my expectations that life was going to unfold in one way and having it go another."

"But wait a minute," Maddie interjected. "There's a lot that's stable in our life—like our marriage and our commitment to the kids. Also, if you talk about holding to agreements, what about our agreement to be concerned with both of us growing—you were willing to let that slide. What's so important about this other agreement?"

Adam thought about it for a minute. "I know, and I totally agree with you logically. I think there's something about our agreement that one of us would stay home that meant a lot to me. I'm probably too traditional or overthinking it, but we've seen so many families around us who are completely stressed out when both parents work. I just want more breathing room in our life, you know? And I don't want to outsource the hard work of parenting too much—it's important to me that one of us does it. I'm embarrassed—it feels sexist to say this, because I'm not willing to give up my job. I *am* committed to your growth and happiness. And I can't justify my feelings, but they're there."

Maddie relaxed. "Thanks for sharing that. I sort of had a hunch that was the case, but it makes a big difference to hear you acknowledge it. Look, honey, I will still be there for the kids, even with part-time childcare. And I get how important the issue of committing to a decision is to you, so we need to be careful when we make final decisions to separate that from 'working agreements.' But it sounds like, for now, the idea of more childcare is the best alternative. Can you live with exploring that?"

Adam nodded in agreement. "Okay. Just having this out there makes me feel better. Let's give it a shot."

Maddie smiled in appreciation. "Thanks. But there's a lot we need to know before we make a decision. I need to explore the feasibility of part-time work and check out childcare options. Let's go over our budget together and see if there are areas we can cut. Okay?"

Adam nodded slowly in agreement. "Whatever we try, let's see it as a trial for a certain period and see how it works out."

MADDIE AND ADAM did a good job in their first pass at problem-solving, avoiding some really common traps:

- Rushing to judgment: Conflict is stressful, and the desire to move quickly past it can lead to premature acceptance of the first option suggested. Complex problems usually have more than one viable solution and often involve issues that each person feels strongly about. Fortunately, Maddie and Adam did not fall into the rush-to-judgment trap. They ensured the discussion *was aimed at solving the problem in a way that satisfied both of them.*
- Either/or thinking: An extreme case of this would have been: "We *either* need to pay for full-time day care *or* it's the status quo." They avoided this when Maddie initially suggested several alternatives. Maddie did most of the heavy lifting here—if they had engaged in a joint brainstorming session, it's possible they would have generated even *more* options, such as seeing if Maddie's mother might cover for them a couple days a week.
- Arguing about solutions rather than focusing on needs: This trap happens when people prematurely focus attention on the upsides and downsides of the solutions rather than stepping back and identifying the core problem. Paying for day care is *a* solution—but not necessarily the only solution—to Maddie's more basic need for intellectual challenge and adult interaction.
- Treating opinions as facts: Adam fell into this trap, believing that

there wasn't a budget for childcare even though he hadn't taken a close look at their finances. Similarly, when he shared his new career opportunity, he explained it would come with more evenings and weekends at work, but how true was that? Had he checked that out with his manager, or was he making an assumption?

- Confusing "trials" with final decisions: What feels right now may not later, as Maddie discovered when she found herself dissatisfied with their previous agreement. A trial agreement is a decision to take action that allows for more data collection. Testing how well the trial decision is working allows modifications before making a final decision.
- Undervaluing personal needs: Facts and logic are important; they point to what is possible. But as we have already stressed, balancing each person's needs is equally important. Adam did a good job acknowledging that some of his feelings of uncertainty weren't logical, but they were there nonetheless. If he hadn't done this, any resolution would have been incomplete and likely unsustainable.
- Not taking account of personal styles: Everyone has habits, needs, and proclivities. Adam appears to be somewhat rigid regarding agreements, and Maddie took that into account in articulating the difference between a trial decision and a final one.
- Deciding who implements what: As there are options (and preferences) in what the decision is, there are also options (and preferences) in how it is carried out. Adam shouldn't tell Maddie how she should go about researching job options, and she shouldn't tell him how to raise issues of work/life balance with his manager. They can jointly agree with *what* has to be done without getting into *how*.

Maddie and Adam, Part 6

The following Wednesday evening, Adam and Maddie sat on the couch for a glass of wine after putting the kids to bed.

"I have to admit something," Adam said. "Even though I agreed with what we talked about on Saturday, I still had some qualms."

Maddie looked worried. "You don't want to open up the whole issue again, do you?"

"Don't worry," Adam laughed, "and I think you're going to want to hear this. I needed to talk about all of this with someone else, so Drew and I had lunch today."

"WHAT? You shared our personal problems with somebody else!"

"Wait a minute," Adam said. "It's all right. You know that Drew and I are close—it's not like I'm telling just anyone. Drew's talked to me about problems he has with his son, and I needed to talk about our decision out loud. I was going around in circles in my own head. And don't worry—I didn't paint you as the bad guy. In fact, he took your side and was very direct with me." Adam laughed. "Some friend!"

"What did he say?"

"Pretty much what you said. In fact, he sort of chewed me out, saying that I was only thinking about myself and not thinking enough about you. He even went so far as to say that I didn't deserve you," Adam said lightly. "It really made me think."

"Well, because you're willing to look at this," Maddie said with a smile, "you very much deserve me!"

"It's not that I didn't listen to you the other day. It was just reassuring to hear another perspective. And the way that he talked about working out his issues with his wife, it didn't make me feel so alone."

Maddie nodded. "I've never thought we have to appear as the perfect couple to the world." After they sat in silence for a bit, she said, "I've been doing some thinking of my own about why it's so important for me to work. I want adult interaction and a chance to continually grow, which we've talked about, but there's something else. Do you remember that my mom dropped out of college when she got married? She had to work to support my dad through engineering school. Not having a degree meant that all she could get was clerical work—not very fulfilling. And she quit even that when my brothers and I came along. She never had a career, and I know she has regrets." Maddie started crying. "And I'm scared of ending up like her."

Adam set down his wine and put his arms around her.

After Maddie regained some control, she continued, "And as I say this, I realize there's something more. Dad loved Mom, but I'm not sure that he really respected her for the whole person she was. Sure, he respected her raising us and keeping a good house, but that isn't the same. I think I'm worried that this may also happen to us."

Adam took it in and was quiet for a minute. "I hate to admit it," he said, finally, "but I see why you're concerned about this. I'm so appreciative of what you do for the kids, but . . . yeah, it might limit what I talk to you about. I don't know if that's the same issue as respect, but I can see where you're coming from." He paused again while both of them processed, then continued, "Okay, I get why this issue is so important—for both of us."

The following weekend, Adam and Maddie pored over the numbers and settled on a budget for childcare, freeing up some of her time. "That should be enough for me to get a part-time job for now," she said, "but I don't want to be locked into this. Let's see how it goes—I may want more or less." After a little more back-and-forth, they agreed to a six-month trial.

"Just to be clear—this is an experiment for both of us, right?" Adam asked.

Maddie nodded. "Absolutely. Thank you for agreeing to try it."

* * *

DURING THE COURSE of the couple's conversations, the framing of the discussion changed. It was no longer "Maddie's problem" but a joint issue the couple needed to solve together. They were both then ready to explore different solutions, which included generating some options and coming up with a joint decision-making process. They succeeded in reaching a tentative solution to the day care problem.

When either or both parties are resistant to giving up on some topic, deep historical issues are often at play. It is important that the conversation be given the time and space for these to surface and be explored. Awareness of ways in which someone is influenced by their past can prevent labeling them prematurely. This was true for both Adam and Maddie. It would have been easy for Maddie to conclude that her husband was a tightwad, but she stepped back, moved into inquiry, and asked, "What is it about this whole money-and-childcare thing that's so difficult for you?"

Asking the question was itself important, but so was Adam's willingness to be self-reflective in his answer. Without having built a climate of support and commitment for each other, they may never have gotten there. What Adam shared about his friend from college wasn't easy, because it could have been logically dismissed. ("Oh, Adam. That's Reed—we would never do anything like that!") Instead, Adam's willingness to be vulnerable and disclose these historical forces made it easier for Maddie to do so later on. Her vocalization about her fears, based on her own upbringing, contributed to their conversation, and to their closeness.

As you put the puzzle pieces of problem-solving in place, paying attention to different time frames—present, past, and future—as Maddie and Adam did, is important. The present identifies sources of dissatisfaction and unmet needs (for example, her need for intellectual stimulation and his concerns over money). The past illustrates what's been lost and informs how you've gotten to where you are. The future keeps you focused on where each of you wants to end up and can break the logjam of mutual recriminations. Often the discussion has to shuttle back and forth among these different time periods in order to get the best outcome.

The Role of the Third Party

People turn to others for help for a variety of reasons. Sometimes, you want to find out how others deal with a similar situation, which is what Maddie did when she asked her friend Teresa how she handled childcare. Sometimes you're looking for a more dispassionate view, which is what Adam needed. After all, Maddie had strong feelings about what she wanted, but Drew didn't have a personal investment in the outcome. Adam thought that Drew could provide a more objective perspective, and perhaps offer new ways of viewing the issue.

But that assumes Drew can be impartial and that he knows both parties. He is Adam's friend, and even though he knows Maddie, he knows Adam much better. It also assumes Drew has all the relevant information. As objective as Adam might want to be, he probably wouldn't tell the story in the same way Maddie would. The extent to which Drew could be helpful depended on his recognition of these limitations.

Those factors didn't seem to constrain Drew's ability to be supportive of Adam and Maddie's shared goals, and his perspective was clarifying. Drew was quite blunt with Adam, but it could have been just as helpful if he had simply let Adam vent or asked open-ended questions to help broaden Adam's view of the situation. We don't advise using a third party to come up with solutions, because they don't have all the relevant information. But they can be very useful thought partners, helping you get clearer about what you most need so that *you* can then productively work the issue out with the other person.

Multiple Outcomes

Adam and Maddie's conflict was tough on both of them. So was it worth it? At the end of the day, they

- reached a working solution to the immediate issue at hand
- emerged with an increased ability to raise and resolve future problems
- strengthened their relationship
- have increased knowledge of each other

As a result of this difficult process, Adam and Maddie understand each other at a deeper level. Their efforts moved them farther on the continuum and firmly into the realm of an exceptional relationship. But perhaps the greatest progress they made was in the second bullet point: their joint ability to deal with other contentious issues in the future. In the process of dealing with the issues of money and childcare, they increased the likelihood that they would raise and resolve future challenges more productively. Maddie agreed not to avoid problems or be shut down by previous agreements that no longer worked for her. Adam agreed to take account of Maddie's needs and not respond solely on the basis of his. Furthermore, he moved beyond the idea that children and home were just Maddie's problems and recognized that he needed to share them as well. Most important, they identified what had previously blocked them.

Agreements like these are important first steps, but they need to be reinforced. One or the other might screw up and neglect to honor their agreement. But more worrisome than the screwup itself is what happens if it isn't acknowledged and addressed. In fact, sometimes a violation—when corrected—actually cements the lesson for both parties and solidifies the recovery. Let's imagine that in the future Adam raises a difficult subject and Maddie starts to avoid it. It would be very helpful if he then said, "We agreed you wouldn't walk away to do the dishes when we're having a hard discussion; what's happening?"

The more complicated a situation (and relationship), the more issues are likely to arise in the process of problem-solving. It's like the proverbial peeling of the onion. The outer skin makes it hard to find out what's going on. Then we discover the presenting issue, and beneath that, the even more personal, vulnerable issues. That might include the impact of significant past experiences. Each person needs to hang in there long enough to find out what's really going on.

All of this was by no means easy. Rome was not built in a day, and the greater the conflict, the longer it's likely to take to resolve. Resolution requires patience, skill, and commitment to both surfacing issues and collaborating to find solutions.

Deepen Your Learning

SELF-REFLECTION

1. Put yourself in Maddie's situation. *There were several times when she and Adam could have given up or gone off course, but she persisted until they were able to reach a working solution. At each choice point, what do you think you would have done? Would any of the actions Maddie took be difficult for you? Any places where you might have trapped yourself?*

2. Key Relationship: It is likely there have been one or more incidents with at least one of your key relationships when it has been difficult to problem-solve. Which of these traps do you and the other person tend to fall into?

    - Either/or thinking
    - Arguing solutions rather than focusing on needs
    - Treating opinions as if they were facts

- Confusing trials with final decisions
- Undervaluing personal needs
- Not taking account of personal styles
- Deciding who implements what

3. Third Party: Have you encountered any of the following problems when you have been a third party or gone to one? The third party

- is unclear about the objective of their role (just listen, broaden perspective, identify untested assumptions, commiserate, etc.)
- thinks they are the person who should come up with solutions
- forgets that they lack crucial information (perspective from the person who isn't there)
- is drawn into taking sides

APPLICATION

If you identified an issue to discuss in one of your key relationships, it's time to use all the skills you have learned to improve your decision-making/problem-solving process.

MAKING SENSE

How did this discussion go? Was the outcome successful in achieving the four objectives of solving the issue, improving problem-solving skills for both of you, getting to know each other better, and further strengthening the relationship?

What do you need to work on, in terms of both improving your competencies and further moving this relationship along the continuum?

14

BOUNDARIES AND EXPECTATIONS

Elena and Sanjay, Parts 5 and 6

A colleague asks if you can drop her off at the airport after work, and you readily agree. It's only slightly out of your way, and the request seems appropriate. But another friend who's strapped for money and doesn't have a car frequently asks you to pick him up at the airport, no matter how late or early in the day. That, too, might feel reasonable because of the importance of the relationship—and then again it might not. If not, how do we determine our boundaries between what feels fair and what feels burdensome? And furthermore, when it is an imposition, how honest can we be? Should we just go along and say nothing for the sake of the friendship?

Everyone carries expectations of what's okay to ask at different stages of a relationship. Your expectations may derive from past experiences or from what you think you would do for the other person. Friends rarely discuss such expectations explicitly but still hold them deeply as "the way people ought to be." The difficulty arises when you have different expectations of what even very close friends should ask for—and do—for each other.

There may come a point when you need to draw a line in the sand, even knowing that it could damage an important relationship. What if the other person feels rejected or distanced? Avoiding the conflict by just going along is oh so tempting. But as the ancient Greek philosopher Plutarch is widely attributed as having quipped, "I don't need a friend who changes when I change and who nods when I nod; my shadow does that much better." In more contemporary terms, we say that a true friend doesn't tell you what you want to hear—they tell you what they believe is best for you. But what if that hurts the relationship? That's the dilemma that Elena faces with Sanjay.

Elena and Sanjay, Part 5

Sanjay and Elena's friendship continued to deepen over the next couple of years. Elena performed well and accepted a higher position in another area of the company. Even though she no longer worked directly with Sanjay, they met regularly for lunch, sharing the ease and comfort of a growing friendship, solidly anchored in knowing and caring for each other. They also broadened the circle to include Sanjay's wife, Priya, and Elena's husband, Eric. The four of them socialized often and became good friends. One day, Sanjay phoned Elena and asked, somewhat cryptically, if they could meet for a drink after work, saying, "There's something business-related that I need to discuss, but not here." She agreed, and they decided to meet at a quiet bar on the other side of town.

Sanjay picked a secluded table away from others. After they'd ordered drinks, Elena said, "So spill. What's going on?"

"Well, first of all, thanks for taking the time. I need a sounding board and don't have anyone else to talk to about this."

"Of course! Sounds important."

"Yeah, it is." Sanjay took a breath, then let the words pour out. "I'm thinking of leaving the company to start my own. Roland, a buddy of mine from college, approached me about joining him as a co-founder. I've always wanted to do this, but it's never been the right time. It may never feel like the right time, though. I've had this dream of doing my own thing ever since I graduated from college and got my first job. Then came marriage and kids and a mortgage and higher-and-higher-paying jobs. You know the story—golden handcuffs and all that. I'm afraid if I don't break free now, I never will. And I *so* want to start up something I truly feel passionate about, not to mention be my own boss and make my own calls."

Elena smiled broadly. "That's so exciting, Sanjay! But yeah, scary, of course. And it doesn't surprise me all that much, because it's seemed like you've been restless for a while now. I'm a bit envious you're willing to take the risk. I'm not sure I could."

"Yeah, it's scary, exciting, and energizing all at the same time. I've always been so conventional and played it safe. You know how much it matters to me to be a good provider. I don't know if it's crazy to even be thinking about tossing aside this solid, high-paying job. But if not now, when? I don't think I've ever pushed myself professionally, and it feels like the right time. Roland's super creative and has been languishing in his job. He's got a really great idea for an educational tech product that could be a game changer, and you know I'm passionate about that area. Do you think I should do it?"

"What does Priya think?"

Sanjay's face fell. "That's the problem. I don't think I can tell her now." Elena looked surprised, so he continued. "You know her. As much as I love her, we both know she's a worrier. She cares a lot about financial security—and the kids are still young. I'm afraid she won't understand, or worse, she'll think I'm being selfish in wanting to pursue a dream at the expense of our family's well-being. I don't want to tell her until I've thought it completely through and have all my ducks in a row. I'll tell her once I know for sure I want to do it. For now, I just want to think it through with you."

Elena's brow furrowed as she looked down at her drink. Once she collected her thoughts, she said quietly, "Sorry, Sanjay, as much as I want to help, it puts me in a bind. I can't do that. It wouldn't be fair to Priya."

"What do you mean? I thought we had the sort of relationship where we could be open and help each other."

"We do," Elena said.

"Obviously not."

Elena winced. "Ouch. That's really painful to hear. First of all, I'm sorry if you feel let down. I *do* think we have that sort of relationship, which is why I can be honest with you. Sanjay, it's hard for me to not give you what you want. I want to support you and I so appreciate your confiding in me. But I don't think this is the best way for me to provide support."

She paused for a minute, considering her words, then continued, "It's because I care so much about you that we can't talk about it until you've talked to Priya. What you're asking of me is at Priya's expense and actually, Sanjay, at yours, too."

"What do you mean? Why is it at Priya's expense? You know her. She's going to get all upset about it. I don't want to unnecessarily worry her when I haven't made up my mind yet. That's why I need to talk about this with you."

"Look, Sanjay. There are actually two issues here. One is your question of whether to try this new venture—and that's actually the easier one—and the other is about how you and Priya are relating to each other."

"That's the marriage we have," Sanjay said with some heat, "and, to be honest, that isn't your business!"

"Absolutely, it is your marriage. Where it becomes *my* business is when you're pulling me in on an issue that really involves Priya. The decision of your possibly starting a business deeply affects her. I care about you, but if I did what you want, it could impact the relationship I have with Priya. She'd be pissed if she found out, and I wouldn't blame her. But more important, doing what you want would be a disservice to you."

"A disservice to me?"

Elena nodded. "This decision is just the first of many important ones if you decide to go for the startup. There will be a lot of other decisions that have financial implications. Are you going to keep those from Priya, too? And if you continue to make these decisions without involving her, she'll feel more and more alienated, and I worry you'd become increasingly distant from each other when you need to feel closer than ever. I totally get that the initial conversation with her will be difficult, but if you have it with me instead, I'd be colluding in the problem—and I don't want to do that to you. That's what I mean by doing you a disservice."

Sanjay took that in and then said, "I just can't talk to her about it now. You know how much she tends to worry. That isn't fair to her."

"Yes, I do know that part of her, and I know you, and my question is, how much of your choice not to talk to her now is about her and how much is it about you?"

"What's that supposed to mean?" Sanjay responded angrily.

"Well," Elena went on, "I've sometimes wondered if you're too protective of her. For example, when the four of us were at dinner the other night, you told her only the very high-level story of your latest conflict with the management committee. You had a calm, matter-of-fact tone when I knew how angry you were from what you told me at lunch that week."

"Yeah, but, Elena, you have to admit, Priya makes mountains out of molehills. If I'd told her the full story, she would have thought that I was about to be fired and it would have taken me an hour to peel her off the wall!"

"I get that, and I can appreciate that the way she tends to respond is difficult. But you're putting all of the problem on her. We've talked before about how you hate conflict, and I just wonder if part of your not wanting to discuss this with Priya is about that. Are you protecting her or are you protecting yourself? In any case, if Eric shared the pros and cons of personal decisions as big as this with someone else before me, I would kill him."

"Well, Priya and I are different, and my marriage is my business. Ugh, I just wish you could support me."

"I hear you're not finding me supportive, and I'm sorry about that. I happen to think I'm being very supportive. I'd be happy at some point to be a sounding board, but not as a substitute for Priya.

If I'm really going to be a good friend, then I have to tell you that I think there are few things more important than talking with her about all of this now—not later, after you have it all figured out."

"I don't know how this suddenly turned into a discussion about my marriage and my difficulties with conflict. I think we should just end this conversation." Sanjay finished his drink and started to get up.

"No, Sanjay, let's not leave quite yet," Elena said. "We don't have to talk more about how you and Priya relate—I've said my piece. But now, whether we intended to or not, we have an issue with *our* relationship and running away isn't going to help. Let's talk this through."

Sanjay sat back down but kept his arms crossed. "What do you mean we have an issue with our relationship?"

"You don't think I'm supporting you, and I think I am," Elena said. "I see support as being as much about challenging your thinking as about agreeing with you. And I want to support you in the way I would want you to support me, which includes telling me when you think I'm making a mistake. If we kept talking about the startup, it might have made us feel closer in the moment, but it could have been at a high cost to you and your marriage. And if I did it this time, you might keep coming to me and not Priya. As a friend who cares deeply about you, I don't want to contribute to potentially bad outcomes."

"So you'll never talk about Roland's idea with me?"

"No, I'm not saying that," Elena said. "I won't talk about it *now*, but I will after you talk to Priya. That's the best way I can support you."

"Boy," said Sanjay, "you aren't letting up on this, are you?"

Elena smiled. "Nope—and I really hope you hear that it's because I care so much about you."

Sanjay smiled ruefully and got up to pay the bill. "My treat. Thanks for taking the time to meet with me." As they walked out together, he added, "This is really hard, and you're being tough on me . . . but maybe I need it. There's a lot for me to think about. I'll let you know what I do."

"YOU'RE BEING TOUGH on me." Sanjay's statement here is correct, and in fact, it's Elena's toughness that has transitioned the relationship to exceptional. They were open with each other about their needs and emotions, honest in their interactions, and eventually able to productively handle conflict. Even though Sanjay didn't think that Elena was on his side early in the conversation, she reiterated that her refusal was primarily coming from what she thought was best for him. At the same time, she didn't deny her concerns for herself—that allowing Sanjay to use her as a sounding board could ruin her relationship with Priya.

Even though this test left their relationship stronger, it easily could have gone the other way—that was the risk Elena took. After she first set a boundary with Sanjay, he could have stormed out of the bar and written off their friendship.

When a close relationship develops, it's likely not only that one person will go to the other for help but also that the other, out of a sense of caring and commitment, will feel a strong sense of obligation to comply. That's the pressure Elena felt. But she chose to push back because she saw the hidden danger and because she thought the upside was worth it. If she hadn't spoken up, she would have signaled a belief that the friendship couldn't handle a conflict.

To achieve this positive outcome, they each had to be open to feedback. That was initially hard for Sanjay to hear, and it took more than one comment from Elena for him to see that what he was doing had major costs. Fortunately, she was willing to be persistent until he understood her position, and then she was able to stop ("I've said my piece"). Her feedback was information, not a cudgel to beat him over the head with. This interaction also had some learning for Sanjay. It's still unclear how much responsibility he'll take for the problematic interactions with his wife, but that issue is plainly out on the table. Equally important is that Elena and Sanjay defined what support really means in an exceptional relationship.

Even though they have made the transition to exceptional, that doesn't mean it's done growing. New situations always arise, and when there's growth in one area, there are potential challenges in another. Will they be willing to raise and resolve them, or has this been so stressful they won't dare risk another? Assume that Sanjay works on his ability to face conflict; will he do that in a way that is productive, or will his actions end up feeling punitive. There is no perfect end state in relationships, and that's part of what makes them both exciting and challenging. The potential for continued learning and growth is not always easy to deal with, but it's also part of what makes exceptional relationships feel magical.

What made this situation even more difficult is that it involved more than Sanjay and Elena. Each person is in a network of relationships. Elena wanted an exceptional relationship with Sanjay. Sanjay wanted an intimate relationship with Priya, and Elena wanted a close friendship with her. If Elena had gone along with Sanjay's request, she would have (at least initially) increased their connection but would have weakened each of their relationships with Priya. Growth in one relationship should not be at the expense of another.

The Importance of Toughness

Because of the high level of trust and care between people in an exceptional relationship, it's likely that each will go to the other with significant requests. But when the other person wants something that you're unwilling to give, how can you say no without their feeling rejected? Being tough is hard when we fear that it will jeopardize the relationship. And yet not being tough can jeopardize it just as much.

If you are a grandparent, you might be getting tired of being asked to babysit all the time, but you don't want to risk the closeness you have with your children. An aging parent might be dangerous behind the wheel, and one of your siblings wants *you* to be the one to tell them they have to stop driving. A friend might ask for a loan, and the idea of saying yes to that might not feel good. But you want to continue to have very close relationships—what to do?

Our friend Brienna's brother is a heavy drinker and, unfortunately, not a jovial drunk. For years, when he and his wife came over for dinner, Brienna tolerated his surly behavior. Then she realized that she'd started to dread his visits. She knew that he was under a lot of stress at work and feared that saying anything to him about his drinking would just add more pressure or put distance between them. She didn't think it was right or fair to talk to his wife about it behind his back, nor did she think that would necessarily help. But the problem had become too prominent to ignore—Brienna feared she would put distance between them if she *didn't* say something.

The day after a particularly unpleasant evening out, she called her brother to tell him there was something important she needed to talk to him about. They agreed to meet for coffee a few days later.

"It was one of the hardest conversations I've ever had with him," she told us. "I basically confronted him with how much I disliked being around him when he's had too much to drink. I told him he was more than welcome to drink as much as he wanted anywhere else or around anybody else, but not when he was with me. I told him I didn't want to be with him in any social situations unless he would agree to curtail his alcohol intake when I was present. I gave him all my reasons, including how worried I was about what would happen to our relationship if I didn't raise this issue. We've always been close, and I'm pretty sure we both want our relationship to remain that way. He initially argued that I was 'making a big deal out of nothing' and being too tough on him, but I held my ground. I told him unless he honored my request, I would not socialize with him anywhere that alcohol might be involved. He eventually agreed to try to honor my request.

"Ever since, when we get together for dinner or are out with mutual friends, he has one scotch on the rocks (instead of four or five). Even though my guess is he still drinks heavily in other situations, he doesn't do it when we're together. I think that if I hadn't said anything—if I hadn't honored an important personal boundary for me—our relationship would have slowly deteriorated. Instead, we remain close—actually we are much closer."

Setting a boundary this way has the potential to feel distancing, but both Brienna and Elena used it to express their wish for even greater closeness. As commonly said, "Good fences make good neighbors." They also make for deep and intimate relationships.

Being "tough"—which is what both Elena and Brienna were accused of—is not the same thing as being mean or rejecting. Elena didn't intend to hurt Sanjay, and throughout their conversation, she continued to focus on his behavior, not on his personality. Being honest and speaking to what you think is in another's best interests can require this sort of toughness, especially when the other wants to go the route of avoidance.

Toughness is also required in receiving feedback. Hearing about the problems caused by your behavior is not easy. But Sanjay was able to eventually do just that. He tried several times to move the conversation away from the subject of his marriage and even started to walk away, but in the end he stuck with it and heard Elena's feedback. Brienna's conversation with her brother followed a similar pattern. It's difficult, if not impossible, to build exceptional relationships with people who are fragile. Both Brienna and Elena understood—and conveyed—that the receiver of the feedback could take it.

Nevertheless, it's still hard to provide disconfirming feedback without the other person's feeling rejected. Elena walked this tightrope in several ways. She could have gotten upset because of the way Sanjay put her on the spot and in response to his angry resistance. Instead, she repeatedly told Sanjay the stance she was taking was intended to help, not hurt, him. She focused on what she believed would be best for him, pointed out granting his request would harm him and his marriage, and reiterated that she saw her efforts as the ultimate in support.

It's important to note that what Sanjay was asking wasn't outrageous. It was possible—even likely—that Elena could have talked the startup issue through with Sanjay without Priya's ever knowing about her role and this could have ended up fine. That's what made it so challenging for Elena to hold to her position. On the other hand, if he'd said, "Hey, I'm joining this risky startup and I need you to convince Priya it's a great idea," he would have crossed a much clearer line. Because his original request appeared reasonable on the surface, it made it that much tougher for Elena to set the boundary she did. And the fact that the situation was so nuanced is what makes this story so important—for these are the situations most likely to trap us.

Just because you have an exceptional relationship with someone, that doesn't mean you're invited into every aspect of their life. Sanjay's angry statement "That's the marriage we have, and, to be honest, that isn't your business!" is valid. Sanjay and Priya can decide how they want to relate irrespective of how Elena feels. Let's imagine that at the meeting over drinks, Sanjay had merely *announced* that he was thinking about this new venture and said that he wasn't going to share the decision with his wife. Elena would have had some concerns and, as a very good friend, would have raised them, leaving it up to Sanjay to do with that as he wished.

However, he didn't just announce his possible plans, he asked for Elena's advice and counsel, and in some sense, for her emotional support. That pulled her in and made her a potential accessory in the process. *That's* what gave her the right to keep raising the issue. She wisely made that distinction in her explanation to Sanjay, increasing the probability of a better reaction from him. Also, note that she was not *ordering* him to share this issue with Priya; she simply told him very directly that she would not be a sounding board until he did.

Elena made three important choices that deepened the friends' connection. The first was her decision not to acquiesce to Sanjay's request. The second was not getting defensive at Sanjay's comment about their friendship, when he suggested she didn't care. And the third was not letting Sanjay prematurely close off their meeting. Throughout, she focused on what she believed was best for Sanjay and their relationship, and her commitment to it.

If she had given way at any of those three choice points, not all would necessarily have been lost. Let's imagine that she initially agreed to be Sanjay's sounding board, but that after several meetings, she realized the trap she was falling into. She could then have stated her concern and said that she was not willing to continue colluding. Likewise, if she had lost her cool when Sanjay accused her of disparaging the relationship, a simple apology might have sufficed, followed by a discussion of what support meant to her. And if they had left the bar with the issue unresolved, they could at their next lunch meeting have talked about what still needed to be discussed. Nobody does it perfectly every time.

Elena and Sanjay, Part 6

Elena and Sanjay met for drinks the following week. As soon as they sat down, Elena asked Sanjay how he was doing and whether he'd talked to Priya. He made a face and said he had, but as he'd predicted, it hadn't gone well. Priya had gotten very upset and claimed that the startup would lead to their financial ruin.

"Did you discuss the other topic?" Elena asked. "About how hard it is to raise issues with her because of how she reacts?"

"No, I didn't know how to. I was afraid that if I went into that, she'd just deny it or get defensive."

"I can see that," Elena said, "but it could have been an opportunity to raise the issue in a way that would be difficult for her to deny. You were experiencing, in that moment, the very response you find so challenging."

"I don't know, Elena. This is hard stuff—I don't want to make things worse."

"You can't expect it to be easy," Elena said. "The two of you have related to each other in one way for years and now you're trying to fundamentally change that."

"You strike a hard bargain, my friend," Sanjay said. "Okay, I'll give it a shot."

It took Sanjay multiple tries over a few weeks, given that Priya initially reacted to these conversations with a great deal of resistance, including anger and accusations that he wasn't being sensitive to her worries. But Sanjay stayed the course once he became convinced that his marriage would be better off for it.

REMEMBER THAT ONCE a relationship qualifies as *exceptional,* it can always continue to grow. Now that Elena and Sanjay's has been tested, it can handle further issues, such as how Sanjay relates to his wife. Though it might appear that Elena is giving advice and intruding in their marriage, her intent is to be a coach, helping him achieve what he wants. This is another example of the third-party role and what two people on their way to an exceptional relationship can do. She is committed to his growth and development and he knows it, but in a different and more productive way than Sanjay initially requested. Coaching him on how to give feedback to Priya did not compromise her relationship with him or with Priya. Embedded in this example is an assumption that Elena knows Sanjay well enough to understand the kind of marriage he most wants.

Elena's refusal to discuss the new venture ultimately deepened her relationship with Sanjay. She took a calculated risk; there was no guarantee that it would work out, but she wagered that the potential benefit made the risk worth it. They learned that their friendship could not only survive but be even richer than it already was. Sanjay saw how deeply Elena cared for him, precisely because she was willing to take that risk, and each of them learned more about themselves in the process. Because they had built a strong foundation and they had the skills and competencies to have a productive though difficult conversation, Elena's gamble paid off. The more commitment there is to the relationship, and the higher the level of skills and competencies two people have when faced with an interpersonal test, the higher the probability that leaning into difficult conversations will be worth it.

Deepen Your Learning

SELF-REFLECTION

1. Put yourself in Elena's situation. *She was in a tough spot. She worried that if she didn't accede to Sanjay's request, he would feel rejected and their relationship would suffer.* What *would you probably do? Review all of the choice points that Elena faced in the story; how would you have likely responded? What would you conclude about how you handle situations like this?*

2. Key Relationship: Take one of your key relationships in which there might be some ambiguity as to what you can expect from the other. Write down what you think is perfectly fine for you to ask for, followed by what is clearly not. Then write down the requests you are not sure about.

APPLICATION

Go to the person you identified in the second question above and share what you wrote. (You might want to first ask them to do the same analysis with regard to what they think they can/can't ask of you.) Then clarify areas where there is ambiguity.

MAKING SENSE

Talking about boundaries is difficult, as setting a boundary can be experienced as rejection. Were you able to raise the topic directly without having the other feel distanced? When they talked about boundaries, how did you feel? What was the effect of your discussion on your relationship? How did it impact your level of closeness?

15

ENTANGLED ISSUES

Mia and Aniyah, Parts 4 and 5

As relationships grow, conversations deepen. How should you handle your aging parents? Should you have children? How are you supposed to come to grips with getting laid off? What do you do about stressful financial obligations or a serious stressor in your marriage? As the topics become more personal, there's a greater chance that the discussion will have emotional resonance, because there's more intensity and *realness* to the interaction. And yet it makes objectivity harder. What to do if the topic raised by the other stirs up personal feelings of how you have dealt, are currently dealing, or will deal with similar situations?

In this chapter, we return to Mia and Aniyah. After their falling-out and then successful repair, they made a point of meeting on a more regular basis. In those get-togethers, each shared a variety of personal issues. Aniyah was able to talk more openly with Mia about the good and the bad in her work. Mia opened up to Aniyah about her concerns with her teenage son's relationship with his girlfriend. These and similar conversations drew the two of them even closer over the following year, as they realized they'd regained the same sort of connection they'd had as college roommates. But then things got complicated.

Mia and Aniyah, Part 4

Over dinner one evening, Mia seemed especially moody and distracted—a pattern Aniyah had noticed in previous dinners, too.

"Mia, you don't seem yourself," she said. "Is something bothering you?"

Mia looked down at her wine. "Yeah," she said, "something is bothering me, but I don't know how much I want to go into it."

"Your choice, of course. But if you do, I'd be glad to listen."

"I don't really know. . . . I'm definitely feeling off . . . and a bit down. I should be happy. Or rather, I have no reason not to be. I have a good job, a beautiful house, and a husband who loves me. And yet I feel little excitement in my life and it's really bothering me. Life just feels so humdrum, you know? Every day looks like every other day. I find myself wondering if this is really all there is."

"I'm so sorry," Aniyah said. "That's a tough place to be. Any sense of what's causing it? Are things okay with Jake?"

"Yes . . . sort of. He's so loving, but to be honest, we feel more like close friends than lovers. It doesn't have the energy that it used to have."

"Well, you've been married for nearly twenty years," Aniyah said. "It's unrealistic to think it's going to be like the first ten. And having kids, no matter how much we love them, always takes a bit away from us as couples. That's certainly true with Christopher and me."

"Yeah, I know that intellectually, but I still want more. Don't you?"

"Sure, at some abstract level. But life isn't all roses. Don't we have to take all the good we have and not expect everything to be perfect?"

"Yes, I guess so. I'm sure I'll get over it," said Mia, and their conversation moved on to other issues.

A month went by before the friends were able to meet again for dinner. Mia was chatty and her demeanor was much lighter. After they ordered and caught up on a number of fronts, Mia said, "I'm so glad we're having dinner."

"Me too. What's going on with you? You seem really 'up.'"

Mia smiled. "You've been right to encourage me to share more. I've realized that I've been trying to sweep my feelings of dissatisfaction under the rug for too long. The more I ignore it, the worse it gets."

"Good to hear. Sounds like things are better."

"Yeah, they are, actually. There's this guy I knew years ago—Tyler—who suddenly friended me on Facebook," Mia said. "He was going to be in town and mentioned it might be nice to reconnect. So we got together for drinks and had a great time. He was so interesting as well as interest*ed*. We talked about all sorts of things, and the longer we sat there, the more I noticed how alive I felt. It was more fun than I've had in years. I can't remember the last time I felt that way with Jake."

Aniyah felt her stomach sink. "Uh-oh . . ."

"Uh-oh what? For goodness' sake, Aniyah. All I'm saying is that it was great to banter and laugh and have a conversation with real depth. I never wanted it to end."

"Hmmm. So how *did* the evening end?"

"Well, nothing happened, of course. We're both married. But we talked about what a great time we had and decided maybe we'd get together for lunch when he's in town again. He's going to be coming here a lot on business."

"Yikes, Mia, I can't help but worry about where this might all lead."

Mia brushed Aniyah's comment aside. "Let's not make a big deal out of this. I just met an interesting man and think it would be fun to have lunch with him. That's all."

Aniyah was dubious that it wouldn't turn into a bigger deal but chose to say nothing more than "Okay." Their conversation shifted to Aniyah's talking about exciting changes in her company.

At their next dinner, a month later, Mia rushed hurriedly to the table, where Aniyah was already seated. Aniyah commented on how happy she looked.

"Thanks! I feel really great. Tyler and I had lunch again yesterday and I'm still flying high from it." She went on to explain that it was their second lunch since she'd seen Aniyah.

Aniyah didn't say anything but frowned slightly.

"Nothing more has happened . . . yet," she said, "but I can see where this might be headed. I find myself thinking about him a lot. Aniyah, maybe this is crazy, but it's what I've been missing in my life—I haven't felt this alive in years."

Aniyah felt her body tense up. She took a sip of her drink and said, "Geez, Mia, this all seems to be happening very fast. I'm not sure being bored is a good reason to toss a marriage overboard."

Mia's face fell. "Well, that's disappointing. You said yourself, I look happy, and for the first time in ages, I am. Why can't you be more supportive?"

"You don't really want me to tell you it's okay to go have an affair, do you?"

"Not exactly—but I do want you to at least empathize with my situation. Haven't you had similar feelings of wanting something more out of your marriage or dreading that the next forty years of your life were going to be one boring day after another?"

Aniyah chose her words carefully. "I can empathize with feeling bored and restless. Yes, there are times I've felt that way. But I think it would be pretty messed up if you went off and had a lovefest with Tyler."

"Aniyah, I don't think you get it. You're being so judgy. I just feel so *trapped*, and every day a little more unhappy. Why can't you understand?"

"There's a difference between understanding and supporting what I think is a bad choice," said Aniyah. "I can't help but think about all the things that could go wrong. Just seems like a line that's really hard to come back from once you cross it."

"What's going on with you? You've been really negative about this from the very beginning. This is *my* life I'm talking about—not yours."

Aniyah put her face in her hands and began to cry softly. "It's about me, too. . . . You don't know how painful all of this is."

Mia's face softened and she reached across the table to hold Aniyah's hand. "What's going on, Aniyah?"

Trying to control herself, Aniyah said, "A few years ago, Christopher had an affair. I never told you about it because it was when we'd drifted apart, and since then the affair has felt like ancient history. Except that hearing you talk about Tyler has taken me back to those old feelings of hurt and betrayal. I guess the pain of it all is still there, just under the surface. . . . It's just so embarrassing. I feel ashamed about the whole thing and afraid you'll think less of me now that I've told you. Christopher said all the words that you're now saying. I worried at the time that it was my fault, somehow, and that I'm inadequate or had done something wrong. Listening to you stirs all that back up."

"Oh no, I'm so sorry—I certainly didn't expect this would be where our conversation went. No, I don't think less of you. I don't think my unhappiness is Jake's fault, and Christopher's affair may not have had anything to do with you."

"In the end, Christopher and I obviously worked things out, but I really wasn't sure we'd get through it. It was all so painful, Mia. I'd hate to see you go through that."

"I hear you, and I'm touched that you're worried about me. But this is *my* life, Aniyah. And I may need to see whether this thing with Tyler is real. You are the only person I can talk about this with."

"I feel deeply conflicted," said Aniyah. "It's so hard to separate my own experience from my reaction to what you're saying. The affair was bad enough, but what was worse was that Christopher didn't say anything to me about being unhappy in the first place. And then his keeping the secret of the affair . . . it was awful. As I hear you talking, I can feel myself reliving my own pain and trying to protect myself from it—and I guess that I want to protect you, too." Then she added, "If only Christopher and I had gone to couples therapy way back at the beginning of it all. I'm glad we eventually did—otherwise we probably wouldn't be married anymore."

"I hear how hard Christopher's affair was and still is for you," Mia said. "But does this mean you can't be here for me to just talk things through with?"

By now Aniyah had stopped crying. "I want you to feel like you can talk to me. But what if you take my support of you as support of an affair? Then it would be like I'm supporting Christopher in having had one. I hate this feeling, and I don't know what to do."

ANIYAH AND MIA are close to having an exceptional relationship. They are increasingly open with each other, honest in their reactions, supportive, and able to raise disagreements. But Aniyah is in a tough spot. Mia's issue struck a raw nerve in her.

It's not hard to imagine this happening in many relationships. Perhaps you're afraid of being laid off, and your best friend has just been fired. Or you just learned that your mother has a terminal illness, but your friend has suddenly lost a parent. Or you're having a hard time adjusting to parenthood, but your friend hasn't been able to get pregnant. It might be that the similarity allows the other to be especially empathetic and understanding, but they might find it traumatic. No matter how close the relationship, it's legitimate to say, "I'm sorry; I really want to help, but this is just too painful for me." Otherwise close relationships can feel coercive.

There are other possibilities, depending on the level of emotional distress. One solution is what Aniyah did, which was to acknowledge and name her feelings. She recognized early in their conversation that she couldn't be objective and said so. That helped Mia hear what Aniyah said more clearly.

Aniyah could go on to say, "Mia, this is going to be hard for me, but I think I can empathize with your feelings if you don't hear that as implicitly supporting your having an affair. I want to be able to raise my reactions as *my* concerns and not have you hear them as admonishment. And maybe expressing my worries can give you a different perspective through the consequences and options."

A third option is for Aniyah to focus on the initial issue: Mia's unhappiness. Even though Aniyah did some preliminary exploration of that the first time Mia expressed her discontent, she in essence shut it down with the logical argument that life isn't all roses. Instead, she could have continued to be curious, to help Mia reflect on the deeper issues behind her moroseness. Focusing on the underlying problem opens up multiple solutions to explore beyond the possibility of pursuing the affair with Tyler.

As Aniyah and Mia moved forward, Aniyah chose elements of all three approaches.

Mia and Aniyah, Part 5

Aniyah was committed to being there as much as she could for her friend and told her so, which Mia appreciated. During their subsequent conversations, Aniyah did her best to help Mia explore the issues behind her unhappiness. She helped Mia examine her options, as well as think about the consequences and potential outcomes of going ahead with an affair. As difficult as it was, Aniyah worked hard to separate her own issues from her friend's proposed solution. That gave her a chance to help Mia explore what an affair meant without Aniyah's having to imply approval.

One afternoon, Mia mused, "Even if Jake knew about it, I don't think a brief affair with Tyler would end my marriage. But does he have to know? Don't a lot of people have little adventures on the side?"

"Well, yeah, you might be able to keep it a secret, but what does that do to your marriage?" Aniyah pressed. "Does that really bring you closer to Jake? And if he does find out, what does that do to future trust? I have to admit, every so often, even now, I feel uneasy when Christopher talks about a female colleague. Is it really worth introducing that uncertainty into your marriage? Plus, what happens if you end up falling in love with Tyler? What then? If your intention is to remain married, aren't you better off figuring out what you want from Jake?"

Aniyah could see Mia struggle with her questions. Mia listened but was resistant to giving up on the idea of a tryst with Tyler. They continued to explore what the underlying issues were. Aniyah asked Mia what she wanted with Jake and what else she could do to get it.

A few bumpy moments cropped up as they continued to talk over the following week. One was when Aniyah reverted to giving Mia advice and warned, "You really need to stop . . . You're playing with fire." Mia responded that the comment wasn't helpful, and they got back on track.

At another point Aniyah said with exasperation, "You're not thinking clearly, and I can't believe you're even considering this!"

Mia was a bit taken aback and then said, "That's hurtful, Aniyah. I don't feel supported or understood. Instead, I feel judged."

"I'm sorry you feel judged," responded Aniyah. "While that is not my intent, I do think it is important for me to be direct with you so that you know what I think and feel. I think that is my responsibility as your friend." They once again returned to the topic at hand.

Aniyah and Mia went back and forth exploring these issues in increasing depth, but at a certain point, they reached an impasse. Eventually, Aniyah said, "I'm not sure I can help you any more than I have. I'm not a professional therapist and there are too many things about this that trigger me, no matter how hard I work at keeping them at bay. Even though I can't keep talking about this, I hope you know how much I care for you and how special our relationship is to me."

To which Mia responded, "Yes, I do."

* * *

Even in exceptional relationships, not every issue can be resolved. But it is possible that dealing with an impasse such as the one these two friends face can further strengthen the bonds between them and cement their friendship at an exceptional level. They achieved this by not blaming each other for the situation. Yes, Mia said, "Does this mean you can't be here for me to just talk things through with?" But that was a question and very different than if she'd aggressively demanded, "Why can't you be there for me?" Likewise, Aniyah didn't say, "How dare you expect me to support you when this is so painful?"

Second, each of them disclosed a great deal: Mia in sharing how important it was for her to feel alive again and how much she needed Aniyah, and Aniyah in telling Mia about Christopher's affair and all that went on with her during that time. And finally, even though Aniyah was in pain, she continued to be there for Mia. That continued effort decreased the chance that Mia would conclude that her close friend didn't care.

Just because you have an exceptional relationship doesn't mean that you have to agree to the other person's every request. It is important to balance two needs. One is to take care of yourself and the other is to be responsive to the other person. That is especially important in the face of entangled issues. The way that Mia and Aniyah handled this challenge provides clues as to how to manage that tension. The key is in being open about your needs, being concerned about the other person's needs, and having that conversation without blame.

Three Additional Considerations

WHAT'S THE DIFFERENCE BETWEEN EMPATHY AND AGREEMENT?

Aniyah wanted to be empathetic and understanding, even if she could not support Mia's proposed solution to her unhappiness. It was a hard line to walk. It required they both be clear that Aniyah's empathy did not imply support for an affair.

A friend of ours, Eve, faced a similar challenge with her father. Alfredo frequently alienated family members and heard all feedback as an attack. Eve tried to connect with him by empathizing with his unhappiness, but he interpreted her empathy as agreeing with his position that he was being mistreated by his family. He always insisted his intentions were good. When Eve tried to point out that it was behavior, not intentions, that affected others, he heard that as just another attack. She didn't know how to get out of that bind. When the other person wants agreement, empathetic understanding may not work. Eve had to accept that what her father wanted she could not give. The cost was a greater distance between them than either of them would have wished for.

WHAT IF SUPPORT VIOLATES MY VALUES?

Aniyah was opposed to Mia's plans less on values grounds and more on the costs that she had personally experienced. But what if she believed that affairs were sinful? Can one truly "hate the sin, but love the sinner"? Would Mia have felt as fully supported by that approach? Pope Francis, when asked about his views on homosexuality, replied, "Who am I to judge?" But when you have strong value beliefs, and you're not Pope Francis, how easy is it *not* to judge?

If Aniyah had strong values about extramarital affairs, and Mia knew that, it is unlikely Mia would have come to her for support. We don't share all issues with one exceptional friend; that's why most of us need more than one.

WHAT IF I'M CROSSING THE LINE AND ACTING LIKE A THERAPIST?

Aniyah encouraged Mia to explore the source of her dissatisfaction with her life and her marriage. She asked open-ended questions to encourage her friend to reflect more deeply about the causes of her unhappiness and consider other possibilities for addressing it. She tried to be nonjudgmental and eventually accepted the fact that Mia knew best what worked for her. But there is only so much a nonprofessional can do, and Aniyah knew her limitations. When Aniyah said, "I'm not sure I can help you any more than I have. I'm not a professional therapist," she was not abdicating her role as a close friend or being judgmental; she was acknowledging her own limits. That said, you can't force someone into therapy. Though Aniyah told Mia how therapy had helped her and Christopher in a similar situation, Mia ultimately rejected the idea. At that point, Aniyah had done all she could.

AN INTIMATE TALK with one person may open doors that can no longer be kept shut with another—for better or worse. In this way, one exceptional relationship can impact another. Aniyah thought that Christopher's past affair had been laid to rest but came to recognize that there were residual feelings beneath the surface, which might reopen a discussion with her husband about further repairs their relationship needed.

There is a potentially double-edged sword to conversations like this. Yes, maybe Aniyah and Christopher ultimately would gain from what Aniyah's conversation with Mia brought up, but Aniyah wasn't looking to have a painful issue brought back to life. Once two people wade into entangled issues, there may be no option but to continue to move forward and deal with them—whether anticipated or not, welcomed or not. Which brings us back to a central tenet of this book: *the importance of a learning mindset.*

Let's assume that Aniyah is stirred up about Christopher's past affair. It's likely that he will not be pleased to be reminded of his dalliance. But if Aniyah can move beyond blame ("How could you have done this to me!") and into exploration ("What do I need in order to find more peace?" or "Where are we now in our relationship?"), there is the possibility for rich learning for both of them. It won't be easy, but it is another choice point.

This is part of what makes exceptional relationships so magical—the experience of being fully known and accepted by another, the chance to be fully human and see the other in the same way, and the chance to learn. It is not easy, but it's part of living a full life.

Deepen Your Learning

SELF-REFLECTION

1. Imagine you are Aniyah. *How would you have handled the situation she was in with Mia? How might you have conveyed your reticence to discuss Mia's issue without her feeling rejected or the relationship's suffering?*

2. Entangled Personally: Have you been in a situation where a close friend/family member/colleague wanted to discuss an issue they were facing with you, but it stirred up strong personal feelings for you? How did you handle it?

3. Entangling Others: Have you been in a situation where you wanted to talk about an issue, but you were uncertain that it would be okay with the other person? For example, perhaps you had a parent who was fading, and your friend had recently lost a parent who had dementia. Maybe your friend welcomed sharing the experience—but maybe not. Whatever the situation was, how did you handle it? Are there aspects of it you wish you'd handled differently?

4. Present Dilemma: Do you currently have a situation in which you want to talk about an issue that might trigger the other person?

APPLICATION

Check out whether there is a way to discuss the issues with the person you identified in self-reflection question 4. How can you have that discussion in a way that allows the other person to decline without making either of you feel rejected?

MAKING SENSE

This discussion required a combination of being forthright and sensitive. How did it go? What did you learn about yourself and about this process? How did taking this risk impact your relationship?

16

WHEN EXCEPTIONAL ISN'T IN THE CARDS

The two of us have been living and breathing exceptional relationships for decades, and yet we don't always get there with people in our lives. From childhood through adolescence, Carole had a very close relationship with her late mother. Flora made it clear that she wanted them to be "best friends" so that Carole could tell her everything, which is pretty much what she did. Flora gave Carole a lot of what Carole took to be good advice on everything from makeup, to boys, to the dangers of premarital sex. Carole wasn't a rebellious kid. She followed the rules, got good grades, and stayed out of trouble.

Everything changed when Carole became an adult, got married, and had her own children. She discovered that their "close" relationship was predicated on Carole's always agreeing with Flora and almost always subsuming Carole's needs to hers—otherwise Carole was "selfish." Flora was very good at giving feedback when she was disappointed or angry but terrible at receiving feedback when anything she did made Carole feel bad. She was one of the most judgmental people Carole has ever met—highly opinionated and exceedingly difficult to influence.

As Carole began to learn more about effective interpersonal dynamics, she wondered whether there was a way she might have a truly close relationship with her mom, as two adult women. When Carole was in the middle of her PhD program, the two had a memorable exchange.

"I don't understand why you're bothering with this whole PhD thing," Flora said. "Your kids and husband are not getting the attention they need."

"Mom, when you tell me you don't understand why I'm bothering to get a PhD at the expense of having more time for my family, I feel bad about myself," Carole said. "Is that your intent?"

"Of course not, I just think you're driving yourself crazy unnecessarily."

"Unnecessarily according to who?"

"Everyone."

"I've had many conversations with Andy about this, and he is one hundred percent behind it. And I have asked him if he thinks he and the kids are having to sacrifice too much, and he has assured me that's not the case."

"I don't believe it."

"So you think he's lying to me?"

Flora was silent for a moment and then said, "I'm just going by my own experience. There was a time when you and I got together all the time—went shopping or just had lunch. We schmoozed on the phone for hours. You don't ever seem to have time for that."

"That's true, and you're right. And it's precisely because I want to focus the spare time I do have on Andy and the kids."

"Which is why I don't understand this whole PhD thing."

"Are you saying you aren't supportive of my getting a PhD because I don't have as much time to spend with you as you want?" Carole asked.

"I said no such thing. I said it's hurting your family unnecessarily."

And so it went. Try as she might to convey the impact of conversations like this, Carole was repeatedly unsuccessful. Carole tried to explain that her inability to influence Flora was distancing them.

She tried to tell Flora how much it bothered her every time she made a definitive judgment about someone else in the family. And Carole told her that it made her want to spend less, not more, time with her when Flora seemed closed to the possibility of being wrong. Carole told her that she was saying all this in hopes they could have a closer adult relationship.

Flora most often responded with tears, saying Carole was being unfair. All she wanted was to be closer, and Carole was the reason they weren't as close as they'd once been, because she was "too busy." Carole tried to point out that their closeness had been a function of how they interacted when Carole was younger (which was characterized by Carole's always deferring because Flora was always "right"), and that no longer worked. Flora dismissed this, argued that wasn't the case, or deflected the conversation.

It was hard for Carole to accept that despite what she'd learned about creating exceptional relationships, she was not going to have one with her mother. When Flora was dying of cancer, Carole tried one last time. She tried to be the best daughter she could through her mother's surgeries, visiting often and driving her to and from the infusion center several days a week for months. In spite of multiple invitations to talk about how she felt about what was happening, Flora would not go there. Carole believes Flora just couldn't engage in a conversation in which there was any chance she might not have the upper hand (and yes, that attribution is over the net). Carole loved her and knows the love was reciprocal. But they did not have an exceptional relationship.

An important outcome from exceptional relationships is the opportunity to grow and develop, but that growth has to be in directions each person wants—not in the direction the other wants for them. But what happens when the other's needs result in their wanting you to develop differently than you want? Flora claimed that she only had Carole's best interests at heart, but Flora wanted Carole to grow (or more accurately, not grow) in ways that would force Carole to regress to the ways they had related when Carole was a teenager. Carole, in turn, wanted her mother to grow but defined that as being able to talk about the fact that she was dying (among many other difficult conversations).

Again, this issue might have been resolved if mother and daughter could have talked about it, but Flora wasn't inclined to have those kinds of discussions. Exceptional requires a willingness to look at issues, allow for the possibility of being wrong, and consider new ways of seeing things. Flora wasn't game because, above all else, she needed to be right. There can be caring, even love, as was the case with the two of them, but that is not what defines exceptional. As much as each might have wanted a more intimate relationship with the other, Carole's loss of autonomy was a price too high for her to pay and the absence of a commitment to growth and learning from Flora precluded theirs from becoming an exceptional relationship.

This chapter covers why, in spite of all your efforts, sometimes more meaningful relationships don't develop. It might be that as you and your counterpart learn more about each other, you discover your views are so different that the effort involved in bridging them is simply too much work. Or perhaps you don't have enough in common—and the costs of building a serious relationship don't outweigh the benefits. But what if your relationship had the potential to become exceptional, and it didn't quite get there? What happened? Was it anything you did or didn't do? What can be learned from relationships that stall along the way?

Phil and Rachel—Only So Far

In chapter 9, Rachel resolved a major frustration with her father, Phil, when she told him his advice-giving and lack of empathy drove her crazy. One confrontation didn't completely address these issues, and Phil sometimes reverted to his previous mode, but they now had a relationship in which Rachel could call him on it. As time went on, Phil curbed his tendencies more and more, and their relationship grew steadily closer.

Emboldened by that success, Rachel realized there was more that she wanted from her father. He didn't share significant parts of his life with Rachel, and she wanted to be let in. Since her mother had passed away, Rachel had wondered and worried about how Phil was adapting. She also had growing concerns about his performance as a surgeon. The hospital didn't have a forced retirement age, and Phil was several years past when he could have collected benefits. When she occasionally brought the subject up, his response was always, "Work is keeping me young," to which he would add that he had no plans to retire. The conversation always ended there. However, Rachel began hearing rumors that her father's surgical skills were not what they'd once been. She was concerned where that might lead. *I'd hate to see him pushed out instead of leaving on his own terms,* she thought, but when she tried to raise the issue delicately, Phil laughed it off and said that his peers were just envious that, at his age, he was still as good as they were.

Rachel yearned to discuss this more and to delve into other personal topics. How did he feel about his career as he reflected on the last four decades? Any disappointments? Did he ever think about paths he wished he'd taken? How was he really doing, having lost the love of his life? She tried to build conditions for that sort of conversation by sharing numerous personal and professional issues that she was facing. Phil seemed to value those discussions, and with his decreased tendency to give advice, Rachel found it easier to disclose her feelings and struggles. But try as she might, this did not lead to reciprocal disclosure. Phil was a closed book.

Rachel decided to be more direct. She made arrangements for them to go out for dinner. As they ate, she laid out the sorts of discussions she wanted to have and what both would gain. "You've said before that you want to pass on your experience; talking about your life is one way to do it," she argued.

"But that isn't me," Phil said. "I don't find reflecting on my life that enjoyable and it seems fruitless to talk about paths I might have taken. I just believe it's best to turn the page." He was silent for a minute and then said softly, "And talking about your mom is just too painful. Can't we just enjoy what we have?"

Rachel persisted. "Look, let's try it and see what it's like. I mentioned several areas. Pick one that you're most comfortable with and we can see how it goes." Phil thought for a moment and said, "I had a choice of two specialties; let me talk about that." He did so for the next half hour, but Rachel could see that his heart wasn't in it, and the discussion felt forced. Phil shook his head. "This isn't working. Look, I love hearing about your life, and I've been good about not giving advice. I would be glad to talk about things we did—trips we took—when you were growing up, but that's all I want to say about the past." Rachel nodded her head and reluctantly agreed to that compromise.

Changing the Basis of a Relationship

What Rachel wanted was more fundamental than she realized. It's one thing to want a change in another's behavior, even when it's as ingrained as Phil's previous tendency to tell others how to lead their lives. But it's another to change the very basis of their relationship, which is what Rachel was asking Phil to do.

She was now an adult and wanting more of an adult–adult relationship. This would have required significant changes for both of them. Rachel would now have to step up to the plate more—which she was starting to do—and Phil would have to do more than just cut down on his advice-giving. He would have to be more vulnerable and self-disclosing. The success of their discussion about Phil's advice-giving moved them in the direction of a more equal relationship, but only so far. It didn't appear that he wanted to go much further—certainly not the distance Rachel wanted. Was this too big a change for him?

Even though Rachel wanted Phil to be more emotionally self-disclosing, he had spent most of his life with a far more analytical style. Furthermore, his training and his professional environment didn't necessarily reinforce the vulnerability she wanted, nor did his home life: Phil's wife had spent years "interpreting" Phil's feelings to Rachel. Change can be very difficult when a central way of relating has been so consistently reinforced.

What, then, are Rachel's options? She could choose to let it be. After all, look at what she's gained. Rachel made a lot of headway in her relationship with Phil over the past year. She was able to share more of herself without Phil's getting into advice-giving. This allowed a closeness that both of them appreciated. One of the potential downsides of focusing on exceptional relationships is devaluing any connection that doesn't reach that level. Sometimes it's necessary to simply be grateful for what's been achieved. We get different needs met from different people. Rachel is in a rewarding marriage and has close friends. She could go to them to get her needs for deeper connection met, while enjoying what she does have with her father.

On the other hand, she could push a bit more. She's seen that Phil can change, so maybe there's more he can do. She'd always had a close relationship with her father, and this next step holds the possibility of an even richer connection for both of them. As for Phil, sharing more about his life (especially with his daughter) could provide a more meaningful way to relate—even if it is difficult for him. And it would also meet his stated goal of passing along his experience.

But how much should Rachel push? Was that thirty-minute attempt at dinner an adequate test? If she picked up on his offer to have nostalgic conversations about her early years, might those morph into the more personal disclosures she's wanted? Or would she just be flogging a dead horse?

The answer comes in the form of a question (we are teachers, after all—it's in our wiring!): *For whose sake would she be persisting?*

Sometimes we just need to accept others for who they are. Is she picking up any real clues that Phil is lonely and wants more intimacy, or is she pushing him because of what she wants?

There's another way to view Rachel's choices. As mentioned at the beginning of this book, Carol Dweck suggests that when identifying a present limitation, it is important to add the word "yet." When a statement like "I can't fully express all my needs with my significant other" gets a "yet" at the end, the meaning changes from hopelessness to possibility. Rachel doesn't know what the future holds for Phil. Maybe a surgery won't go as well as it has in the past, and it will be easier for him to discuss that with Rachel than with another surgeon. Or perhaps Phil will see a colleague who is over the hill but won't recognize that reality, and Phil will realize he doesn't want to go that route. At those times, Phil might be more amenable to self-disclosure.

There is a danger that the harder we push, the more we risk alienating the other person. Holding desires too tightly can squeeze the life out of a relationship. Instead, sometimes meeting the other person where they are increases the chance they'll join the journey at a later time. Rachel can value and appreciate what she's gained without giving up awareness that conditions might change and that more might become possible. Indeed, she herself might change. Perhaps more personal self-disclosure from Phil will become less important to Rachel as she reflects on all that she has gained over a lifetime with her father.

Ben and Liam—a Failed Attempt

When we left Ben and Liam in chapter 4, the two friends had made some progress. Ben said he would work on not pushing with personal questions as much, and Liam promised to raise issues he had with Ben rather than just shutting down. He also said he'd try to share more.

Over the following year, their friendship grew. Liam met and fell in love with a woman named Brittany, whom Ben thought was great—and perfect for his friend. Ben loved the way that she held her own with Liam, who, at times, could be dominating.

Because Liam spent quite a bit of time with Brittany, the two men didn't see each other as often. One night when they met up for drinks, Ben asked Liam how it was going, and Liam divulged that he thought Britt might be the one.

"That's awesome!" Ben said. "She's great, and I'm really happy for you." Liam looked pensive and wouldn't meet Ben's eye, so Ben followed up. "Is there something going on?"

Liam laughed and shook his head. "I can't slip anything past you . . . which I guess is good. The problem is her mother. Nancy drives me nuts. She thinks she has the answer to everything—she gives her opinion about things she knows nothing about." Liam got more agitated as he continued. "Just last week she started lecturing me about buying a house, even though she knows nothing about my finances and nothing about the housing market."

Ben shook his head sympathetically. "Ugh, that's annoying. What do you think's behind it?"

"For one thing, she is incredibly needy. Her husband died about four years ago, and she can't seem to move on with her life. Nancy calls Britt *every* day. Britt and I occasionally take her out to dinner since Britt feels bad that she's so lonely, but those dinners put my teeth on edge. She spends most of the time interrogating Britt about her life and then telling her how she should lead it. For Christ's sake, Britt's an adult, and a competent one at that. It drives me crazy! Why does Nancy think she's God's gift to people's issues?" Liam took a deep breath. "And I think what bothers me even more is how Britt responds to her—or, more accurately, *doesn't*. She just says, 'Thanks, Mom. That's something to consider,' to all that advice and then changes the subject. Why doesn't she tell Nancy to back off? I'm starting to lose respect for her. I want a wife who has backbone."

"Boy, you're really upset about all of this!"

"Of course I am," said Liam. "Wouldn't you be?"

Ben felt conflicted. On the one hand, he wanted to support Liam, but on the other, he sensed that there was more going on. He had never met Nancy, but Liam was painting a very one-sided picture. It was hard to believe that she was as horrible as Liam described. Also, Britt had impressed him as a self-assured and grounded woman. She didn't appear to be weak or overly compliant. He wasn't sure what to say that might be useful. So he nodded and said, "Yeah, probably." He let a moment pass, then asked, "Why do you think they act that way?"

"Look, I'm not their therapist! And I don't need you to play therapist. I just want to blow off steam. Not sure I have anyone else I'd be comfortable doing that with."

"Got it," said Ben. "I hear you—this sounds really tough. Especially given how much you care about Britt."

Liam leaned back and relaxed a bit.

"And I'm glad you're venting to me," Ben said. "I want you to feel like you can do that with me. But I have to be direct here—you're describing the situation pretty narrowly. It might not be so black-and-white, and it would suck if you broke things off with Britt because you're thinking that way. We don't need to talk about it if you don't want to, but I needed to say this."

Liam was quiet. Then, somewhat hesitantly, he nodded and said, "Go ahead. What are you thinking?"

"I don't know Nancy, but I wonder if she's as much 'the Wicked Witch of the West' as you've described her. And I do know Britt a bit, and she doesn't strike me as a person without backbone! She sure stands up to you. So why are you labeling her as so passive? Seems to me she's found a good way to handle her mom."

"Yeah, but it's the way Nancy holds court all the time. Britt should just shut her down."

"But that's your way. You say that Nancy thinks she knows the right way to do things; aren't you doing the same thing? Anyway, why are you so worked up? Britt seems to let it roll off her back—why can't you?"

"That pisses me off, Ben. Why do you always turn it back on me? So it's my fault?"

"No, that's not what I'm saying. All I'm saying is that the only person you really have control over is yourself. I'd be annoyed by Nancy, too, but I don't think I'd be as bent out of shape as you are. And I actually respect how Britt's handling the situation. She's not letting herself be controlled, but she's also not attacking her mother. I just wonder if you've asked yourself what's behind all of this for you."

"What good would that do?"

"You're talking about marrying Britt, so Nancy will be your mother-in-law. You need at least a decent relationship with her. Can you figure out what's going on with you so that you don't find her impossible?"

"I don't know," Liam said. "This introspection stuff isn't my thing, but I'll think about it."

In the subsequent months, Liam and Britt's relationship continued to blossom, and Ben and Liam met up less frequently. But their friendship grew stronger as Liam shared more of his feelings about Britt. Ben was sensitive about not asking how things were going with Nancy, although he worried about it.

Then Liam told Ben that he and Britt were engaged and were planning the wedding for the coming June. The friends found a time to meet up for a celebratory drink. After they caught up on work and general life, Ben asked Liam how the wedding plans were going. Liam rolled his eyes and took a swig of his beer.

"We should have just eloped," he said. "Predictably, Nancy has taken over and Britt has let her. This feels like Nancy's event, not ours."

"Ugh, that sucks. Must be hard on Britt."

"I actually don't think it is," Liam said. "The most maddening thing about this is that Britt seems to be just fine with all the decisions Nancy is making. Drives me nuts."

"I thought things had gotten a bit better between you and Nancy."

"Nah, I just don't talk about it."

Ben stopped for a minute to reflect. "Liam, I still don't get why this bothers you so much—especially since it doesn't sound like it bothers Britt. Do you think there's something about you and your dynamic with Nancy that's the problem?"

Liam exploded. "Ben, I'm sick and tired of this psychoanalysis crap every time I'm upset about something, and I'm not going to have another one of those touchy-feely conversations. It makes me not want to tell you anything."

Ben backed off. "Sorry. I was trying to help. Let's talk about something else."

The conversation moved on to other topics—work, Ben's training regimen for an upcoming marathon, an apartment that Liam and Britt were considering renting, and the woman Ben had been seeing and planned to bring to Liam and Britt's wedding.

At subsequent get-togethers, both before and after the wedding, Liam continued to express his frustration with Nancy, and Ben limited himself to sympathetic comments but didn't try to explore the underlying issues. Liam mentioned that he'd found Ben's recent comments helpful and said, "Thanks for just letting me vent instead of getting all touchy-feely."

"Guess we like different things." Ben shrugged. "As I've said before, I sort of like digging deeper into these things."

Liam shook his head. "Yeah, and that sort of navel-gazing is not for me."

As time went on, Ben and Liam saw less and less of each other. Liam focused on his marriage, and Ben realized he got less out of their relationship. They remained friends and would periodically get together for drinks, but Ben found other relationships more satisfying, so that's where he put more of his time and energy.

When People Want Different Things

At first blush, it looks like what kept Ben and Liam's relationship from being exceptional was that they wanted very different things. Liam appeared to want a connection based on "being a buddy" where he could just share the ups and downs of his life. Ben wanted a connection that was more deeply personal. Earlier on, they had enough shared experiences around work and sports to grow a friendship, but over time these were overshadowed by the disconnect between what they were each looking for in a relationship.

Wanting different things out of a relationship doesn't necessarily have to be an obstacle, but it does have to be addressed. People can grow in different directions and in the process want something different. That doesn't necessarily mean they will grow apart. Close relationships aren't dependent on wanting exactly the same things. The basic problem that Ben and Liam have is their inability to discuss these differences. Without that, they can't reconcile them.

They have fallen into the "either-or" trap. Either Ben stops asking personal questions or Liam tolerates them. That has blocked them from getting clear about what each wants and doesn't want. Did Liam not want *any* introspection? Or was it about Ben's approach? Would it have been okay with Liam if Ben wanted to explore his own issues and use Liam as a sounding board, as long as Ben didn't expect Liam to do the same? We don't know, but neither do they. They never got that far.

For example, Ben could have asked, "What's getting in our way? Why are we having such difficulty?" Liam might have squashed that line of questioning as "too touchy-feely," but he might not have. The point is that Ben didn't ask, and they weren't able to get into figuring out how to talk about the disconnect more productively.

Not being able to discuss this limited the potential of their relationship. At best, it will stay where it is, with the two periodically getting together to catch up on events, but they might just drift apart. It's unlikely that they'll forge a truly meaningful relationship.

Exceptional Relationships at Work

Both of us have spent much of our professional career applying the competencies in this book in work settings. We have coached executives and managers in for-profit and not-for-profit organizations, in educational and medical settings, and in governmental organizations at the national and local levels. We have helped employees, managers, senior executives, and CEOs learn how to deal more directly and honestly with each other. We have helped teams develop so that conflict can be dealt with productively, interpersonal problems resolved, and strong relationships built. In this process, we have seen great individual growth, better work conditions, and higher performance.

We have also seen and experienced exceptional relationships in a work setting. They have the same characteristics we have described throughout the book. These relationships can occur whether you are the boss, a direct report, or a peer, though an organizational setting poses its own set of challenges in building them.

There are significant constraints that don't exist outside of work. You might be able to pick your friends and partner, but less so your colleagues. Simon might be a royal pain in the neck, but your work is interdependent, so you have to find a way to build a productive relationship. Even when you do have strong work friendships, there is only so far you are going to go to help others advance if it is at your expense. Yes, you want to support them, but hierarchies are inherently competitive—there's only so much room at the top. If one of the dimensions of exceptional relationships is that you're committed to the other's development, you may feel conflicted supporting a colleague in getting the special assignment you both want. You're not going to sabotage them, but how much are you going to sacrifice your own advancement?

Good working relationships can develop into close friendships. That is important because doing so can motivate both parties to be more honest and transparent with each other as well as decrease the risk in raising difficult issues. But there are limits. This was vividly illustrated in a talk that Jeff Immelt, CEO at General Electric, gave at Stanford several years ago: "I was one of the three senior vice presidents reporting to Jack Welch. Jack and I were good friends; our families would often have barbecues together. One time, I had missed making my numbers for two quarters in a row. At an executive retreat, Jack took me aside, put his arm around my shoulder, and said, 'Jeff, I really like you, but another quarter like the last two and you are out.' I made sure to make my numbers next quarter." Organizations can be positive places to work and supportive of employee development, but the needs of the organization are inherently placed ahead of the needs of the individual.

In your role as a manager, you are faced with another constraint. You want to develop your employees, and you now know how to give developmental feedback. You also know that providing stretch assignments is another important way for them to grow. But as we have said, your primary responsibility is the organization's success. You might think twice before giving a crucial task to an employee who might fail, even if it would be a learning opportunity for them. Balancing developmental needs with organizational success is an important managerial competence, and it involves risks.

Strong, high-trust relationships are ones where we can be open with each other. But it's not easy for a direct report to admit self-doubts to his manager if it decreases the chance of getting a choice assignment—even though such an admission could be valuable in getting needed coaching. Furthermore, even if the employee might know what their boss does well and not so well, they are likely to have concerns about offering honest feedback or even strongly disagreeing with the person who signs their paycheck. Sam Goldwyn, the famous Hollywood movie mogul, reportedly said, "Tell me the truth, even if it costs you your job." Bosses may say they want honest interactions, but how much and how often?

None of these factors inherently block exceptional relationships at work. It is possible to have those with co-workers who, like you, are looking to advance; with your direct reports as you balance concern for them with obligations to the organization; and with your manager, despite the power discrepancy. We have provided a number of examples on how to do that in this book. Moving a relationship at work toward exceptional requires the competencies you have learned. Disclosure, being direct, dealing with pinches, giving and receiving feedback, raising difficult issues, speaking to the other person's interests, and addressing power differences all lay the foundation. Most work relationships can probably reach the meadow. Once there, you need mutual commitment, a steady and ongoing process of increasing self-disclosure, continually stretching 15 percent beyond your comfort zone, and seeing setbacks as something to explore and learn from rather than as a reason to retreat.

In spite of organizational constraints, our experience is that most managers and employees *want* more open and direct conversations than they often have. In the programs we conduct for executives, we have found it fascinating that when we ask, "How open can you be with your boss?" the responses are most often, "Oh, I have to be very careful," "I need to watch my words if I disagree," and "It's best to make bosses think the new ideas are theirs." These answers are irrespective of the participants' level of management.

Then we ask a follow-up question: "If your direct reports disagree with one of your ideas, what do you want them to do?" The responses are again similar across all levels of management. Except this time the answer is, "I want them to be direct, to lay it out, not to beat around the bush. I want to know the truth."

We then observe, "Isn't that interesting? All the people in this program are secure and centered, but all have bosses who are fragile and insecure. Clearly, we need to get your managers, not you, to these programs!" As we noted above, if you use the lessons from this book, you can be direct and straightforward. You can help your boss see that you are on their side and your intent is to be their ally.

You are likely not only to gain more respect but also to end up with stronger and more functional relationships. With that as a basis, it is possible that many work relationships can grow to be exceptional.

Our intention is not to be flip and imply that any of this is easy. Nothing in this book is easy! But then again, you already knew that. Applying this material in an organization is far more complex than we could do justice to in this chapter. For a deeper dive, we recommend two books David co-authored with his colleague Allan Cohen: *Power Up: Transforming Organizations Through Shared Leadership* and *Influence Without Authority*.

Deepen Your Learning

SELF-REFLECTION

1. Checking Progress: At the beginning of the book, you identified relationships you wanted to develop further. Where are you now with them? Of course, these still have the potential for further growth, but are you satisfied at this point in time? Are some similar to the significant progress that Rachel experienced with her father? Are you satisfied with having reached the meadow? Or do you want to make the final ascent to the summit?

2. Work Settings: Are there a couple of work relationships that you would like to significantly improve or move further along the continuum? For each of them, be specific about what would make them stronger. What concerns come up for you as you think about raising these wishes with that person?

APPLICATION

For those relationships in which you're happy with the progress made (be they at the meadow or beyond), to what extent have you fully expressed your appreciation to those people for joining you in the journey? If not, do so!

For those with whom you have stopped at the meadow, what have you decided to do? If you choose to stay there, have a conversation in which you share how much you value the progress, and make sure that in doing so you do not diminish what you have accomplished. If you still want to encourage them to go further, ask for what you want in a way that is compelling without being coercive.

Choose one of your work relationships from your self-reflection in question 2 on page 259. What can you do to explore ways in which the two of you can make your relationship stronger than it is now.

MAKING SENSE

What did you learn from the conversations you had above? What did you do that was successful, and what was less so?

17

AN EXCEPTIONAL RELATIONSHIP GONE AWRY—AND BACK AGAIN

The two of us have had a long and close relationship. We first met at Stanford over twenty years ago, when David ran the Interpersonal Dynamics course as well as the training for its facilitators. Carole went through the training and eventually joined the other faculty in teaching the course. We quickly developed a close mentoring relationship and moved along the continuum to exceptional.

We tended to agree on general goals but came at issues in slightly different ways, producing better solutions than either of us would have achieved alone. We were able to raise and resolve disagreements easily, resulting in a great working relationship. Our friendship deepened, and we used each other as a resource for personal and professional problems. We believed we knew each other very well given our high degree of mutual openness and great trust. Furthermore, we both lived much of what we have discussed in this book—mutual self-disclosure, giving and receiving both affirming and developmental feedback, resolving pinches, and jointly solving major problems.

Then an incident occurred that neither of us saw coming and that nearly ended our high-trust, caring relationship. Our issues became deeply entangled, and we had to know which strand to pull to unravel the knot—we did so with the help of a third party and by using the competencies in this book. It was a close call, though, and goes to show just how difficult the work of building exceptional relationships is—even among its most fervent teachers.

The specifics of the disagreement itself boiled down to a scenario that will sound familiar, if not universal (and we've changed the details, in any case!): Carole asked for something from her employer that she didn't get and learned that David hadn't gone to bat for her.

From David's perspective:

> I had been coordinating the Interpersonal Dynamics faculty for many years and was getting ready to step down. Touchy-Feely had been the pinnacle of my professional career at Stanford and was now my legacy there. I had been grooming Carole for over a decade and was impressed with how her Stanford career had blossomed. She had taken on more and more responsibilities, throwing herself into the work. She taught multiple sections of the Interpersonal Dynamics course, developed several new courses in both the MBA and executive programs, and overhauled what became the school's signature, the Leadership Fellows Program. In spite of the courses' and programs' successes, there was little recognition from management for her contributions. But I highly valued her and believed she was my obvious replacement.
>
> She indicated a willingness to be my successor, and I was confident that I'd be leaving the course in excellent hands. That was reassuring since I was in the middle of a budget fight. The business school was facing financial constraints and was cutting course support. Interpersonal Dynamics was already, by far, the most expensive course taught, and I was afraid some necessary funding would be taken away. Saving that was my highest priority.

From Carole's perspective:

When David announced he was going to step down and conversations began about my taking over his responsibilities, I asked management that Interpersonal Dynamics be given the designation of "program," not "course." The specifics of why this mattered so much are complex, but in a nutshell, programs were given more infrastructure support, in part because they were recognized as being complicated to run, which Interpersonal Dynamics undeniably was. With the designation of "program," I'd also be eligible for a director title, which I believed would give me more credibility with the faculty and administration.

I feared that, unlike David, who had been in that role for decades, I needed these two conditions to be as effective as he had been. Without them I wouldn't be able to honor his legacy as fully as I wanted. We also worked in a highly male-dominated arena, and as a woman, I felt disadvantaged. Having experienced discrimination for years in the private sector, I had hoped academia would be different, only to find out it was just as bad. I was counting on David, my mentor, to help me make this happen.

I went to management to make my case, but they turned down my two requests. I was furious. I had given everything I had to the school, and though I was appreciated by my students, I rarely felt appreciated or acknowledged by management for my contributions. Instead, I was consistently asked to do more. I had long believed that being a "good soldier" in service of the system would eventually pay off but was growing dubious that would be the case. I never had asked for much for myself before, and now, when I wanted something that I believed was essential for the course's success, they were unwilling to grant my request. The result was that I was growing increasingly resentful. I no longer believed "good things come to those who wait." I told management that unless Interpersonal Dynamics was categorized a program and they announced that I was officially running it, I wouldn't do it. I went to David to ask for his support.

The First Conversation

After pleasantries, Carole explained what she wanted from David. He replied, "Carole, why are you pushing so hard for the program and title? I just don't get what's the big deal."

"The big deal is that I'm going to have to fight the very battles you are fighting right now. Without the recognition I'm asking for, I don't think I'll be successful."

David thought for a moment, then said, "I don't think that's true; you have built a strong reputation for all that you've done. Management recognizes that, and the Interpersonal Dynamics faculty is behind you."

Carole argued back, "The course is at a critical juncture in its evolution. Running it has become extremely complex, given its many moving parts. It's also much more interdependent with people and departments throughout the school than any other course. It's reached a point where it *needs* to be acknowledged as a program. And I need the credibility in order to lead it well."

David assured Carole he would still be around and happy to help. He also reiterated how much confidence he had in her.

"I need more than that," Carole said. "I want you to go fight for me and ask management to give me what I've asked for. There is no way I am going to succeed in this system as you have if you don't, especially as a woman, and one who isn't tenured, at that!"

"Sorry, Carole," David said. "Given how well you have done in the past in building the program, I don't think you need this. Furthermore, I have to use all of my credit on saving our budget. If they cut that, as they are considering, *that* will have a significant negative impact on the course and put you in a bind. I have to put everything into that fight right now and don't want to jeopardize the outcome."

Carole said, "But why can't you tell them how crucial *both* of these things are for the future of the course?"

David agreed that he'd raise the request and support it but said that he wouldn't fight for it. "That's all I'm willing to do."

Carole left feeling angry and misunderstood. *How does he not recognize why this is so important to me* and *the ongoing success of his life's work?*

David felt annoyed. *Why can't she see that she can succeed without those labels? And why can't she accept that she will never get appropriate recognition? I never did and learned to live with that. I figured out how to run Interpersonal Dynamics without a program designation—she can, too.*

To put it mildly, the conversation had gone nowhere. And from there things got even worse.

At David's next budget meeting with management, he made the case for Carole's requests. He was asked whether they were crucial for her to lead the other faculty. David hesitated for a moment. "Well, not getting these things certainly makes her job harder, but she can do it," he said. He added that the real challenge was her legitimacy and influence with management. They assured him that was not an issue. David then asked why the program designation and title were such a problem for them, and they said that they were totally consumed with the financial issues and that had to be their first priority. They also wanted to conduct a full and thoughtful review of programs and titles after the crisis was over and were very reluctant to make a one-off decision at that time. David then let it go.

When David told Carole what had happened at the meeting with management, and that he had chosen not to push further, even knowing how much this meant to her, she was furious and deeply hurt.

"This is a real slap in the face, David," she said. "What's the point in busting my ass the way I have if, when the chips are down, it doesn't matter?" He responded that her work had mattered and she was underestimating the influence she had built. She then reiterated the damage she feared this would do to the Interpersonal Dynamics course in the long run and added: "If the situation had been reversed, I would have gone to bat for you in an instant, even if as a man you might not need the support as much as I do."

"Carole, I wouldn't want that. Why would you do that?"

"I would want to do right by you," she said, "because of all you've done for the school. And I expect you to do the same. I can't believe you don't think doing right by me *is* doing right by the organization. And I just can't believe you're doing this, after all I have done for *you* and your Interpersonal Dynamics 'baby.' "

"You've done a lot for the school and for the course, and I—and others—very much appreciate you for that," David said. "But I don't agree that any of that should factor into what is ultimately best for the course. This budget issue is crucial, and I think it is important to respect their process when it comes to program and title designations. Furthermore, I wouldn't want anyone to think I was advocating on your behalf because of our friendship—that wouldn't be fair to you."

At that point, our discussion ended.

Carole's perspective:

> In that moment, David represented the entire institution and all the ways in which I had felt expendable and marginalized for years. I thought, *If I can't count on him to see the injustice and show me appreciation by doing right by me, I can't count on anybody.*
>
> I completely wrote him off. I wasn't sure I'd ever be able to trust him again. I thought our worldviews were just too different. I have a very high value around loyalty, and it seemed

> clear he didn't—or that he defined it differently. I thought our differences were irreconcilable. I wanted nothing to do with him . . . ever again.

David's perspective:

> At this point, I felt helpless. I felt written off, which was painful, but I didn't know what to say. We had gone around and around with the same arguments. I hoped with the passage of time that Carole's anger would somewhat dissipate and we could reconnect.

Even though our relationship was severely strained, we still had to work together for the rest of the year. We barely exchanged a word outside of what was necessary. Staff meetings were as short as possible, and our interactions were down to a minimum. While we were polite and able to work together as professionals, we did not go to each other for advice or to talk about issues, much less banter as we once had.

A critical element of the Touchy-Feely course is learning to repair, and several colleagues pushed Carole to live what she taught and meet with David. Carole felt so wronged, so hurt, and so betrayed that she refused. She continued to believe that if the situation had been reversed, she would have fully supported David. She wanted nothing to do with him. David, knowing this, didn't know what to do.

Repair Begins

Months later, Carole was encouraged to try a repair. Her negative feelings were still strong, but she was also feeling the loss of the relationship. She reached out to David and asked him to meet with her in her office to see if there was anything to be done to salvage it.

David leapt at the invitation since he hadn't seen any other way to connect. He didn't know what new might be said, but he was hopeful.

After a cool and somewhat awkward greeting, Carole told David she hoped they could have a real repair conversation. David expressed the same wish. At first, the conversation seemed a repeat of the first, to little avail.

But then David expressed that he was puzzled that Carole was so upset, and she was incredulous that he didn't understand why, knowing her as well as he did.

"It makes me really nervous," David said, "to think I might not know where the next land mine is going to be with you."

"It's not an issue of land mines," Carole said. "It appears that we have significantly different values, and that makes me question just how well we really do know each other."

After reiterating how hard it was for her to accept David's choice not to strongly advocate for her, Carole talked more about why the title and the acknowledgment of Interpersonal Dynamics as a program were so very important to her and how her feelings of being devalued by a system she'd given so much of herself to, and a life of having to fight harder for everything as a woman, were mixed up with it all. She shared how vulnerable she had felt in taking such a strong stance for fear of being misunderstood. And she expressed how deeply disappointed she felt after all she had done to support David and his life's work for decades, only to learn that when the chips were really down, she couldn't count on him.

David began to understand the depth and importance of her concerns. At one level, there were no new facts, but he was starting to more fully appreciate what was going on for her. It wasn't that he changed his mind about prioritizing the budget conversation, but he now moved into empathizing with what this whole situation meant to Carole. At that point, he said, among other things, "I'm seeing what has been going on for you, maybe for the first time. And I'm sorry."

It was a big breakthrough for Carole. It was the first time since the rupture that she felt heard, and not looked at as though there was something "wrong" with her for reacting the way she had. Because David was empathetic to why she was so upset, it was a little easier for her to hear that David disagreed with the basis of her stance. It was the first time she felt emotionally met. She experienced David's empathy and willingness to just be with her, in her upset-ness, without trying to talk her out of it or make her wrong for feeling it. It opened her up to believing they could have this conversation from an emotional-based place instead of through thoughts and opinions.

Carole asked, with genuine curiosity, "Why couldn't you support me *and* push for the budget?"

"Carole, you were worried about being successful in running the course. If I hadn't used all my credit to prevent the cuts, you would have had one hell of a time being successful. Also, if I got you what you wanted, it wouldn't have given you the status you thought you needed."

David explained that he was afraid it would actually hurt her credibility down the road if the only reason she'd gotten her requests granted was because he'd insisted. He shared the tremendous pressure he had felt, given the trade-off he'd made about what to push for. Finally, he talked about how he himself had lived with the lack of full recognition for decades and had just come to accept it as part of working in the system. He also talked about his anger and disappointment at her refusal to take over the program unless her conditions were met.

Our issues were highly entangled. We spoke for hours. Even though we explored these issues in much greater depth and gained a clearer understanding of why each of us had responded as we had, everything was not all wrapped up in a neat bow. There had been too much pain in this incident for it to be completely resolved in one sitting. But we had broken through, and enough trust had been restored that we could truly hear each other once again.

Analysis: What Went Wrong—and Why?

Why did two competent people get so stuck? How did everything go so sideways? In this situation, too many factors became too intertwined. It was like a big knot that, when pulled on, just got tighter and tighter. We had to know which string to pull on first.

Throughout this book, we've stressed the importance of fully understanding other people, of trying to get to the underlying issues through curiosity and inquiry. Yes, each of us asked questions of the other, but there wasn't real curiosity. Why?

In David's case, there were several reasons. He truly believed Carole was so good at her job that she didn't actually need a title or a program designation to be effective. He thought he knew what was going on with Carole, that it was mainly her ego and insecurity. So why ask? And since he was so sure of his assessment, and his over-the-net attributions of her motives, any "asking" on his part would have been more of an accusation, possibly inflaming Carole even more. There was no genuine curiosity. David also had put up with lack of recognition during his entire career. He'd learned to cope, so why couldn't she? Then there was his own anger at all the mentoring he had invested in her and, last, the worry about what would happen to the course now.

For Carole's part, she felt wholly justified in her anger and hurt, and was unable to see anything else. She was a professional and considered herself a person of the highest integrity. She rarely asked for anything for herself and had taken a risk in doing so, which made her feel vulnerable. Her feelings of marginalization ran very deep. Carole had said little to none of this to David in prior conversations.

Thus, logical arguments (from either of us) not only didn't work but were counterproductive. We had also gotten stuck because of a fundamental difference in values.

At the very core of Carole's intense reaction was that one of her most fundamental values—loyalty—had been crushed. Carole defined loyalty as "faithfulness to commitments or obligations and allegiances." That's why she told David she would have supported him had their places been reversed, full stop. Because she was so clear about what she would do under the circumstances, she never considered that David would act differently.

David valued loyalty, too, but defined it differently. He saw it as "commitment to another's growth and success"—and the stronger the relationship, the greater the commitment. That's why he had gone all out to mentor Carole. And because he so believed in her, he didn't think what she wanted was necessary for her to be successful.

We had another values difference, in that we both saw ourselves behaving with the utmost integrity and believed we were doing what was best for Touchy-Feely and the school. This certainty led each of us to become judgmental and see the other as wrong. With each of us feeling negatively judged, neither of us felt compelled to understand the other.

What Broke the Impasse?

Our colleagues played a crucial role in pushing us to talk to each other, but we think we could have broken through regardless. It probably would have taken more time but would still have been possible for the following reasons:

We did not "demonize" each other. We did not make up stories that imputed malevolent intentions or bad character. (Carole said that even though she didn't understand why David had done what he did, she knew it was not his intention to hurt her.) Likewise, each of us was disappointed in the other, but neither jumped to the conclusion that the other was an evil or terrible person. Avoiding those extreme positions made it possible, eventually, for us to understand each other.

Neither of us got locked into false pride. It would have been easy for someone in Carole's position to be trapped by a stance that reaching out to David would mean losing face. Fortunately, Carole's pride did not impede her. Also, neither of us had a difficult time saying that we were sorry—whether for something we did or in order to demonstrate understanding of the other's pain.

We differentiated *understanding* from *agreement.* David never agreed that Carole's position was objectively right. The breakthrough occurred when he was able to separate that from being able to understand *why* she was so hurt. Accepting her feelings as valid, and conveying that acceptance, made the difference. Here, again, it took Carole much longer, but she, too, eventually came to understand (and respect) why David made the choices he did.

We let go of logic to explore the deeper personal issues. One of the reasons the first two meetings turned out so poorly was that each of us argued the logic of the issues. And we each wanted to be, first and foremost, "right." We also had very different opinions about what was best for the course, and each had a logical reason for them. Things may not make *logical* sense, but they can make *psycho*logical sense.

Our outcome met the four criteria of successful conflict resolution. We found a way to go back to really (vs. barely) speaking to each other, we understood each other at a deeper level, our ability to problem-solve improved (so it's unlikely we will get as stuck again), and our relationship ended up even stronger than it had been before the conflict.

Recovery and Repair: Highlighting the Breaks

Kintsugi, or "golden repair," is a Japanese art form for fixing broken pottery. Lacquer mixed with powdered gold, silver, or platinum is applied in such a way as to highlight the breaks while also serving the practical purpose of mending the pot. It is also a philosophy; if an object has been damaged, then it has a history that should be celebrated rather than hidden, covered up, or discarded. The rare-metal powder aggrandizes the break to say that when something has been subjected to damage, it becomes more beautiful. We believe the same orientation applies to the "breaks" in a relationship and how they're repaired. That has certainly been true for us. Even though we regret our painful impasse, we value what we got out of it.

Going to the brink of a ruined relationship and recovering gave us confidence that we could handle any future disagreements. We had built an even deeper "emotional bank account." We came to realize we had held untested assumptions, including a belief that because we had known each other for so many years, we fully and deeply understood each other. That sobering experience prompted us, since then, to move more into inquiry and away from certainty that we knew exactly what was going on with each other.

Our conflict resulted in one more crucial outcome, and that was rebalancing the power relationship between us—illustrating the complexity of exceptional relationships in a work setting. Carole had been in awe of David from the very beginning and felt incredibly fortunate to have been mentored by him. In spite of finding it easy to disagree with David, Carole still had a tendency to defer to him even after she took over some of David's courses and responsibilities in Interpersonal Dynamics. This power differential was not very evident to either of us, in spite of how much we knew about the costs of power discrepancies. This dynamic, and the fact that we almost always agreed on key issues, meant we had never had a major conflict. In finding our way through this one, Carole came to see and accept David as a mere mortal who can and does make mistakes. This equalized the power differential that had previously existed in our relationship. It was empowering for Carole and freeing for David. Without this shift in power, Carole is not sure she would have agreed to partner with David on the book you hold in your hands.

It was a long road back for both of us, and we were able to not only recover but also emerge closer than ever. We went from distant, formal interactions, to gradual warming, to back to where we had been before, and then to having an even stronger relationship. It was not an easy journey. But it was well worth the pain and effort, and we have the golden repair to prove it.

EPILOGUE

O wad some Pow'r the giftie gie us
To see oursels as others see us!

—ROBERT BURNS

We want to end this book by talking about fear. That may seem like an odd choice, but it's only by talking about fear that we can help you see what's possible *without* it.

We all hold back sharing significant parts of ourselves because we fear being negatively judged. Don't think you're the exception—in all the T-groups we've led, participants consistently struggle with, "Do I dare show these parts of myself that I've worked so hard to keep hidden?" Think about it: You've probably resisted making a commitment to someone else because you were afraid they wouldn't reciprocate. Perhaps you've been hesitant to try something new because you're afraid of making mistakes. You may not have asked for what you needed, or confronted others when they hurt you, because you feared damaging the relationship. Even more basic is the fear that if someone really knew you—all of you—they would reject you.

We all know people who hold a self-image that is very different from how others see them. Is that partially true for you? Is it really a gift to "see ourselves as others see us," especially if it destroys a self-image that you've worked hard to develop? You may fear losing your self-esteem and sense of personal worth if you take in another's feedback.

These fears limit growth and learning and reduce willingness to take risks and experiment with new behavior. They keep you stuck in unhappy situations you are loath to confront, and they consume a huge amount of energy. They cost you real connection. "Fear" is sometimes an acronym for "false expectations appearing real."

Most of all, these fears limit your likelihood of moving your relationships to exceptional. As we have illustrated time and again, it is only when we can manage our fears and take the necessary risks that exceptional becomes possible. And that results in a paradox. Just as fear can limit you, the risks you take as you build and maintain an exceptional relationship can free you from much of that fear. That is partly because you have tested those fears, only to discover they were false expectations. The process of building deep relationships has increased your interpersonal competence and given you the confidence you need to speak your truth and be more fully yourself.

All of this frees you from constantly asking, "Do I dare say . . . ," "What does she think of me when I . . . ," or "How does he feel about my doing . . ." Instead of wasting energy on self-doubt, you can focus it on curiosity and learning. Sure, you may still worry about how things will turn out, but that's different from worrying about being rejected for who you are. In this way, exceptional relationships help you shift from living in black and white to living in full color.

At the heart of an exceptional relationship, then, is a unique experience of freedom that feels almost magical. Because you know the other cares for you and will be honest, you can hear their feedback. This results in knowing *yourself* in a much fuller way. You know specifically what you do well and how to leverage those strengths. You see your weaknesses not as something to beat yourself up about, but as a part of being human that gives you opportunities to grow. Exceptional relationships allow you to pressure-test your beliefs. Maybe some assumptions that served you well in the past don't anymore. Another's feedback and perspective offer you the chance to broaden the way you see situations and even influence your understanding of the choices you have.

But most of all, those you care about accept you, in all of your flawed humanness. You have narrowed any gap between how others see you and how you see yourself. Their acceptance helps you accept yourself. The freedom that results is unparalleled.

Knowing yourself and accepting yourself allows you to develop an internal gyroscope—you know, like one of those inflatable toys that can be hit but always comes back to center. You aren't upended by feedback or controlled by another's reactions. You're solidly connected to who you are and to your worth, which allows you to take in others' perspectives. Learning and growing always require risk-taking, but now you have a strong foundation. You're perfectly positioned to be a lifelong learner. And you have the capacity to profoundly connect with another human being.

You've reached the top of the mountain. You've a much wider view of the world than you had when you were in the valley or even the upper meadow. You know that being there with someone else will give you plenty of opportunities to see new vistas from different vantage points. And having made this climb several times, you know it's possible to make it again, with others. Much more connection and magic await.

ACKNOWLEDGMENTS

IT IS UNLIKELY we would have written this book were it not for Daniel Crewe of Penguin Random House, who called us to ask if we were interested in writing a book based on the famous "Touchy-Feely" course at Stanford. First and foremost, we thank him for inviting us to embark on this journey, believing in us, and providing constant support along with many editorial suggestions over three years. Additionally, a big thank-you to our Crown editor, Emma Berry, for her exceptional responsiveness, improving one draft after another with her gifted editor's eye, and for making this work that much stronger.

We are deeply grateful to Jenna Free for her patient guidance as she took our original manuscript and helped turn it into something far more readable. She was masterful at flagging redundancies, clarifying content, cutting through unnecessarily dense material, and helping bring the book more fully to life. Her rigorous editing taught us that often less is more. And a big thank-you to our wonderful agent, Howard Yoon, for guiding us through this process.

Our appreciation extends to Mary Ann Huckabay, to our good friend and frequent informal advisor Max Richards for his extensive input on the manuscript and stellar work on references, and to Adele Kellman and Vanessa Loder, each of whom read the manuscript at different times and made specific suggestions that helped advance our thinking.

Numerous people provided us with feedback and sage counsel at different points along the way. We thank our Interpersonal Dynamics colleagues Ed Batista, Leslie Chin, Andrea Corney, Collins Dobbs, and Yifat Levine, and our dear departed friend Lanz Lowen, who went over our original proposal and helped us set the direction of the book.

Over the ensuing three years, we gained invaluable suggestions from Alan Briskin, Gary Dexter, Basya Gale, Mary Garber, Susan Harris, Tony Levitan, Edgar Schein, and Roger Scholl. All of their ideas and input, whether we accepted them or not, invited us to pause and consider more deeply what we wanted to say. The book greatly changed over the years we worked on it. *Connect* would have undoubtedly been a lesser work without their input. We take full responsibility for any limitations in the final product.

Thank you Patricia Will for Casa Taupa; Roy Bahat, Ricki Frankel, Cynthia Gorney, and Wendy Cavendish for commiserating, cheerleading, and providing enthusiastic support; and the gang at Leaders in Tech for picking up the slack time and time again.

We want to acknowledge and thank our thousands of students and clients who not only shaped our thinking but also impacted each of us personally. We hope to have done justice to what they taught us about developing meaningful relationships. During the writing of this book, we had hundreds of conversations with many, many people, and while it is impractical to name them all, we apologize for our failure to acknowledge them specifically.

Lastly, in addition to our spouses, to whom we have dedicated this book, we are immensely grateful to our children and our grandchildren—Jeff Bradford (Sophia Lau), Winry Bradford, Kendra Bradford (Todd Shuster), Lev Shuster, Gail Shuster, Nick Robin (Alex Robin), and Molly Robin—who have played such significant roles in our lives and helped us understand what it takes to build exceptional relationships.

APPENDIX A

Vocabulary

	happy	caring	depressed	inadequate	fearful
Mild Intensity	*glad good contented satisfied gratified pleasant pleased fine*	*warm toward friendly like positive toward*	*unhappy down low bad blah disappointed sad glum bummed*	*lacking confidence unsure of yourself uncertain weak inefficient*	*nervous anxious unsure hesitant timid shy worried uneasy bashful embarrassed ill at ease doubtful jittery on edge uncomfortable self-conscious*
Moderate Intensity	*cheerful up neat serene wonderful light-hearted aglow glowing in high spirits jovial riding high elevated*	*fond of regards respectful admiration concern for hold dear trust close*	*distressed upset downcast sorrowful demoralized discouraged miserable pessimistic tearful weepy rotten awful horrible terrible blue lost melancholy*	*whipped defeated incompetent inept overwhelmed ineffective lacking unable incapable small unfit unimportant incomplete no good immobilized*	*afraid scared apprehensive jumpy shaky threatened distrustful risk alarm butterflies awkward defensive*
Strong Intensity	*thrilled terrific ecstatic overjoyed excited blown away fantastic exhilarated sensational on cloud nine elated enthusiastic delighted marvelous great on top of the world liberated*	*loving infatuated enamored cherish idolize worship tenderness toward affection for captivated by attached to devoted to adoration*	*gloomy dismal bleak in despair empty barren grieved grief grim desolate dejected hopeless alienated*	*helpless impotent crippled inferior emasculated useless finished like a failure worthless good for nothing*	*terrified frightened intimidated horrified desperate panicky terror-stricken vulnerable stage fright dread paralyzed*

# of Feelings

confused	hurt	guilt/shame	lonely	angry
uncertain unsure bothered uncomfortable undecided	*put down neglected overlooked minimized let down unappreciated taken for granted*	*regretful wrong embarrassed at fault in error responsible for blew it goofed lament sheepish*	*left out excluded lonesome distant aloof*	*uptight disgusted bugged turned off put out miffed irked perturbed ticked off chagrined cross dismayed impatient "pinched"*
mixed up disorganized foggy troubled adrift lost at loose ends embroiled disconnected frustrated in a bind ambivalent disturbed helpless going around in circles	*belittled shot down overlooked abused depreciated criticized defamed censured discredited disparaged laughed at maligned mistreated ridiculed devalued scorned mocked scoffed at used exploited debased slammed slandered impugned cheapened*	*ashamed guilty remorseful crummy to blame lost face demeaned*	*alienated estranged remote alone insulated apart from others isolated from others*	*resentful irritated hostile annoyed upset with agitated mad aggravated offended antagonistic exasperated belligerent mean vexed spiteful vindictive*
bewildered puzzled baffled perplexed trapped confounded in a dilemma befuddled in a quandary full of questions	*crushed destroyed ruined degraded pained wounded devastated tortured disgraced humiliated anguished at the mercy cast off forsaken rejected discarded*	*sick at heart exposed unforgivable humiliated disgraced degraded horrible mortified*	*isolated abandoned all alone forsaken cut off*	*furious enraged seething outraged infuriated burned up pissed off violent indignant hatred bitter galled vengeful hateful livid repulsed*

APPENDIX B

Furthering Your Learning

The most important and long-lasting skill we hope you take away from this book is that you have *learned how to learn*. Research on T-groups shows that participants who have acquired the competencies in this book continue to learn after the course is over, thanks to a positively reinforcing cycle. Take advantage of this cycle, of this ability to stretch yourself, by reminding yourself of what you've learned:

- How to be more fully yourself, including seeing the power in expressing your emotions. You have learned how to use the 15 Percent Rule for increasing self-disclosure in building relationships. Even though there can be risks in being vulnerable, in most cases the benefits far exceed the costs. Being willing to be more fully known takes courage, and you have learned that vulnerability can come much more out of strength than out of weakness.
- How to build conditions where the other person is willing to disclose and be more themselves. Listening for their feelings and encouraging their full expression is crucial in that process. Likewise, you have learned not to rush to judgment but instead to be curious when you don't initially understand the other or they do something that upsets you. You also have learned to value the

other's uniqueness as opposed to requiring that they be just like you.

- The limitation of giving advice and the power of open-ended questions. You have increased your ability to be empathetic, and just as you want to be more fully known and accepted, you have learned to do the same for the other person.
- How to give and receive behaviorally specific feedback, to both raise and resolve difficulties, and to help the other see what they do well and might build on. The difficulties between you and the other might range from minor pinches to some major conflicts, but irrespective of where the issue is along that range, you see that feedback, although challenging at times, doesn't have to be an attack. Instead, it can be a way to surface the core issues so that both of you can jointly resolve them. Feedback truly is a gift when you are both invested in each other's growth and in your relationship.
- Appreciating the power and range of emotions, you have become aware of your capacity to feel many at the same time, as well as all the ways you can block yourself from recognizing and appropriately using them.
- Support comes in many forms, but being supportive sometimes requires raising difficult issues that can be uncomfortable for both the giver and the recipient. In doing so, you have learned how to be more honest than you thought possible. That honesty starts with sticking with your reality—how the other person's behavior is affecting you—not in providing your psychological interpretation of their motives or character.
- You have many more choices than you previously thought. It is not that you "can't" do or say something, but that you choose not to. Sometimes saying nothing is the best alternative, but it's important to recognize that's nonetheless a choice.
- Conflict need not be destructive. If you use the feedback model, difficult issues can be raised and resolved in a way that actually strengthens the relationship.

- Relationships rarely develop in a straight line. It's often "two steps forward and one step back." Building meaningful relationships requires persistence; difficulties are just temporary barriers that can be resolved, and damage can be repaired.
- You have learned more about yourself—what you do well and how you limit yourself. Perhaps most important, you see the multiple sources of learning. You can learn from your emotions, since they can signal what's important to you. You can learn by asking yourself, "*Why* am I reacting as I am?" You can learn from feedback, since others know, and tell you, the impact of your behavior. And you have learned what situations are likely to trigger you.

But perhaps most important of all, using these competencies has helped you learn from your experiences, as you've taken action to improve your relationships. You have seen what works well for you and another person and, rather than denying problems, have learned from glitches so that you and the other can do better next time. Strengthened by these competencies, you are less afraid of taking risks. That's what gives you the freedom to continue to learn.

A CALL TO ACTION

1. Based on the summary above and now that you have read this book, what stands out as most important for you to work on?
2. Setting Specific Learning Goals: You are more competent and comfortable with some of these competencies than with others. You can't work on all of them at once, so remember the 15 Percent Rule and pick the ones that are more important. Likewise, are there ways that you tend to limit and trap yourself? Being aware of what you want to work on and what is successful increases the chance that you will see opportunities to put your skills to the test.

3. Getting Assistance: Others are instrumental in helping you reach your learning goals, as it's hard to significantly change all on your own. For example, you might not see that you're backing down, even though one of your objectives is to give greater voice to your opinions. Share what you want to work on with someone you trust and ask them to be aware of times when you fall into one of your traps or have missed an opportunity to work on one of your change goals. They might also help you further clarify your goals and think through ways to achieve them.

4. Recording and Reflecting: Earlier in the book, we encouraged you to keep a journal, not just to record progress made, but as a place to reflect. Let's say you had an unsuccessful experience where, once again, you didn't lead with your feelings. What was going on that led to that? Did you have trouble with certain emotions? Were you caught in an ego trap that made it difficult to be vulnerable?

There is a story, perhaps apocryphal, of a patient who asked a therapist, "How do I know when I'm cured?" The response was "When you catch yourself before I do." Long-held habits are difficult to erase. You might continue to have difficulty with conflict. Make the goal less about being *comfortable* with confrontation than about being *competent*. It takes practice and persistence to lay down new behavioral pathways. But keep at it and honor your progress. Don't be thrown by temporary setbacks.

In closing, we come back to Auguste Renoir's dying words: "I think I'm beginning to learn something about it." We wish you a lifetime of continued development in which there are constant discoveries until the very end. That's what life should be about.

NOTES

2: A WORLD-CLASS COURSE, ONE CHAPTER AT A TIME

17 **"Your assumptions are your windows":** Alan Alda, commencement address, Connecticut College, June 1, 1980.

3: TO SHARE, OR NOT TO SHARE

25 **Self-disclosure creates more opportunities to connect and increases trust:** Nancy L. Collins and Lynn Carol Miller, "Self-Disclosure and Liking: A Meta-Analytic Review," *Psychological Bulletin* 116, no. 3 (1994): doi.org/10.1037/0033-2909.116.3.457; Susan Sprecher, Stanislav Treger, and Joshua D. Wondra, "Effects of Self-Disclosure Role on Liking, Closeness, and Other Impressions in Get-Acquainted Interactions," *Journal of Social and Personal Relationships* 30, no. 4 (2013): doi.org/10.1177/0265407512459033.

28 **not take in any new disconfirming information:** Confirmation bias was first described by Peter Wason in the context of an experiment examining the extent to which people seek confirming evidence to draw conclusions. P. C. Wason, "On the Failure to Eliminate Hypotheses in a Conceptual Task," *Quarterly Journal of Experimental Psychology* 12, no. 3 (1960): doi.org/10.1080/17470216008416717. Confirmation bias is defined by the American Psychological Association as "the tendency to gather evidence that confirms preexisting expectations, typically by emphasizing or pursuing supporting evidence while dismissing or failing to seek contradictory evidence." *APA Dictionary of Psychology,* American Psychological Association, accessed March 11, 2020, dictionary.apa.org/confirmation-bias.

34 **plenty of other options to choose from:** For a fuller list of emotions, see Appendix A.

36 **hold sway as the coin of the realm:** For a deeper look at the impact of differing cultures on emotion, see Keith Oatley, Dacher Keltner, and Jennifer Jenkins, "Cultural Understandings of Emotion," in *Understanding Emotions,* 3rd ed. (New York: John Wiley & Sons, 2013).

37 **key determinant in leadership success:** Daniel Goleman, *Emotional Intelligence* (New York: Bantam Books, Inc., 1995).

39 **belief in our ability to act in the world:** For a deeper look at the concept of "agency," see Martin Hewson, "Agency," in *Encyclopedia of Case Study Research*, eds. Albert J. Mills, Gabrielle Durepos, and Elden Weibe (Thousand Oaks, CA: Sage Publications, Inc., 2010), dx.doi.org/10.4135/9781412957397.n5.

44 **helps the leader be seen as more human:** Katherine W. Phillips, Nancy P. Rothbard, and Tracy L. Dumas, "To Disclose or Not to Disclose? Status Distance and Self-Disclosure in Diverse Environments," *Academy of Management Review* 34, no. 4 (2009); Kerry Roberts Gibsona, Dana Hararib, and Jennifer Carson Marr, "When Sharing Hurts: How and Why Self-Disclosing Weakness Undermines the Task-Oriented Relationships of Higher Status Disclosers," *Organizational Behavior and Human Decision Processes* 144 (2018); Lynn Offermann and Lisa Rosh, "Building Trust Through Skillful Self-Disclosure," *Harvard Business Review,* June 13, 2012, hbr.org/2012/06/instantaneous-intimacy-skillfu.

45 **the real me is undesirable:** In "Changing Faces," Laura Roberts explores the intrapsychic and interpersonal consequences of impression management while drawing on numerous studies related to the detrimental impact of masking authentic internal feelings, values, and social identities, and the positive impact of expressing them. Laura Morgan Roberts, "Changing Faces: Professional Image Construction in Diverse Organizational Settings," *Academy of Management Review* 30, no. 4 (2005).

4: HELPING OTHERS BE KNOWN

63 **women in male-dominated fields and people of color:** Katherine W. Phillips, Nancy P. Rothbard, and Tracy L. Dumas, "To Disclose or Not to Disclose? Status Distance and Self-Disclosure in Diverse Environments," *Academy of Management Review* 34, no. 4 (2009).

64 **be open and direct with one another:** David L. Bradford and Allan R. Cohen, *Power Up: Transforming Organizations Through Shared Leadership* (New York: John Wiley & Sons, Inc., 1998).

5: INFLUENCE IN BALANCE

72 **couple has children and only decreases after those children have left home:** Jean M. Twenge, W. Keith Campbell, and Craig A. Foster, "Parenthood and Marital Satisfaction: A Meta-Analytic Review," *Journal of Marriage and the Family* 65, no. 3 (2003); Gilad Hirschberger, Sanjay Srivastava, Penny Marsh, Carolyn Pape Cowan, and Philip A. Cowan, "Attachment, Marital Satisfaction, and Divorce During the First Fifteen Years of Parenthood," *Personal Relationships* 16, no. 3 (2009); Sara Gorchoff, John Oliver, and Ravenna Helson, "Contextualizing Change in Marital Satisfaction During Middle Age: An 18-Year Longitudinal Study," *Psychological Science* 19, no. 11 (2008).

73 **We are also influenced by comparison with others:** L. Festinger, "A Theory of Social Comparison Processes," *Human Relations* 7 (1954), pp. 117–140.

77 **often results in a dysfunctional cycle:** Allan R. Cohen and David L. Bradford, *Influencing Up* (New York: John Wiley & Sons, 2012).

6: PINCHES AND CRUNCHES

86 **"Own your feelings or they will own you":** Douglas Stone, Bruce Patton, and Sheila Heen, "Have Your Feelings (or They Will Have You)," in *Difficult Conversations: How to Discuss What Matters Most* (New York: Penguin Books, 2010).

86 **initially felt a pinch:** John J. Sherwood & John J. Scherer, "A Model for Couples: How Two Can Grow Together," Journal for Small Group Behavior, February 1975.

93 **everyone is subject to confirmation bias:** *APA Dictionary of Psychology,* American Psychological Association, accessed March 11, 2020, dictionary.apa.org/confirmation-bias.

93 **As our colleagues Jennifer Aaker and Naomi Bagdonas's:** Jennifer Aaker and Naomi Bagdonas, interview by David Needle, "Humor in the Workplace," *Gentry Magazine,* September 2017, https://www.gsb.stanford.edu/experience/news-history/humor-serious-business.

8: CHALLENGES IN USING FEEDBACK EFFECTIVELY

122 **important elements of emotional intelligence:** Daniel Goleman, *Emotional Intelligence* (New York: Bantam Books, Inc., 1995).

123 **select confirming data:** Jennifer Aaker and Naomi Bagdonas, interview by David Needle, "Humor in the Workplace," *Gentry Magazine,* September 2017, https://www.gsb.stanford.edu/experience/news-history/humor-serious-business.

10: OWN YOUR EMOTIONS OR THEY WILL OWN YOU

160 **"when we numb anger, sadness, and fear, we also numb gratitude, love, and joy":** Brené Brown, "The Power of Vulnerability," TEDxHouston lecture, 2010, www.ted.com/talks/brene_brown_on_vulnerability/transcript?language=en#t-640207.

162 **adversely affect our health, our happiness, and the quality of our relationships:** Douglas Stone, Bruce Patton, and Sheila Heen, "Have Your Feelings (or They Will Have You)," in *Difficult Conversations: How to Discuss What Matters Most* (New York: Penguin Books, 2010).

12: USING CONFLICT PRODUCTIVELY

190 **stonewalling is infuriating:** To learn more about the phenomenon of stonewalling and the emotional flooding associated with it, see John Gottman, *Why Marriages Succeed or Fail: And How You Can Make Yours Last* (New York: Simon & Schuster, 1995).

13: RESOLVING CONTENTIOUS ISSUES

206 **rather than stepping back and identifying the core problem:** Across two studies, Maier and his colleagues found that the quality of problem-solving increased when participants explored alternative solutions instead of sticking with the first they arrived at. Norman R. F. Maier and Allen R. Solem, "Improving Solutions by Turning Choice Situations into Problems," *Personnel Psychology* 15, no. 2 (1962): doi.org/10.1111/j.1744-6570.1962.tb01857.x; Norman R. F. Maier and L. Richard Hoffman, "Quality of First and Second Solutions in Group Problem Solving," *Journal of Applied Psychology* 44, no. 4 (1960): doi.org/10.1037/h0041372.

16: WHEN EXCEPTIONAL ISN'T IN THE CARDS

250 **Carol Dweck suggests:** Carol Dweck, *Mindset: The New Psychology of Success* (New York: Random House, 2006).

259 **we recommend two books:** Allan R. Cohen and David L. Bradford, *Power Up: Transforming Organizations Through Shared Leadership* (New York: John Wiley & Sons, 1998); David L. Bradford and Allan R. Cohen, *Influence Without Authority,* 3rd ed. (New York: John Wiley & Sons, 2017).

INDEX

ABOUT THE AUTHORS

DAVID BRADFORD, PHD, is the Eugene O'Kelly II Senior Lecturer Emeritus in Leadership at Stanford Graduate School of Business, where he has taught for over fifty years. He was the primary architect for the legendary "Touchy-Feely" course (aka Interpersonal Dynamics), which is one of the school's flagship offerings. He introduced leadership to the GSB curriculum at the MBA and executive levels by developing multiple courses and mentoring colleagues for nearly four decades.

He founded the Organizational Behavior Teaching Society, a professional organization dedicated to experiential learning, and was its journal's first editor. He has co-authored seven other books, including the classic *Influence Without Authority* and *Power Up: Transforming Organizations Through Shared Leadership*.

In addition, he has provided executive coaching and consulted numerous organizations in the for-profit and not-for-profit sectors, including Levi Strauss, IBM, Genentech, and the Whitney Museum of American Art.

He lives in Berkeley with Eva, his wife of more than fifty years. They have two children and three grandchildren.

CAROLE ROBIN, PHD, was the Dorothy J. King Lecturer in Leadership at Stanford Graduate School of Business, where she helped to further develop the Interpersonal Dynamics course, including co-developing the executive version. She also became the director of the Arbuckle Leadership Fellows Program. She was known as the Queen of Touchy-Feely and received the MBA Distinguished Teaching Award. When she retired in 2017, a scholarship was established in her name. Subsequently, she cofounded Leaders in Tech, a nonprofit that brings two decades of lessons to Silicon Valley startups.

Prior to joining Stanford, she was a partner in an international consulting firm and a senior manager in a Fortune 500 company. She has provided executive coaching, leadership development, and executive team building to a wide range of business, government, and nonprofit clients ranging in size from startups to global and Fortune 500 organizations, and is currently an advisor on several boards. She is the recipient of two Congressional Awards for community service.

Carole was raised in Mexico City, Mexico, where she lived for seventeen years. She now lives in Palo Alto, California, with her husband of thirty-five years, and has two children.

connectandrelate.com

ABOUT THE TYPE

This book was set in Dante, a typeface designed by Giovanni Mardersteig (1892–1977). Conceived as a private type for the Officina Bodoni in Verona, Italy, Dante was originally cut only for hand composition by Charles Malin, the famous Parisian punch cutter, between 1946 and 1952. Its first use was in an edition of Boccaccio's *Trattatello in laude di Dante* that appeared in 1954. The Monotype Corporation's version of Dante followed in 1957. Though modeled on the Aldine type used for Pietro Cardinal Bembo's treatise *De Aetna* in 1495, Dante is a thoroughly modern interpretation of that venerable face.